CYBER 2022

The Seventh International Conference on Cyber-Technologies and Cyber-Systems

November 13 - 17, 2022

Valencia, Spain

CYBER 2022 Editors

Steve Chan, Decision Engineering Analysis Laboratory, USA

Kevin D. Jones, University of Plymouth, UK

Printed from e-media with permission by:

Curran Associates, Inc.
57 Morehouse Lane
Red Hook, NY 12571

Some format issues inherent in the e-media version may also appear in this print version.

Printed with permission by Curran Associates, Inc. (2023)

International Academy, Research, and Industry Association (IARIA)
412 Derby Way
Wilmington, DE 19810

Phone: (408) 893-6407
Fax: (408) 527-6351

petre@iaria.org

Additional copies of this publication are available from:

Curran Associates, Inc.
57 Morehouse Lane
Red Hook, NY 12571 USA
Phone: 845-758-0400
Fax: 845-758-2633
Email: curran@proceedings.com
Web: www.proceedings.com

Table of Contents

CYBER 2022

Forward

The Seventh International Conference on Cyber-Technologies and Cyber-Systems (CYBER 2022), held between November 13 and November 17, 2022, continued the inaugural event covering many aspects related to cyber-systems and cyber-technologies considering the issues mentioned above and potential solutions. It is also intended to illustrate appropriate current academic and industry cyber-system projects, prototypes, and deployed products and services.

The increased size and complexity of the communications and the networking infrastructures are making it difficult the investigation of the resiliency, security assessment, safety and crimes. Mobility, anonymity, counterfeiting, are characteristics that add more complexity in Internet of Things and Cloud-based solutions. Cyber-physical systems exhibit a strong link between the computational and physical elements. Techniques for cyber resilience, cyber security, protecting the cyber infrastructure, cyber forensic and cyber crimes have been developed and deployed. Some of new solutions are nature-inspired and social-inspired leading to self-secure and self-defending systems. Despite the achievements, security and privacy, disaster management, social forensics, and anomalies/crimes detection are challenges within cyber-systems.

The conference had the following tracks:

- Cyber security
- Cyber infrastructure
- Cyber Attack Surfaces and the Interoperability of Architectural Application Domain Resiliency
- Embedded Systems for the Internet of Things
- Cyber resilience

We take here the opportunity to warmly thank all the members of the CYBER 2022 technical program committee, as well as all the reviewers. The creation of such a high quality conference program would not have been possible without their involvement. We also kindly thank all the authors that dedicated much of their time and effort to contribute to CYBER 2022. We truly believe that, thanks to all these efforts, the final conference program consisted of top quality contributions.

We also gratefully thank the members of the CYBER 2022 organizing committee for their help in handling the logistics and for their work that made this professional meeting a success.

We hope that CYBER 2022 was a successful international forum for the exchange of ideas and results between academia and industry and to promote further progress in the domain cyber technologies and cyber systems. We hope that Valencia provided a pleasant environment during the conference and everyone saved some time to enjoy the charm of the city.

CYBER 2022 General Chair

Steve Chan, Decision Engineering Analysis Laboratory, USA

CYBER 2022 Steering Committee

Carla Merkle Westphall, Federal University of Santa Catarina (UFSC), Brazil
Rainer Falk, Siemens AG, Corporate Technology, Germany
Anne Coull, University of New South Wales, Australia
Daniel Kästner, AbsInt GmbH, Germany
Barbara Re, University of Camerino, Italy
Soultana Ellinidou, Cybersecurity Research Center | University Libre de Bruxelles (ULB), Belgium
Patrik Österberg, Mid Sweden University, Sundsvall, Sweden
Steffen Fries, Siemens, Germany

CYBER 2022 Publicity Chair

Mar Parra, Universitat Politecnica de Valencia, Spain
Sandra Viciano Tudela, Universitat Politecnica de Valencia, Spain

CYBER 2022

COMMITTEE

CYBER 2022 General Chair

Steve Chan, Decision Engineering Analysis Laboratory, USA

CYBER Steering Committee

Carla Merkle Westphall, UFSC, Brazil
Rainer Falk, Siemens AG, Corporate Technology, Germany
Anne Coull, University of New South Wales, Australia
Daniel Kästner, AbsInt GmbH, Germany
Barbara Re, University of Camerino, Italy
Soultana Ellinidou, Cybersecurity Research Center | University Libre de Bruxelles (ULB), Belgium
Patrik Österberg, Mid Sweden University, Sundsvall, Sweden
Steffen Fries, Siemens, Germany

CYBER 2022 Publicity Chair

Mar Parra, Universitat Politecnica de Valencia, Spain
Sandra Viciano Tudela, Universitat Politecnica de Valencia, Spain

CYBER 2022 Technical Program Committee

Aysajan Abidin, imec-COSIC KU Leuven, Belgium
Shakil Ahmed, Iowa State University, USA
Cuneyt Gurcan Akcora, University of Manitoba, Canada
Oum-El-Kheir Aktouf, Grenoble Institute of Technology, France
Khalid Alemerien, Tafila Technical University, Jordan
Usman Ali, University of Connecticut, USA
Aisha Ali-Gombe, Towson University, USA
Mohammed S Alshehri, University of Arkansas, Fayetteville, USA
Alina Andronache, University of West of Scotland, UK
Abdullahi Arabo, University of the West of England, UK
A. Taufiq Asyhari, Coventry University, UK
Morgan Barbier, ENSICAEN, France
Sébastien Bardin, Université Paris-Saclay | CEA LIST, France
Samuel Bate, EY, UK
Vincent Beroulle, Univ. Grenoble Alpes, France
Clara Bertolissi, Aix-Marseille University | LIS | CNRS, France
Khurram Bhatti, Information Technology University (ITU), Lahore, Pakistan
Michael Black, University of South Alabama, USA
Davidson R. Boccardo, Clavis Information Security, Brazil
Ravi Borgaonkar, SINTEF Digital / University of Stavanger, Norway
Florent Bruguier, LIRMM | CNRS | University of Montpellier, France

Enrico Cambiaso, Consiglio Nazionale delle Ricerche (CNR), Italy
Nicola Capodieci, University of Modena and Reggio Emilia (UNIMORE), Italy
Pedro Castillejo Parrilla, Technical University of Madrid (UPM), Spain
Steve Chan, Decision Engineering Analysis Laboratory, USA
Christophe Charrier, Normandie Universite, France
Bo Chen, Michigan Technological University, USA
Mingwu Chen, Langara College, Canada
Lu Cheng, ArizonaState University, USA
Ioannis Chrysakis, FORTH-ICS, Greece / Ghent University, Belgium
Anastasija Collen, University of Geneva, Switzerland
Giovanni Costa, ICAR-CNR, Italy
Domenico Cotroneo, University of Naples, Italy
Anne Coull, University of New South Wales, Australia
Heming Cui, University of Hong Kong, Hong Kong
Monireh Dabaghchian, Morgan State University, USA
Dipanjan Das, University of California, Santa Barbara, USA
João Paulo de Brito Gonçalves, Instituto Federal do Espírito Santo, Brazil
Vincenzo De Angelis, University of Reggio Calabria, Italy
Lorenzo De Carli, Worcester Polytechnic Institute, USA
Noel De Palma, University Grenoble Alpes, France
Luigi De Simone, Università degli Studi di Napoli Federico II, Italy
Jerker Delsing, Lulea University of Technology, Sweden
Nicolás E. Díaz Ferreyra, University of Duisburg-Essen, Germany
Patrício Domingues, Polytechnic Institute of Leiria, Portugal
Paul Duplys, Robert Bosch GmbH, Germany
Soultana Ellinidou, Cybersecurity Research Center | University Libre de Bruxelles (ULB), Belgium
Rainer Falk, Siemens AG, Corporate Technology, Germany
Omair Faraj, Internet Interdisciplinary Institute (IN3) | UOC, Barcelona, Spain
Umer Farooq, Dhofar University, Slalalah, Oman
Yebo Feng, University of Oregon, USA
Eduardo B. Fernandez, Florida Atlantic University, USA
Steffen Fries, Siemens Corporate Technologies, Germany
Somchart Fugkeaw, Thammasat University, Thailand
Damjan Fujs, University of Ljubljana, Slovenia
Steven Furnell, University of Nottingham, UK
Gina Gallegos Garcia, Instituto Politécnico Nacional, Mexico
Huangyi Ge, Purdue University, USA
Kambiz Ghazinour, SUNY Canton, USA
Konstantinos Giannoutakis, University of Macedonia, Greece
Uwe Glässer, Simon Fraser University - SFU, Canada
Mehran Goli, The University of Bremen - Institute of Computer Science / German Research Centre for Artificial Intelligence (DFKI), Bremen, Germany
Ruy Jose Guerra Barretto de Queiroz, Federal University of Pernambuco, Brazil
Ekta Gujral, Walmart Global Tech, USA
Chunhui Guo, San Diego State University, USA
Amir M. Hajisadeghi, AmirkabirUniversity of Technology, Iran
Arne Hamann, Robert Bosch GmbH, Germany
Zecheng He, Princeton University, USA

Lorenzo Musarella, University Mediterranea of Reggio Calabria, Italy
Maria Mushtaq, LIRMM | Univ. Montpellier | CNRS, Montpellier, France
Vasudevan Nagendra, Stony Brook University, USA
Roberto Nardone, University Mediterranea of Reggio Calabria, Italy
Klimis Ntalianis, University of West Attica, Greece
Jason Nurse, University of Kent, UK
Riccardo Ortale, Institute for High Performance Computing and Networking (ICAR) of the National Research Council of Italy (CNR), Italy
Jordi Ortiz, University of Murcia, Spain
Patrik Österberg, Mid Sweden University, Sundsvall, Sweden
Richard E. Overill, King's College London, UK
Antonio Pecchia, University of Sannio, Italy
Eckhard Pfluegel, Kingston University, London, UK
Mila Dalla Preda, University of Verona, Italy
Muhammad Haris Rais, Virginia Commonwealth University, USA
Paweł Rajba, Hitachi Energy / University of Wroclaw, Poland
Massimiliano Rak, Università della Campania, Italy
Ramesh Rakesh, Hitachi India Private Limited, India
Alexander Rasin, DePaul University, USA
Danda B. Rawat, Howard University, USA
Barbara Re, University of Camerino, Italy
Antonio J. Reinoso, Alfonso X University, Spain
Leon Reznik, Rochester Institute of Technology, USA
Jan Richling, South Westphalia University of Applied Sciences, Germany
Giulio Rigoni, University of Florence / University of Perugia, Italy
Andres Robles Durazno, Edinburgh Napier University, UK
Antonia Russo,University Mediterranea of Reggio Calabria, Italy
Peter Y. A. Ryan, UniversityofLuxembourg, Luxembourg
Asanka P. Sayakkara, University of Colombo School of Computing (UCSC), Sri Lanka
Florence Sedes, Université Toulouse 3 Paul Sabatier, France
Abhijit Sen, Kwantlen Polytechnic University, Canada
Shirin Haji Amin Shirazi, University of California, Riverside, USA
Luisa Siniscalchi, Aarhus University, Denmark
Daniel Spiekermann, Polizeiakademie Niedersachsen, Germany
Srivathsan Srinivasagopalan, AT&T CyberSecurity (Alien Labs), USA
Ciza Thomas, Government of Kerala, India
Zisis Tsiatsikas, Atos Greece / University of the Aegean, Greece
Tobias Urban, Institute for Internet Security - Westphalian University of Applied Sciences, Gelsenkirchen, Germany
Eric MSP Veith, OFFIS e.V. - Institut für Informatik, Germany
Simon Vrhovec, University of Maribor, Slovenia
Stefanos Vrochidis, ITI-CERTH, Greece
James Wagner, University of New Orleans, USA
Khan Ferdous Wahid, Airbus Digital Trust Solutions, Germany
Gang Wang, Emerson Automation Solutions, USA
Ruoyu "Fish" Wang, Arizona State University, USA
Zhiyong Wang, Utrecht University, Netherlands
Zhen Xie, JD.com American Technologies Corporation, USA

Copyright Information

Security Analysis of Embedded Systems Using Virtual Prototyping

Yasamin Mahmoodi
Forschungszentrum Informatik
Haid-und-Neu-Str. 10-14
D-76131 Karlsruhe, Germany
mahmoodi@fzi.de

Sebastian Reiter
Forschungszentrum Informatik
Haid-und-Neu-Str. 10-14
D-76131 Karlsruhe, Germany
sreiter@fzi.de

Alexsander Viehl
Forschungszentrum Informatik
Haid-und-Neu-Str. 10-14
D-76131 Karlsruhe, Germany
viehl@fzi.de

Oliver Bringmann
Universität Tübingen
Sand 13 72076 Tübingen, Germany
bringman@informatik.uni-tuebingen.de

***Abstract*—Connected embedded systems have a significant role in modern life. Prominent benefits of this new concept and how it eases our life is irrefutable. However, as this technology provides users remote connection, it opens new opportunities for attackers to get access to the system and perform malicious activities. In order to get full benefits of connected embedded systems, security should be considered during system design. As a proposed approach to produce secure embedded systems, we offer a comprehensive attitude based on security by design concept. The proposed solution is inspired by Secure System Development Life Cycle (SSDLC) models and employs virtual prototyping to present an early security evaluation during development process of embedded systems.**

Keywords: Security analysis; IoT; Security requirement; Virtual prototyping; Security-by-design.

I. Introduction

Embedded systems are an essential part of modern life. Transportation systems, from automotive to airplanes, increasingly apply embedded system to elevate performance and comfort. Medical instruments, on the other hand, profit from embedded systems for monitoring applications. Smart home is another area in which embedded systems showed up to offer light and temperature controlling, pet and baby care, smart kitchen and many other applications. Connected embedded systems including connected automobiles, connected smart homes and wearable technology bring up the capability of remote monitoring and functioning.

Alongside the distinguished roll of connected embedded systems in our modern life, security challenges which may be turned up by these new technologies should be considered. Security flaws in embedded systems may lead to privacy and financial problems or endanger people's life. A vulnerability in embedded systems may give attacker the opportunity to access critical information and perform malicious activities.

In order to make a profit of outstanding advantages of connected embedded systems, security measures should be considered during design and development phases. Security by design [1] is a proper solution, which helps system designers produce the system from the ground up to be secure. In this method, security aspects of the system will be considered in the entire life cycle of system development, from system specification and modeling to system development and assembly. Corresponding to each development phase, several test and analyses will be considered. As the ultimate destination, penetration testing on the final product will take place. Therefore, security considerations should play an equal role in system development process alongside functional and usability features.

As a solution, we propose a comprehensive model-centric methodology to consider and evaluate security during the design process in the form of a Virtual Prototype (VP). The approach offers automated security consideration which enables early architectural analyses and provides preparation of penetration testing by architectural analyses, as well as searching for already known weaknesses.

In recent years, virtual prototyping has been applied in system development process in the automotive industry and other industrial products. In this area, virtual prototyping is applied as a platform for software development, architecture modeling as well as system implementation. We believe that virtual prototyping has the capability to play a significant role in security analysis and security assurance for embedded system design. A VP represents the preliminary stage of a physical prototype in the design process and denotes the complete or partial provision of system sub-components as executable models. With VP, different security analyses such as penetration testing or structural analyses, including dynamic data flow analyses during the design and development process are possible.

The paper is structured as follows: Section II highlights previous works which focus on secure system development approaches. Section III introduces considering security during design and development phases of embedded systems development cycle. The proposed solution in order to design and develop secure embedded systems is explained in Section IV. In Section V, techniques and methods to support the proposed framework are mentioned. Finally, in Section VI, a conclusion of the paper is presented.

II. Related work

Current system development approaches, such as [2] and [3] do not consider security features in system design and development life cycle. Several works [4], [5] integrated security considerations into development life cycle; However, these works are limited to software systems and embedded systems features are still missing.

MILS (Multiple Independent Levels of Security) platform introduced in [6] is based on security by design approach which break the system into partitions and defines partition categories based on their criticality. The focus of this work is on system architecture and does not offer security consideration for all development steps. ESSAF (Embedded System Security Assessment Framework) [7] offers collaborative security assessment in embedded systems development. The focus of this work is to document the assets, threats and security mechanisms. Security evaluation of the embedded systems is divided into tree phases, System Modeling, Security Modeling and Mitigation Planning. ESSAF provides a well defined documentation approach for security evaluation of embedded systems during design and development phases. Yet, no mechanism is offered to cover hardware features during security assessment.

In [8], a secure-by-design process for cyber-physical systems is represented which integrated secure software engineering practices into a discipline spanning engineering process for cyber-physical systems. In this paper, the authors added platform-independent features to security requirements in software design processes in order to consider hardware characteristics of the system. Threat models, misuse case and anti-requirements with platform consideration are added to the existing model-based system engineering. However, lack of a comprehensive security assessment during the system development life cycle, from requirement specification to the final prototype development is visible.

[9] suggests a design methodology to integrate and evaluate security mechanisms into design process of embedded systems. In this paper security requirements are defined, then suitable security mechanisms based on the requirements will be offered and evaluated. The results of security mechanisms integration are assessed based on proper metrics. However, comprehensive evaluation during all design and development phases is not consider in this work.

To sum up, several works focus on security evaluation of embedded systems. It should be mentioned that most of them do not consider security analysis during design and development life cycle. However, a few approaches which bring security evaluation into development cycle do not offer comprehensive approaches. More important, the gap between current development state and final system prototype is noticeable in most of the works. To be specific, at each step of design and development, evaluation and tests will take place only on parts of the system which are already developed and characteristics of physical parts of the system are missing. This issue specially for embedded systems which lay on hardware environment is important.

III. Security by design

Security by design is a methodology which offers considering security features during all design and development phases of the systems, from planing phase and requirement analysis to final prototype. Secure System Development Life Cycle (SSDLC) [10] as security by design technique integrates security measures throughout design and development cycle and brings up security assessment corresponded to each development step [11]. SSDLC is in fact adapted version of traditional System Development Life Cycle (SDLC), which includes security assessment capability.

Several models for SDLC are presented and each model traces a set of phases unique to its type to ensure expected outcomes in system development process. Waterfall model, agile model, V-shaped model, iterative model, Spiral Model and big bang model [2] are some of the popular techniques for SDLC. V-shaped model and iterative model draw our attention as potential models to offer security during design and development phases of the system. V-shaped model at very first step of system design starts with planing and requirement specification and goes deeper with high level design, then low level design and the final implementation. In this model, corresponding to each design and implementation phase a set of tests is considered. On the other hand, iterative model begins with implementation of a simplified version of the system and at each iteration add more details to it until the implemented system is sophisticated enough to ensure the requirements. In this model, at the end of each iteration developed system will be tested and refined.

By addressing security measures to the SDLC pipeline, security evaluation will be presented from the outset. Proposed security analysis approach is inspired by V-shaped and iterative model to offer security by design for embedded systems. V-shaped model makes a profit of mapping development phases to test packages and iterative model suggests refinement after each iteration. Bringing both models into practice enhances security by design approach.

IV. Proposed approach

We offer an analysis process based on virtual prototyping to support comprehensive security evaluation of connected embedded systems. The process enables security assessment of the system, security mechanisms estimation and architectural evaluation of the system under development and supports the designers to make efficient design decisions during the design phases. The presented approach closes the gap between initial design and security tests on the final prototype. It enables applying abstract models in preliminary design stages to evaluate rough security aspects of the system. During the design process the model is refined and will be more accurate. Each refinement step provides the opportunity to perform associated security analyses of the current design phase. When software prototypes are developed it is possible to attach and assess them in combination with the simulated parts of the system. The virtual prototype of the system is beneficial even when the physical prototype is ready. Monitoring internal states of the system when the complete system is halted in physical prototype is cost and time intensive in comparison to virtual prototype.

Envisioned design flow

Figure 1 represents the proposed approach for security analysis of embedded systems during system development phases. The generic idea lays on the security-based V-model. It also inherits the iterations from iterative model for system development. Exploring overall view of the framework at a glance, comparable to V-model system design begins at very abstract level on the left side and passes through the next steps by defining more detail to the design until producing final prototype. At the right side of the flow, set of security evaluation and tests corresponding to the development level is defined. It follows a sequential design process on the vertical axe and system verification is planned in parallel with a corresponding stage of development in horizontal manner. Security specifications of the system present validation factors for the security analyses through the design process. In an overall view, after defining security requirements this framework follows several phases in a vertical axe starting from top. Each phases consists of three steps in horizontal axe which starts with design and development on the left side, performs tests and compares the results with validation factors on right side.

After specifying security requirements of the system, modeling phase is the next step. For this phase of system design, we defined an approach to assure that design decisions are consistent with security requirements. At the end of each analysis on the right side of the flow the results will be compared with the validation factors. Moving forward to the design flow happens only when the results of the current analyses pass validation factors. Otherwise the next iteration will begin from top of the flow. Each iteration starts with requirements specification, refines the model to resolve security weaknesses and as long as passes the requirements validation, proceeds through design progress.

Each iteration not only is sophisticated enough to perform corresponding analyses of the current abstraction level, but also provides information for penetration testing of the final virtual/ physical prototype. Information such as potential attack vectors as well as the must be protected assets extracted from models of the system can be considered as guidelines to steer penetration tests. Dynamic and static analyses on the architectural design on the other hand sound the alarm of hidden dependencies and potential vulnerabilities for penetration testers.

Subsequently, each part of the presented framework will be explained in this order: Security specification, Model designing and evaluation, architectural design and assessment, software analysis and penetration testing as the final goal.

At the first step system designers will define security requirements and specifications. To carry out this phase, system designers may discus with stakeholders about their prospect security features of the system. Security specifications in this phase may vary from general features to well detailed requirements. The outputs here are utilizable for security validation in next phases. Well specified security features and requirements come up with more precise specification validation for next steps.

In the next step designing phase will be started from very abstract level with modeling. The first model of the system will be sketched considering security requirements. The modules and their relations, data type and methods of the modules as well as required hardware and software for the system will be specified here. At the end the model will be augmented with security features and mechanisms. We defined a security profile which helps the designers to integrate security relates information to the model [12]. Specification validation is the next step of this phase which applies the output of modeling analyses and assesses security measure of the system based on the specification from the first phase. If the specification validation passes the expected standards, the development process can proceed through the layout. Otherwise, the next iteration will be launched.

In the next phase, designers will design a secure architecture for the system. Accomplishing this objective, an abstract model of system architecture will be simulated with the help of architectural modeling techniques such as Transaction Level Modeling (TLM). More detail will be added to the system model from previous phase and the transaction between the modules will be simulated. This phase carries on the procedure by a static/ dynamic analysis threat modeling to find out data dependencies and potential threats. Threat models will be facilitator in the next phases for the penetration testing. Based on the results of the analyses, specification validation step will check if defined security specifications are endangered. If not, the next iteration will be started and the model will be modified. Otherwise, designers can go to the next phase.

When software prototype is available, thanks to the Virtual prototyping it can be attached to the simulated parts of the system in order to perform analyses. In this way, we not only can perform penetration testing on the solid software, but also try to penetrate the software which is laid on simulated hardware. The output of the penetration testing will be compared with the security specifications and based on the results, designers decide to launch the next iteration or go to the next phase.

The final goal in this process is to integrate the software to the real hardware and perform penetration tests on the final prototype. This phase helps the developers to analyze final prototype and resolve the last security flaws before producing the product in the huge amount. Even in this phase that physical prototype is available, applying virtual prototype to

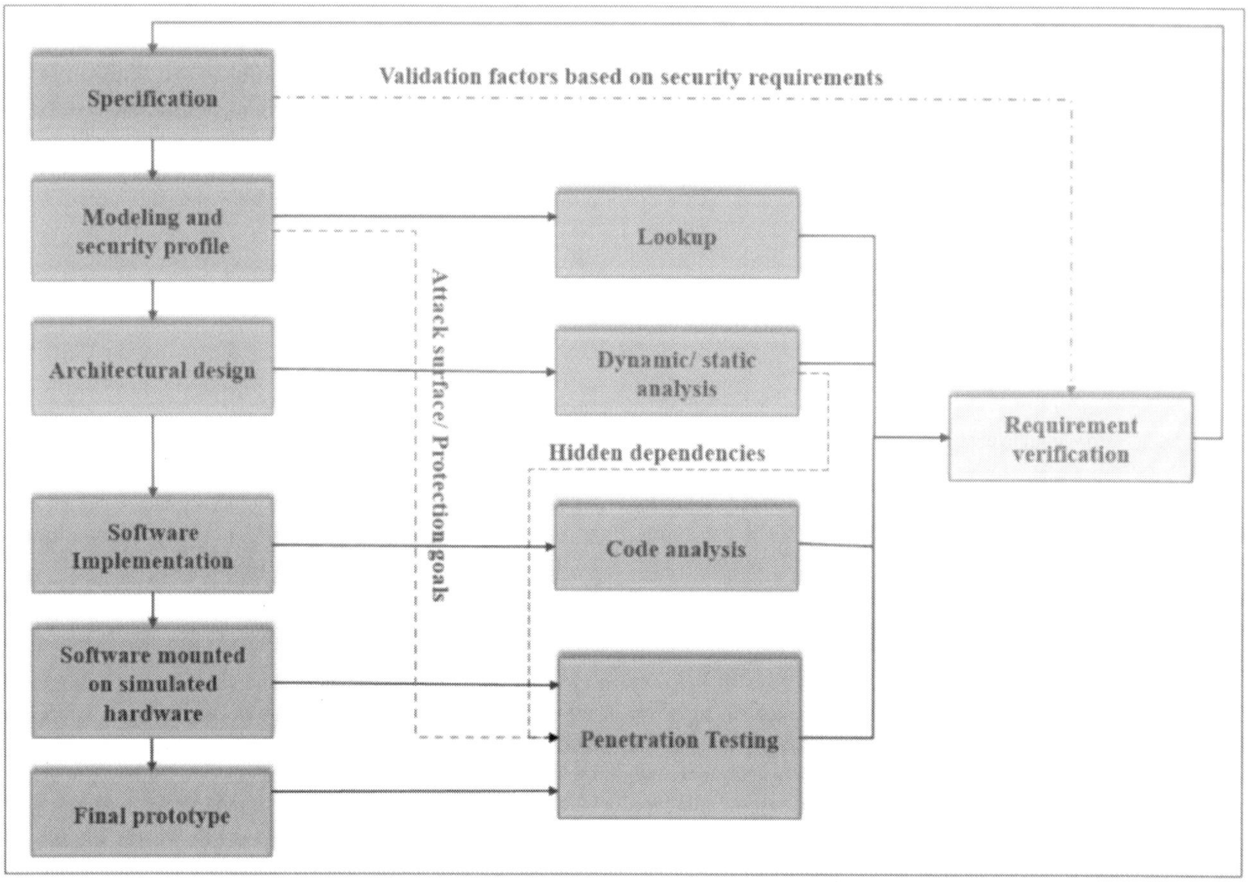

Fig. 1. Proposed approach

perform the tests in several situation has benefit over physical prototype. In the scenarios which may lead to crash the whole system or may damage parts of the system, monitoring behavior of the system on virtual environment has advantage over system evaluation in physical prototype.

V. IMPLEMENTATION

In order to support presented security analysis framework, several techniques are offered. As mentioned earlier, specifying security requirements plays an important role in designing secure systems. By a well defined security specification stakeholders, designers and security experts are able to properly address their desires. We propose three-step method to specify and manage security requirements from coarse system aspects to detailed technical features. As the next step in our security analysis approach, supporting modeling, a security profile based on UML (Unified Modeling Language) with the focus on connected embedded systems are offered which goes along with a look-up function to search in vulnerability databases to find vulnerable parts of the system. Architectural analysis of the system is the next step in our proposed process and in order to bring it into practice, we applied SystemC to simulate the system in TLM (Transaction-Level Modeling) level, afterward taint propagation analysis as a dynamic analysis technique is employed. As the last step we employed output results of previous parts to provide information for guided penetration testing on the final virtual and physical prototypes. In the following, the applied techniques are described in detailed.

A. Security Specification

Requirement specification is the entry point of a system development process. Following section explains the proposed approach for a consistent and guided security requirements modeling. We provide a three-step requirement modeling, which supports system designers to define security requirements from general specifications to fine-grained system architecture's security features. At very first steps of design process, security specification starts with general security aspects of the system. As the design process goes into more detail, security requirements will be shaped more clear and go to detailed categories. The requirement modeling concludes with a detailed specifications and assign security information such as protection goals (assets and data which should be protected from attackers) and attack surface (points of the system which may offer access to the system for potential attackers) to single entities in the system. The revealed information in last step is advantageous for architectural analysis as well as penetration testing. Because this last step should ensure a seamless transition into the system development process, we applied it to a traditional UML modeling approach by a developed security profile.

As mentioned, the first step in security specification brings up general questions about security issues regarding the system. The stakeholders discuss about their desire system with the system designers as well as with security experts to make a security checklist. Questions such as What are the important parts of the system which should be protected from attackers, Who are the potential attackers, Which security measures are needed and so on should be answered during security requirement analysis. The answers to these questions give an overall perspective about the security aspects of the system. However, this information is qualitative and subjective and in order to apply this knowledge to design and development process, well-defined classifications and security metrics are needed.

In the second step of security specification, protection goals and potential attack surfaces of the system will be derived and categorized in the three classes of the CIA triad: Confidentiality, Integrity, Availability. To illustrate, confidentiality for assets refers to system properties which should be protected in order to assure their confidentiality. On the other hand, confidentiality in attack surface discloses parts of the system which are potential attack point to endanger confidentiality of the system. From this general specification, all relevant information will be extracted in the next step.

The last step maps the information from the second layer about security requirements to a well-defined schema. The goal is to map detailed security information to system architecture. Accordingly, several fine-grained categories as well as parameters are defined which fulfil system architecture with well-defined information about assets and potential attack vectors. Figure 2 depicts proposed security requirement method in three levels.

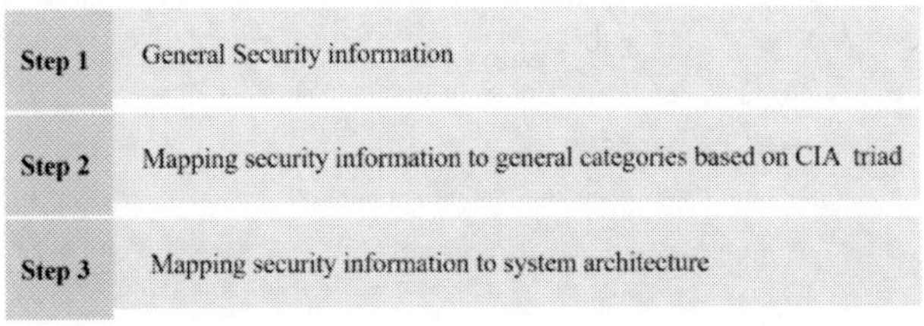

Fig. 2. Three steps of proposed security requirement analysis model

B. Security specification modeling

Presented model-based specification describes the system to be analyzed structurally, safety concepts and security mechanisms, attack surface, as well as protection targets. The modeling is also used for documentation of the analyses. The specified information is automatically integrated into the analysis to reduce the manual effort for the user. In this section, we highlight a modeling approach used to guide the security analysis with VPs. We use UML as modeling language. The goal is to have a well-defined, easy-to-handle user interface to manage the analysis and document the system's security features. In addition, the model eases manual analyses, such as penetration testing, by enhancing the documentation and highlighting potential design flaws.

As Figure 3 shows, the proposed model-based security analysis approach consists of two components: Graphical modeling environment, which is composed of UML models augmented with security features as a security profile and a lookup function which can be connected to a vulnerability database. This approach enables the designer to refine security requirements in the same development environment as the system design. Our proposed security modeling approach provides models for security requirements of the system and helps to discover the inherent weak points of the system architecture or chosen implementations by specifying the protection goals of the system, potential attack points as well as additional security related documentation.

Our presented security profile offers three categories of stereotypes and tags to add security-related information to the model. The first category consists of five stereotypes and related tags which help the designers to mention protection goals on the model. Second category suggests five stereotypes and their related tags to add information about potential attack vectors to the model. Finally, with the aim of offering documentation-based information such as indicated security mechanisms and software version our last category of stereotypes is suggested. The proposed security profile can be attached to the UML models to entitle the information about protection goals and assets, weak points and attack surfaces, as well as documentation-based information. These models can later on be beneficial for validation, e.g., with static analysis and vulnerability assessment. In addition, the model simplifies manual analysis, such as penetration testing, by boosting the documentation and helps identifying underlying potential design flaws, e.g., by enabling an automatic lookup in well known security vulnerability databases.

Drawing the advantage of documentation-based information form presented security profile, our model-based security analysis approach offers connection to vulnerability data bases which provide latest discovered security vulnerabilities for embedded systems. We presented this function in our lookup function. Vulnerability database describes vulnerabilities, affected assets, and the solutions to mitigate the issue. There are several vulnerability databases such as as the ISS (Internet Security Systems) X-Force database [13], Symantec / SecurityFocus BID (Bugtraq ID) database, and the Open Source Vulnerability Database (OSVDB) [14] which aggregated a broad range of publicly disclosed vulnerabilities, including Common Vulnerabilities and Exposures (CVE) [15]. CVE, run by MITRE collects vulnerabilities and puts them in a standard format. for the sake of connection to up-to-date vulnerability databases, the influence of design decisions on the actual system will be evaluated in very early stages.

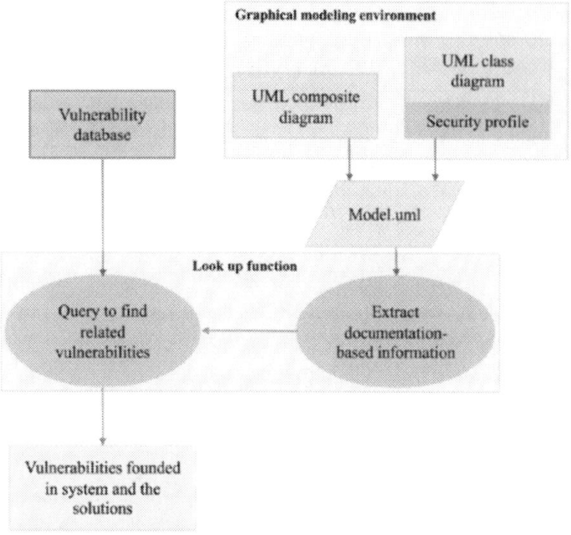

Fig. 3. Proposed modeling environment

Clarifying lookup function, security-related information will be extracted from the security profile and the function searches for probable vulnerabilities in vulnerability database based on this information. Information such handshaking protocols, applied cryptography methods, Encryption protocols and software version enables finding potential vulnerabilities based on published vulnerabilities and exposures. The designers will be able to find out vulnerable parts of the system at modeling phase and to rectify the model to sketch secure layout for the system.

C. *System Architectural Analysis*

System architecture is an important aspect in the design of trustworthy systems. We can develop security level by means of a suitable architecture and thus logical structuring, even in early development phases. The proposed approach offers system architecture assessment in design phases and as a result, prevents architectural weaknesses. However, in embedded systems design and development, hardware is only available at the latest phase.

With the help of abstract virtual prototypes, which represent the architecture of the system to be developed and target-platform-specific IP components, analyses for architectural security issues are to be carried out. Due to the fact that the virtual prototypes describe the hardware / software structure in a software-based model, analyses which have traditionally been applied to the pure software evaluation can now be applied to the virtual total systems (hardware / software). There are methods such as Dynamic Taint Propagation or Symbolic Evaluation. By applying these methods on VPs, analyses that are currently used for input validation and filtering in software implementations are used for hardware architecture analysis e.g. to inspect gateways or controllers.

The aim of this section is to verify the effectiveness of security models such as access rules, input validation, or filtering of potentially counterfeit messages. This means that correctly functioning security mechanisms are adopted and modeled and their correct use verified in this type of analysis. From the point of view of system architecture, for example, the effectiveness of compartmentalization, the separation of critical and uncritical system parts, is to be checked. Several techniques such as static and dynamic analysis in this step facilitate architectural assessment of the system. In static analysis methodology the source code will be assessed at rest in order to detect security flaws such as input validation, numerical errors, path traversals, and race conditions. Dynamic analysis procedure on the other hand assesses the application during run time with the focus of detecting conditions during which the application can be exploited. Various tools and techniques are offered in these areas which let security experts find out security condition of the software. As a capable method, we offer taint propagation analysis [16] to perform dynamic analysis on the simulated system.

1) Simulation approach in virtual prototype framework: The presented approach uses a subset of the UML to specify VP and its security analysis related information. In this section, the link between modeling and VP should be described. An overview is given in Figure 4. The simulated model is generated from this specification. The simulation contains all system components required for one simulation run. This simulated model is compiled and for each simulation run a configuration file is given that determines the simulation instance. This configuration file is again generated from the UML-based model-based VP specification. Different security analyses, such as dynamic data flow analysis or manual penetration testing are based on the executable simulation.

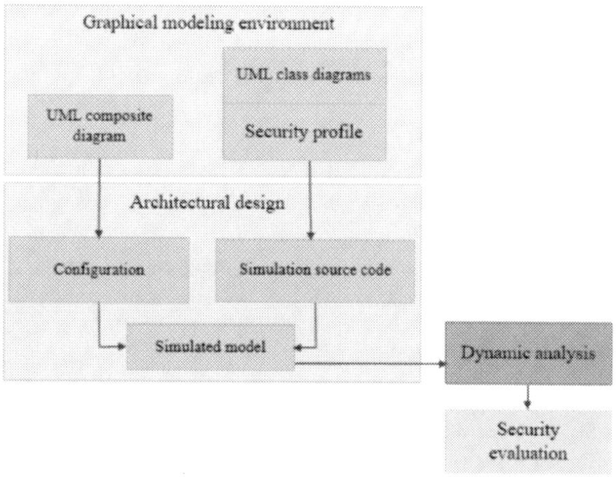

Fig. 4. Modeling framework for the VP-based security analysis

The presented approach uses event-driven SystemC [17] simulation language, a standardized modeling language with a lot of EDA (Electronic Design Automation) vendor tools support. SystemC covers different abstraction levels of hardware and software systems and enables both the modeling of software applications as well as digital/analog electronic components. SystemC provides abstract TLM to specify the interaction of system components and enables a very early structural analyses of the complete system.

As SystemC is a C++ class library it is possible to integrate actual application code that is compatible with C++. This reduces the overhead required to create the VP and enables the analysis of the actual implementation. Flaws can be found that would lead to security vulnerabilities. The overall goal is to execute security analyses combined with risk assessment.

D. Penetration Testing

By the time that final software is available, testing pure software will be started. Several software security analysis techniques with the purpose of vulnerability detection may be performed in this phase. An appropriate software test is structured around elements such as the risks, assets, potential threats and vulnerabilities. Our evaluation framework facilitates software analysis by providing needed information extracted from previous steps.

However, the advantages of presented framework are not limited to pure software testing; Instead, the framework proposes significant gain by offering security analysis for the software in combination with simulated hardware. Integrating already developed software into the virtual prototype offers an overall view of the system in a way that general penetration testing will be possible.

In order to perform a successful penetration testing the following six phases are critical: Recognition, Scanning, Gaining access, Maintaining access, Exploitation, Clean up and Reporting

Security analyses performed in previous stages of presented evaluation framework, in addition to major benefits in reaching efficient design decisions in early stages, propose information to guide final penetration testing. The rest of this section is devoted to describe penetration testing phases separately and to represent how proposed approach provide information to these steps.

1) Recognition: In recognition phase penetration testers try to get as much information about the target as possible. Information such as the scope of the system, network and interconnection architecture as well as the software and hardware features should be extracted.

Our proposed approach offers comprehensive and well-defined information to penetration testers. Proposed security requirement specification sidelong system requirement specification gives general information about the system, potential attackers, data and assets which should be protected and desired security features. Our security profile on the other hand with its documentation-based information offers knowledge about the software, encryption algorithms as well as other security mechanisms such as authentication and authorization methods.

2) Scanning: In scanning step, testers try to identify vulnerabilities of the target. Scanning the network with scanning tools, identification of open share drives and running services are the measures which will take place in this phase. static and dynamic analysis alongside vulnerability scanners are powerful techniques to detect vulnerabilities.

Presented security requirement specification, modeling approach and architectural analysis offer information as guideline to find vulnerabilities. Attack surfaces give testers the first impression about weaknesses as entry point to penetrate the system. On the other hand, protection goals mentioned in the model, guide testers to concentrate on the assets with essential data or the services which should be available all the time as the target of attack. Lookup function reveals known vulnerabilities for chosen software or protocols. By detecting any know vulnerability in modeling phase designers modify the model in early stages before penetration testing; However the information extracted from know vulnerabilities give direction to tester to find more vulnerabilities. Further considerations for the testers derive from architectural analysis to sound the alarm about hidden dependencies and possible track between attack point and the targets.

3) Gaining access: Once the weaknesses are identified, the next step is gaining access to the system by exploiting vulnerabilities. It should be mentioned that not all of detected vulnerabilities are exploitable and the ones which are vulnerable enough to provide the access into the target should be identified. Integrating already available software with simulated hardware will be the first detailed development of the system which proposes the chance to penetrate the prototype. In this step the entry points to the system, authentication and authorization mechanisms and the security protocols are developed in the software. The network, the hardware as the environment to mount the software and all the connections is simulated now. By performing tests on this virtual prototype weaknesses of the system as entry points for unauthorized user will be disclosed.

4) Maintaining access: Maintaining access as the next step of penetration testing is possible on the final virtual prototype by rebooting, resetting or modifying the system to find out if the access will be maintained under different conditions.

5) Exploitation: Exploitation phase is the point that actual damage to the system will be brought up. When the penetration testers attain access to inside of the compromised system, they try to promote their access privilege within the environment, subsequently performing any number of additional actions. With the administrative privilege the testers are able to find security weaknesses in other areas and resources, such as weak connections, unguarded access to critical data, implementation's weakness in gateway and control devices which interfere on several buses and inner network or ineffective account or password management. Final virtual prototype presents an environment for the penetration tester to exploit the system without concerning about the potential expensive damage to the system. Simulating time behavior of virtual prototype helps to evaluate the system under timing-related attacks such as denial of services. By integrating product-related software prototypes, implementation errors or weak points, such as incorrect, insufficient checking of value ranges, use of copy operations without validated, fixed upper limits can be checked. Further implementation aspects such as the use or generation of random values, e.g. in the case of key streams in stream ciphers, can be analyzed. Sometimes, the mechanism used is fundamentally correct, but implementation weaknesses, such as reuse of generated random values, reduce the effectiveness of applied mechanisms. Other aspects of the system security model can only be verified with the presence of the partially manually optimized binary code. These include, for example, buffer overflows with effects on the stack structure and change of return addresses. Virtual prototype as the latest step of this approach assists security analysts to evaluate these features.

6) Clean up and Reporting: Once the penetration testing is completed, the tester will find a way to clear any evidence and trace of compromising the victim system including event logs in order to remain anonymous. Eventually, as the final goal of the penetration testing, a detailed report will be written. Detailed information about vulnerabilities, sensitive data accessed during the test, complexity and the amount of the time to exploit an asset and the way to delete the evidences should be reported in this step. Well-defined information in a standard manner which will be comprehensible to designers is beneficial to refine the design. With the help of proposed three steps for security specifications, security profile in modeling environment as well as offered solutions for known vulnerabilities this intention will be achievable.

VI. Conclusion

In this paper, we applied virtual prototyping to present a security by design approach with the intention of security assessment in each design and development phase. This approach is based on two SSDLC models: V-shaped model and iterative model. The proposed framework gains benefits from both V-model and iterative model of SDLC, however provides advantages over applying each of the models separately. Design and development process takes place in sequential manner from very abstract level to detailed developed product. It also derives a benefit of verification and validation perspective of V-model by providing a associated testing phase for each corresponding development stage. Proposed framework inherits the iterations from iterative model. However unlike the iterative model, in each iteration as well as the requirements are satisfied development process goes further into design flow and more detail will be added.

Yet, the strength of the presented approach is based on employing virtual prototyping to fill the gaps between already designed and developed system modules at each step and final prototype. Virtual prototyping supports simulation in different abstraction levels; moreover, it offers detailed simulation as the final prototype. These features in combination with SDLC models enable system designers to evaluate design decisions at very early stages, to analyze system architecture from security point of view, to perform penetration testing way before that physical prototype is ready and as a result present a cost and time efficient approach. This approach has profits even when the final physical prototype is ready. Sometimes, performing tests on physical prototype may damage parts of or even the entire system. In these situations final virtual prototype could be a practical alternative to prevent loss during the tests.

Acknowledgement

This research is partially funded by the German Federal Ministry of Education and Research (BMBF) within the project COMPACT (grant number 01|S17028C) and project Scale4Edge (grant number 16ME0126).

References

[1] L. A. Bygrave, "Security by design: Aspirations and realities in a regulatory context," *Oslo Law Review*, no. 3, pp. 126–177, 2022.

[2] M. A. Rather and M. V. Bhatnagar, "A comparative study of software development life cycle models," *International Journal of Application or Innovation in Engineering & Management (IJAIEM)*, vol. 4, no. 10, pp. 23–29, 2015.

[3] K. Pohl, M. Broy, H. Daembkes, and H. Hönninger, "Advanced model-based engineering of embedded systems," in *Advanced Model-Based Engineering of Embedded Systems*. Springer, 2016, pp. 3–9.

[4] N. M. Mohammed, M. Niazi, M. Alshayeb, and S. Mahmood, "Exploring software security approaches in software development lifecycle: A systematic mapping study," *Computer Standards & Interfaces*, vol. 50, pp. 107–115, 2017.

[5] M. U. A. Khan and M. Zulkernine, "Quantifying security in secure software development phases," in *2008 32nd Annual IEEE International Computer Software and Applications Conference*. IEEE, 2008, pp. 955–960.

[6] S. Tverdyshev, "Security by design: Introduction to mils," in *MILS*, 2017.

[7] F. Köster, M. Klaas, H. Q. Nguyen, W. Brenner, M. Brändle, and S. Obermeier, "Collaborative security assessments in embedded systems development," *NSTICC Pr.*, 2009.

[8] J. Geismann, C. Gerking, and E. Bodden, "Towards ensuring security by design in cyber-physical systems engineering processes," in *Proceedings of the 2018 international conference on software and system process*, 2018, pp. 123–127.

[9] A. Ferrante, J. Milosevic, and M. Janjušević, "A security-enhanced design methodology for embedded systems," in *2013 International Conference on Security and Cryptography (SECRYPT)*. IEEE, 2013, pp. 1–12.

[10] E. Mougoue, "What is the secure software development life cycle (sdlc)?— synopsys," 2016. [Online]. Available: https://www.synopsys.com/blogs/software-security/secure-sdlc/

[11] M. E. Whitman and H. J. Mattord, "Principles of information security, course technology," *Google Scholar Google Scholar Digital Library*, 2012.

[12] Y. Mahmoodi, S. Reiter, A. Viehl, O. Bringmann, and W. Rosenstiel, "Model-guided security analysis of interconnected embedded systems." in *MODELSWARD*, 2018, pp. 602–609.

[13] Ibm internet security systems. x-force. [Online]. Available: https://www.ibm.com/x-force

[14] Open source vulnerability database. [Online]. Available: http://www.osvdb.org

[15] Cve list. [Online]. Available: http://cve.mitre.org/

[16] M. G. Kang, S. McCamant, P. Poosankam, and D. Song, "Dta++: dynamic taint analysis with targeted control-flow propagation." in *NDSS*, 2011.

[17] I. S. Association *et al.*, "Standard systemc language reference manual," *IEEE Std*, pp. 1666–2011, 2011.

Mitigating Against a Succession of Hidden Failure Accelerants Involved in an Insider Threat Sequential Topology Attack on a Smart Grid

Devising a Defensive Paradigm via a Bespoke Convolutional Adversarial Neural Network Module and Particle Swarm Optimization-based Enhanced Reinforcement Learning Component

Steve Chan
Decision Engineering Analysis Laboratory, VTIRL, VT
Orlando, USA
e-mail: schan@dengineering.org

Abstract—**Protection System Hidden Failures (PSHF)-induced sequential events have been shown to have higher impact and greater likelihood of segueing to major outages. Hence, a pragmatic mitigation approach is to intercede in the outage-related successive event stream. From a cyber perspective, as pertains to the power grid, PSHF are comparable to a Zero-Day attack (a.k.a. "0-Day"); accordingly, adequate mitigation is not yet in place. This problem is particularly interesting because of the involved paradox; although widely accepted to be comparable to a 0-Day, some form of apriori architected mitigation is crucial so as to prevent a major outage. This can be construed as contributory toward resiliency. Accordingly, a pseudo-inverse approach is taken to the optimal controllability problem (in this case, non-optimal controllability is sought, particularly in the case of an Insider Threat Paradigm or ITP) as a form of mitigation. In essence, the maximal optimum Control Signal Energy Cost ($CSEC_{opt}$) and reduction of the diffusion of malicious Control Signals (CS) and/or Augmented CS (ACS) is sought. The described problem space is non-trivial, as Efficient Controllability Problems (ECP) have been shown to exhibit Non-deterministic Polynomial-time Hardness (NP-Hard), and likewise, countermeasure non-ECP are NP-Hard. This paper advances matters by leveraging a bespoke Machine Learning (ML) paradigm, comprised of a multi-Convolutional Adversarial Neural Network (CANN) Module and Particle Swarm Optimization (PSO)-based Enhanced Reinforcement Learning (RL) Component (ERLC), to better orchestrate Defensive Circuit Breakers (DCB) and leverage ML-based Protection Relay Selection (MLPRS) for more optimal Defensive Grid Re-configuration (DGR) so as to better obviate a PSHF-based ITP Sequential Topology Attack (STA). Although previously thought to be a High-Impact, Low-Frequency (HILF) event, PSHF studies have shown that the associated distribution has an unusually fat tail; by endeavoring to reduce the fat tail, a principal contribution of this paper is to lessen the impact of the involved event.**

Keywords-Cyber; supply chain vulnerability; insider threat; zero-day type vulnerabilities; hidden defects/failures; protection system hidden failure; sequential topology attack; cascading failure; blackout; resiliency; control signal energy cost; artificial intelligence; machine learning; reinforcement learning.

I. INTRODUCTION

Despite the numerous advancements in power grid protection systems, in many cases, these systems have constituted the actual problem and caused cascading failures resulting in power outages; in essence, they induced undesired effects in the very power grids they were tasked to protect. To further this irony, Protection System Hidden Failures (PSHF) are now recognized as a key amplification factor and cause of several recent major disturbances and outages. Although previously thought to be a High-Impact, Low-Frequency (HILF) event, PSHF studies now show that the associated distribution has an unusually fat tail; in essence, the frequency of manifestation has been much higher than its current classification. Some PSHF researchers construe the paradigm to actually be Very High-Impact, Medium-Frequency (VHIMF) events. To compound this issue, for contemporary times, wherein cybersecurity is a prevailing societal issue, several research studies have shown that in the counterpoising between dependability (e.g., clearing a fault on a protected element) and security (e.g., mis-operating, such as clearing a fault when a fault has not yet occurred on a protected element), the bias is skewed towards dependability/reliability. On the surface, this seems quite reasonable. However, as the Operational Technology (OT) PSHF is the equivalent of the Information Technology (IT) "0-Day," the dearth of robust progress in mitigating against PSHFs makes for a specious paradigm — PSHFs not only remain a critical security issue, but should PSHFs manifest, the involved power system reliability will experience a non-graceful degradation and likely be subject to a Bak–Tang–Wiesenfeld (BTW) cascading effect resulting in a cascading failure (i.e., outage).

Among other "perfect storm" events in the cyber threat ecosystem, particularly as pertains to the power grid, a particularly ominous one is the triumvirate of: (1) an Insider Threat Paradigm (ITP), (2) a PSHF(s) paradigm known to the involved ITP actor(s), and (3) the requisite knowledge/ability to launch a targeted (based upon knowledge of the PSHF paradigm) ITP Sequential Topology Attack (STA) to effectuate a cascading failure paradigm (e.g., outage) of the involved power grid. The described scenario would be of tremendous concern to the involved system operators, power engineers, reliability engineers, protection engineers, cyber practitioners, and resiliency engineers, among others. Each of these three paradigms, collectively comprising the undesired triumvirate amalgam, is described below.

A. The ITP for the Smart Grid

The ever-expanding modern "Smart" Grid (SG) creates an ever-larger attack surface area, as it incorporates a plethora of IT, the IT subset of Information and Communications Technology (ICT), the adjacent realm of OT, the OT subset of, among others, Industrial Control Systems (ICS), and the various nexuses. According to Accenture's "State of Cybersecurity Resilience 2021," cyber security-related attacks increased 31% from 2020 to 2021; more specifically, according to the Kaspersky ICS Computer Emergency Response Team (CERT), 39.6% of ICS were targeted in the second half of 2021. According to Claroty's "Biannual ICS Risk & Vulnerability Report" and its Team82, ICS vulnerabilities increased by 41%, 61% of the vulnerabilities were remotely exploitable, and 71% were classified as high/critical vulnerabilities. To aggravate matters, according to ID Watchdog, 60% of data breaches in 2020 were from ITPs. According to Techjury, 66% of organizations consider IPTs a more likely paradigm than external attacks. Also, according to Ponemon Institute's "Cost of Insider Threats: Global Report," over the last two years, the number of ITP incidents has increased by 47%. Suffice it to say, the ITP/ICS/SG amalgam within the cyber ecosystem seems to constitute a prevailing paradigm.

B. PSHF within the SG

In addition to the ITP, the SG is also beset with the equivalent of "Zero-Day" or "0-day" vulnerability exploits, which is used to describe a software, hardware, firmware, or paradigm-related vulnerability for which no mitigation yet exists; the ICS manifestation is referred to as Hidden Defects/Failures (HDF) and these include, among others, PSHFs that are not able to be detected under current Condition-Based Maintenance (CBM) instantiations. To compound the ominous nature of PSHF, according to Insights (as well as various contributors to the Carnegie Mellon University Software Engineering Institute), based upon statistics from the CERT National Insider Threat Center (NITC) Incident Corpus, "the percentage of insider incidents perpetrated by 'trusted business partners' typically ranges between 15% and 25% across all insider incident types and industry sectors." According to MITRE and DTEX Systems, there has been a 72% increase in ITP incidents between 2020 and 2021. The implication is clear; if the "trusted business partner" (that provided the protection system-related device/component, which is also known as a Security and Stability Control Device or SSCD) constitutes the ITP, then the PSHFs could, potentially, be intentional and by design. For this case, the encompassing Security and Stability Control System (SSCS) or Electric Power Alarming and Coordinated Control System (EACCS) (for which the SSCD is a constituent component) could be considered compromised. The ensuing implications could potentially be quite profound. The North American Electric Reliability Corporation (NERC) has asserted that more than 70% of major disturbances, which segue to system cascading collapses (e.g., outages), are caused by PSHF. In addition, Yankson et al. demonstrated that a 0-day can amplify the negative impact of a disturbance event by a factor of 86 with a major disturbance outcome [1]. Suffice it to say, the ITP-PSHF/ICS/SG amalgam within the cyber ecosystem seems to constitute an ominous threat.

C. STA as a Targeted ITP Attack

It was previously shown in [2], as well as by studies, such as by Guo et al. and others, that while certain Cyber Physical Systems (CPS), such as Cyber-Physical Power Systems (CPPS), can provide a modicum of resilience for high-indexed nodes, they are much less resilient to targeted attacks (e.g., ITP attacks) [3][4]. From a Supply Chain Vulnerability (SCV)/Cyber-Physical SCV(CPSCV) perspective, if a "trusted business partner" has intricate knowledge of the involved power grid (e.g., CPPS topology, EACCS, SSCS, SSCD, PSHF, etc.), then the associated CPPS (and involved EACCS and/or SSCS) resiliency against a targeted ITP attack could dramatically shift from a more desirable higher resilience number (e.g., resilience = 10 for a minimally vulnerable CPPS, EACCS, SSCS, etc.) to an undesirable lower resilience number (e.g., resilience = 0 for a maximally vulnerable CPPS) in a fashion alluded to by Silveira, et al [5]. Moreover, with such intricate knowledge, the targeted ITP attack might leverage the capability for sequential control to exploit the phenomenon in a fashion that, as Zhu et al. and others have noted, "the sequential attack is demonstrated to be statistically stronger than the simultaneous attack" [6]. Yan et al. and others seem to concur that the impact of the STA could be much more devastating than a concurrent attack and further point out that "sequential attacks require less concurrent resources to coordinate" and therefore have a lower effectuation cost (e.g., Control Signal Energy Cost or CSEC). It was previously discussed in [2] that sufficiently low CSEC for Large Complex Networked Systems (LCNS), such as CPPS or SG, may yield to an optimal controllability paradigm (in this case, advantageous for the ITP attacker to operationalize an STA); hence, the maximal optimum CSEC ($CSEC_{opt}$) is sought to block the Malicious Command and Control (C2) (collectively, MC2) of the ITP. Suffice it to say, the ITP-PSHF-STA/ICS/SG amalgam within the cyber ecosystem seems to constitute a "perfect storm."

Contending with this "perfect storm" amalgam is a non-trivial feat. After all, mitigation actions, such as leveraging defensive SSCDs (e.g., Defensive Circuit Breakers or DCBs) and facilitating Defensive Grid Re-configuration (DGR), are non-trivial to effectuate. However, a mitigation module — to maximize CSEC at certain key nodes in the form of $CSEC_{opt}$) (so as to, indeed, effectuate a non-optimal controllability paradigm for the ITP attacker), obviate (via degrade, perturb, or disrupt) the involved "perfectly planned" STA strategy, and somewhat mitigate against the involved PSHF — is explored. Accordingly, the main contribution of the paper is to introduce a multi-Convolutional Adversarial Neural Network (CANN) (i.e., CANN1 and CANN2) mitigation module designed for handling certain PSHF, whose potency can be somewhat blunted with the mitigation module's Particle Swarm Optimization (PSO)-based Enhanced Reinforcement

Learning (RL) Component (ERLC), which can better orchestrate DCBs and leverage ML-based Protection Relay Selection (MLPRS) for more optimal DGR so as to better obviate a PSHF-based ITP STA. The paper is structured as follows. Section I introduces the "ITP-PSHF-STA" challenge. Section II presents relevant background information and discusses the current operating environment. Section III delineates the experimental strategy behind the multi-CANN mitigation module and its subordinate PSO-based ERLC, which collectively endeavor to contend with the referenced challenge, and compares certain solvers; some preliminary experimental findings are provided. Section IV concludes with some reflections, puts forth some envisioned future work, and the acknowledgements close the paper.

II. Background Information

Contemporary society relies upon reliable and resilient Critical Infrastructures (CI), such as the power grid [7]. The advent and prevalent usage of ICTs has led to more connected and "smarter" CPS, such as CPPS and SG. Standards are still evolving, such as exemplared by the fact that International Electrotechnical Commission (IEC) 62351 addresses some of the security issues not addressed by IEC 61850, which has been hitherto utilized to address some of the security issues of yet other standards (e.g., IEEE C37.118). Suffice it to say, the rapid convergence of IT and OT has revealed gaps in both the security and reliability paradigms. For example, The OT threat landscape presents challenges, as various cyber security professionals have noted that the current Common Vulnerability Scoring System (CVSS) is more suitable for IT than OT. According to Tenable Research, 56% of current vulnerabilities are scored as High (i.e., CVSS score of 7.0-8.9) or Critical (CVSS score of 9.0-10.0); however, more than 75% of the vulnerabilities with a score of 7 or above have "never had an exploit published against them." Meanwhile, while there are indeed robust IT domain-centric projects, such as the 0-day Tracking Project (a.k.a., Project Zero), which keeps track of 0-days with assigned Common Vulnerabilities and Exposures (CVEs) (e.g., for 2022, it lists 17 known 0-days, which have been subsequently patched, in 2021, it lists 58, in 2020, it lists 25, etc.), much more work needs to be done in the OT domain (e.g., ICS), particularly in the area of identifying, understanding, and mitigating against PSHFs (the OT equivalents of IT 0-days), which could lead to cascading failure of an involved SG. Without properly addressing PSHFs, security will remain problematic and reliability assessments can be specious; in essence, vulnerabilities in the OT domain may need to be re-prioritized — with PSHF receiving a renewed emphasis. The current operating environs is delineated in subsections A through I below.

A. *The Notion of SG*

Cecati et al. noted that the SG is a "concept for transforming the electric power grid by using advanced automatic control and communications techniques and other forms of information technology" [8]. Wang et al. and others have reviewed SG communications architectures [9]. Fang et al. well noted that the U.S. Energy Independence and Security Act of 2007 directed the National Institute of Standards and Technology (NIST) to coordinate the research and development of a framework to achieve interoperability, efficiency, and reliability of SG systems (e.g., EACCS, SSCS) and devices (e.g., SSCD) [10]. Kawoosa et al. and others have reviewed SG cyber security [11], and Zhao et al. and others have reviewed PSHF in the context of security and stability of the SG. However, with regards to security and stability/dependability/reliability, Barnes et al. assert that the prevailing bias is skewed towards reliability, which may be quite specious in actuality, as the associated vulnerability paradigm actually makes the involved SG quite brittle [12].

B. *SG Reliability*

Indeed, whether it be a SG or non-SG, reliability (i.e., "keeping the lights on") has been central for the power grid. NERC was originally formed as the North American Electric Reliability Council in 1968 (prompted by the 1965 cascading failure and ensuing blackout in the northeastern part of the U.S.) to promote reliability standards within electric utility systems. Among other NERC promoted standards is TPL-001-1 "System Performance Under Normal (No Contingency) Conditions," wherein Category A equates to "No Contingencies," Category B equates to "Events resulting in the loss of a single system element," Category C equates to "Event(s) resulting in the loss of two or more (multiple) elements," and Category D equates to "extreme event resulting in two or more (multiple) elements removed or cascading out of service." A Category B event (with continued performance after the loss of a single component) is known as an N-1 contingency. A Category C event (with continued performance after loss of two components) is further subdivided with regards to timing: (1) N-k (where k>=2) contingency for nearly simultaneous losses, and (2) N-1-1 contingency for consecutive/sequential losses.

C. *Sequential Events in the SG*

Perhaps, in a counter-intuitive fashion, sequential events (e.g., attacks) turn out to have greater impact than simultaneous/concurrent events. In addition, Chen et al. illuminated the fact that the loss of one element immediately raises the likelihood of losing another element under the "cluster" probability distribution [13]. Along this vein, Salim et al. also noted that adjacent/neighboring lines or exposed lines (particularly those sharing the same bus) would have a higher probability of incorrect tripping (induced by the loss of the first element) [14]. Zhu et al. utilized an IEEE 39 bus system to show that the sequential failure of two links caused an 80% power loss, while the simultaneous failure of the links caused less than 10% power loss [6]. Yan et al. noted that, as an extension of the N-1-1 contingency, the specific targets, number of attacks, and timing of attacks (i.e., STA) could be determined by the attackers (e.g., who had knowledge of an involved PSHF paradigm) to maximize damage [15]. For this STA scenario, the involved [SCV/CPSCV] vulnerability chain (which represents the threats due to the manifestation of an existing vulnerability, such as PSHF, as well as the threats added due to the impotency of the available mitigation controls — none in the case of "0-day" or PSHF [5]) is likely to yield to the BTW cascading effect and an ensuing outage.

D. *Cascading Failure of the SG Induced by PSHF*

Prourbeik et al. have noted that "cascading outages are among the most severe threats to power grid stability." [16]. One of the main causes of cascading outages for the most recent series major Western Systems Coordinating Council (WSCC) events, interestingly, involved PSHF that are not able to be detected under current CBM paradigms [17]. Salim et al. have noted that most of the major cascading collapses, have been caused by PSHF [14]. Elizondo et al. have described a PSHF as "a relay that is misconfigured or fault such that it will cause the inappropriate removal of system assets during an event" [18]. Others, such as Ree, et al. have delineated PSHF as "a permanent defect that will cause a relay or a relay system to incorrectly and inappropriately remove a circuit element(s) as a direct consequence of another switching event" [19]. Yet, in a broader sense, PSHF do not simply reside within relays; the PSHF phenomenon also resides with the various protection system-related components – SSCDs, in general.

While contemporary power grids are fairly resilient against N-1 contingency single element issues, they remain highly vulnerable to N-k contingency (particularly where k>=2) multi-element issues [20]. Forensic examinations have found that several major outages were indeed caused by the PSHF of the involved Special Protection Schemes (SPS) or Remedial Action Schemes (RAS) (which are measures specifically designed to preserve the integrity of the CPPS or SG during aberrant operating conditions [21]) within the involved EACCS, SSCS, etc. The PSHF referenced are caused not only by inherent Protection Element Functionality Defects (PEFDs) within the SSCDs, but also by associated human factors (e.g., relay settings), which can lead to a degradation of the involved SPS.

E. *Classifying PSHF*

PSHF can be classified in a variety of ways, but they are often divided into: (1) the causes (e.g., hardware faults, software errors, logic errors, improper operation, improper maintenance, improper protection setting values, etc.), (2) the characteristics (e.g., static, dynamic, etc.), and (3) the defects — PEFDs — which are further classified as device-related faults (a.k.a., PEFD-A) and human-related faults (e.g., protection setting-related) (a.k.a., PEFD-B) [22]. PSHF have also been organized by their positioning and functional role within the EACCS or SSCS: (1) Measuring, (2) Strategy, (3) Setting, (4) Communication, and (5) Voting pattern [22]. Taking the latter issue of voting patterns, there are typically three: (1) 2 out of 3, (2) 2 out of 2, and (3) 1 out of 2. Currently, (3) is the most adopted. However, it is not able to prevent the mal-operation of the EACCS or SSCS, via the PSHF. (2) can be quite effective, as the involved SSCDs are serially connected and will only trip when both SSCDs act; this will effectively mitigate against PSHF in either of the SSCDs, but protection action failures are still possible. (1) can also be quite effective, as demonstrated by Sandoval et al. [23], but it is the least adopted due to the high cost, architectural intricacies, Operation and Maintenance (O&M) complexities, etc. Even if (1) were utilized, Albinali et al. demonstrated that it would not eliminate all PSHF mis-operations [24]. In essence, current SGs are not architected to mitigate against PSHF.

F. *Ascertaining the Probability of PSHF*

To ascertain the possibility of PSHF manifesting, two distinct approaches are often used to ascertain the probability of its/their existence in the involved EACCS or SSCS: (1) probability statistical method, and (2) probability model method. The probability value obtained from (1) is a fixed value, which has a notional value at a particular snapshot in time, but unfortunately, a fixed value is not able to adequately reflect the changing probability of PSHF amidst real-time operating conditions. The probability value obtained from (2) is a non-fixed/variable value, which does indeed change to reflect different operating conditions (e.g., power flow, bus voltage, system frequency). (1) is utilized more often, as it has a lower computational cost and is more timely. However, it is not as accurate as methods utilized for (2), such as the Markov model method. Yet, the Markov model method, among other methods, requires many samples to ensure accuracy, is less timely, and an assumption is made that future states do not depend on past states (which may not necessarily be true).

PSHF may also be inclusive of multiple SSCD, SSCS and/or EACCS, such as in the case of a [Protection System] Coordination Hidden Failure (PSCHF). It is difficult enough to detect PSHF by the occurrence of a single element issue, but when complicated multi-element issues occur (e.g., such as in the case of PSCHF), the involved fault judgment circuit is likely to be ineffective and cascading failures may follow.

G. *Attempts to Mitigate against PSHF and/or PSCHF*

To mitigate against potential PSHFs and/or PSCHFs, one approach, among others, is to identify the key lines affected by the potential PSHFs and implement mitigation measures to inhibit cascading failures and their ensuing wide-area disturbances. Artificial Intelligence (AI) has been brought to bear to help mitigate against these scenarios, with various Defect Diagnosis/Prediction Models (DDPM) proposed. AI approaches, such as those centered upon retraining, have been studied. By way of clarification, EACCS or SSCS and the involved SSCD functions — let us say, Protective Relaying (PR) — can be construed to be a Decision

Engineering (DE) problem with a clear decision – to trip or not trip. Hence, Intelligent Protective Relays (IPR), which can retrain themselves so as to not trip inappropriately, reside within the realms of AI and DE; however, this research area is still nascent, and much works remain to be done. In brief, mitigation approach vectors for PSHF and/or PSCHF are far from robust.

H. The Intensifying Protection Challenge and PSHF

The literature shows that AI and DE research has been performed in the area of islanding detection (which endeavors to ascertain when the involved microgrid is disconnected from the main grid), which is just one of the various protection issues (e.g., undesired nuisance tripping, blinding problem involving a delay or non-tripping, etc.). Various Islanding Detection Techniques (IDT) are presented in the literature and have been reviewed by Khan et al. and others; however, IDT is, likewise, still a nascent area (as are other more complex protection issues, such as PSHF and PSCHF), and failed IDT are of critical concern for system operators, power/resiliency/security engineers, etc. [25].

To aggravate matters, the increase in highly distributed Renewable Energy Sources (RES) is increasing the need for IDT, thereby necessitating more EACCS, SSCS, and their constituent SSCD; in the case of high RES, because of the varying intermittencies, fault levels will vary, and this complexity has led to an increase in nuisance tripping (as well as associated sympathetic [nuisance] trippings) when in grid mode (i.e., false positive) and a decrease of requisite tripping (e.g., blinding problem) when in islanded mode (i.e., false negative); this is known as a loss of coordination from sequentially false operations (e.g., nuisance, sympathetic, blinding, etc.) of the relays from downstream to upstream feeders [26]. This might also involve reverse power conditions [27]. In essence, cascades can be comprised of a mixture of taxonomic (i.e., upstream to downstream) as well as folksonomic (i.e., downstream to upstream) effects.

By way of contextualizing information, the International Energy Agency (IEA) asserts that by 2026, the global renewable electricity capacity is forecast to rise dramatically from 2020 levels. RES are set to account for a substantive portion of the global power capacity through 2026, and Solar PhotoVoltaics (PV) is expected to be a principal contributor. Some areas have increased their Renewable Portfolio Standards (RPS) target to 100% renewable before 2045 (e.g., California, Hawaii) [28]. The United Nations (UN) Conference of the Parties (COP) 26 Summit accelerated action towards the goals of the Paris Agreement and the UN Framework Convention on Climate Change (UNFCCC), which places an urgency on RES to operationalize the reduction of greenhouse gas emissions/concentrations (e.g., carbon dioxide) in the spirit of the Sustainable Development Goals (SDGs). The adoption of RES (a.k.a., "green energy") has made matters, regarding CPPS or SG, more complex; after all, the RES Distributed Generation (DG) aspect introduces topological paradigms, such as islanded mode. Accordingly, the varied topology (e.g., grid mode, islanded mode) will affect the magnitude and direction of the fault currents within the microgrid in differing ways, and "the low fault current during islanded mode can lead to difficulties in fault detection or long tripping times for [Over Current] OC elements" [28]. Hence, the protection challenge, and that of the involved EACCS, SSCS, and their constituent SSCD, becomes much more complicated.

To meet this challenge, an Adaptive Protection Scheme (APS) seems prudent, as APS endeavors to ascertain the state of the CPPS or SG and make adjustments to its configuration (e.g., changing relay settings), accordingly; after all, settings likely need to be different for different network operating topologies/different operating modes due to a large difference in fault currents [26][28]. Horowitz et al. and others point out the merits of APS. Others, such Gao et al. point out that even though APS might be able to reduce the potential for mis-operation (e.g., incorrect settings), such approaches will not help to protect against PSHF (and PSCHF), which are not detectable via self-tests (a.k.a., self-diagnostics) and are extremely difficult to detect even centrally/externally.

The very real underlying danger of PSHF (which should be of interest, pursuant to the spirit of Critical Infrastructure Protection (CIP)-002-4 "Cyber Security – Critical Cyber Asset," particularly as it relates to intentional/unintentional compromises of the power system [9]), is that they are hidden during normal CPPS, EACCS, SSCS, as well as SSCD operating conditions and only manifest when disturbances occur (e.g., overloads, faults, etc.). In a sense, they are comparable to the classically understood "0-day" vulnerabilities, as no mitigation is yet in place. PSHF are particularly ominous, as they can induce unnecessary outages of functional/operational SSCD, SSCS, EACCs, etc. upstream as well as downstream and are particularly pervasive; Zhang et al. provide an example of an SSCD — remote zone 3 protection relays (wherein the protection relay setting covers the first line, the longest second line, and 25% of the third line) — as being essential to power systems, but their false trips are also one of main causes related to cascading outages [29]. PSHF variations have also been increasing at an alarming rate.

By way of background, Liptak et al. nicely articulate the fact that the "the IEC 61850 logical device model allows a single physical device to act as a proxy or gateway for multiple devices[,] thus providing a standard representation of a data concentrator" [30]. The underpinning basic element, for devices and functions, is the Logical Node (LN). As the LNs are associated with a Substation Configuration Description (SCD) file, any shift in the SCD may result in Configured [Intelligent Electronic Device] IED Description (CID) changes, thereby increasing the potentialities of PSHF.

I. Devising a Detection Schema for Certain PSHF

To adequately contend with the burgeoning corpus and potentialities of PSHF, we first look at the gamut of SSCDs.

The NERC Standard Protection and Control (PRC)-005-6 organizes the SSCDs as follows: (1) Protective Relay (Table 1-1), (2) Communications Systems (CS) (Table 1-2), (3) Voltage and Current Sensing Devices Providing Inputs to Protective Relays (Table 1-3), (4) Protection System Station Direct Current (DC) Supply (PSSDCS) (Table 1-4), and (5) Control Circuitry Associated with Protective Functions (Table 1-5) (includes CBs — which includes DCBs —and other interrupting devices) [31].

First, for the Protective Relay (and constituent Time Delay Relays or Delay Timers), when the operating condition of the overarching SSCS changes, and the setting of the involved Relay does not change accordingly (e.g., thereby resulting in an outdated Relay setting), the Relay may not be able to accurately detect the status of the SSCS and mis-operate; with regards to the delay timers, they could fail in the "closed" position [12]. Second, for the CS, Gao et al. pointed out the heavy dependence on CS greatly reduces the reliability of the involved EACCS, SSCS, etc. [31]. Third, for the Voltage and Current Sensing Devices, we first take the Current Transformer (CT); for the CT, after a fault occurs, fault currents may cause the CT core to segue to a saturation situation, wherein the secondary current of the CT is no longer a viable proxy for the primary current. Next, we take the Voltage Transformer (VT); for the VT (e.g., Capacitor Voltage Transformer or CVT/Coupling Capacitor Voltage Transformer or CCVT), after a fault occurs, the system voltage may decrease dramatically from its prototypical baseline level to a very low-level paradigm, wherein, the secondary voltage level of the VT is no longer a viable proxy for the primary voltage level. Fourth, for the PSSDCS, were it to fail, there would likely be no power provided to the involved SSCDs in the event of an fault/outage. Fifth, for the "Control Circuitry Associated with Protective Functions, we take the Circuit Breaker (CB) (and CB's subordinate trip circuit) among others; Yang et al. explored Circuit Breaker Trip Mechanisms (CBTMs) and found that CB-related PSHF dramatically decrease the involved EACCS, SSCS, et al. reliability level; PSHF in the CBTM can cause CBs/DCBs to fail to open (i.e., trip) when required, which would obviate their usefulness [32].

The commonality of (1) through (5) is that they are all subject to, among other attack vectors, a code attack, data attack, or PSHF. It is critical that (1) and (3) provide accurate measurement data (i.e., analog data). It is also vital that (2), (4), and (5) provide an accurate status of their operational health (i.e., status data). In essence, analog data equates to measurement of system states (e.g., voltage, frequency), which are emblematic of system dynamics (which can be affected by a data attack). Status data equates to topological measurements describing the connectivity of the SG (which can be affected by a code attack). Analog and status data are both used for operational DE. A mal-operation that induces deceptive analog and/or status data can be construed as a contingency event [33]. The proper orchestration of (1) through (5) is what allows the involved EACCS, SSCS, and SSCD to operate as intended.

For this paper, the devising of a mitigation module will be limited to the Protective Relay-related Paradigm (PR2P), as various researchers, such as Cheng et al. have noted that the majority of outages have been PSHF/protective relay-related. Moustafa, et al., have noted that PSHF cause about 75% of EACCS and SSCS-related events [35]. Salim et al. concurs by noting that PSHF "have been identified as one of the main causes of system cascading collapse resulting in power system instability" [14]. Furthermore, NERC data underscore the prior assertions by illuminating the fact that the distribution of cascading failures have a "fat tail instead of an exponentially falling tail, as in a normal distribution" — meaning that it occurs far more often than thought [36].

III. EXPERIMENTATION

To contend with the ominous PR2P paradigm, Wang et al. and others have posited that RL can be advantageous when contending with these Multi-Stage DE Problems (MSDEP) (e.g., to trip or not to trip), particularly in those cases involving a high degree of uncertainty (e.g., potential ITP) [9]. However, prototypical instantiations of RL necessitate a reward function, and studies have found that it is difficult for an RL agent to avoid stagnation at local optima.

It was previously shown in [37], as well as by certain other studies, that PSO could be advantageous (given the reduced number of hyperparameters to tune while providing "good enough" near-optimum solutions in relatively few iterations for solving the involved Mixed Integer Non-Linear Programming or MINLP problems), if Adaptive Inertial Weighting (AIW) (such as effectuated via a modified GNU Octave numerical computational platform, as discussed in [38]) is utilized to prevent stagnation at local optima. This approach helps to overcome the challenge of instantiating PSO aboard a Deep Convolutional Generative Adversarial Networks (DCGAN), wherein the continuous or discontinuous hyperparameters must be converted to discrete values (e.g., integers) [39], but rounding the calculated velocities to discrete integer values lends to creating an artificial paradigm, whereby particles may stagnate prematurely at local optima [40]. As the AIW-PSO approach has a suitably high efficacy for avoiding local optima and attaining a more globally optimal solution, the utilization of modern RL techniques, such as Multi-Agent RL (MARL) and Asynchronous Actor-Critic (AAC) (wherein multiple actors are efficiently trained in parallel with varying exploration policies [e.g., Novelty Search or NS, Quality Diversity or QD, etc.] [41] and whose parameters are globally contextualized by the collective actors/agents), among others, becomes viable with relatively high efficacy. Given the PSO-based ERLC, we now refer to the involved schema as AIW-PSO-ERLC.

Efficient support for MARL, ACC, etc., with the overarching MSDEP, often necessitates contending with nonconvex optimization problems; these are, in essence, nonconvex MINLPs, which need to be transformed to convex optimization problems, via certain relaxation techniques. However, the involved transformations may spawn yet other nonconvex optimization problems, thereby necessitating the use of an Enhanced Robust Convex Relaxation (ERCR) framework for the tightest possible relaxation (as previously delineated in [2] and [37], among others). Interestingly, preliminary findings indicate that a specific APS IPR schema with ERCR & AIW-PSO-ERLC atop CGAN-CANN1-CANN2 (with the Bespoke Numerical Stability Implementation or BNSI discussed in [2] and [37]) well supports MARL, AAC, etc. for $MSDEP_{opt}$ (as well as Non-Efficient Controllability Problems or NECP for $CSEC_{opt}$ and AI/ML DDPM for DCB_{opt}+$MLPRS_{opt}$+DGR_{opt}), as shown in Figure 1 below. This seems to be in tandem with the posits of Ly et al., Alhazmi, et al., and Namei et al.; they contend that leveraging DCBs, [MLPRS], and DGR can mitigate against MC2 and enhance the overall SSCS, EACCS, and CPPS/SG reliability, security, as well as resiliency [42][43][44].

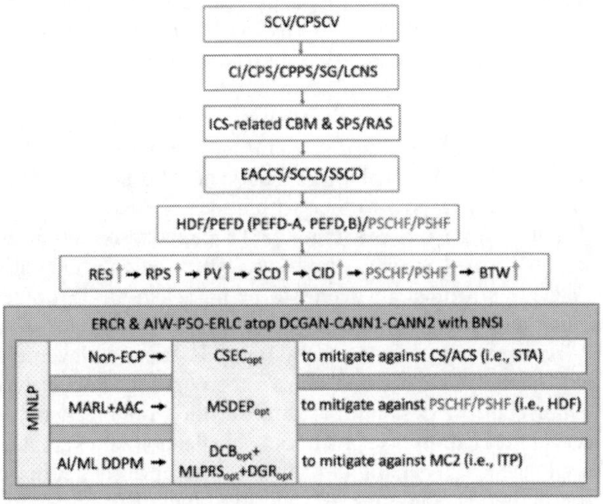

Figure 1. ERCR and AIW-PSO-ERLC atop DCGANN-CANN1-CANN2 with BNSI Framework

In essence, $CSEC_{opt}$, $MSDEP_{opt}$, and DCB_{opt}+$MLPRS_{opt}$+DGR_{opt}, among others, are — for all intents and purposes — MINLP to be resolved by the ERCR & AIW-PSO-ERLC atop DCGAN-CANN1-CANN2 with a BNSI Framework (hereinafter, referred to as the "Experimental Testbed" or ET). In resolving these particular MINLP, some mitigation of STA (for which Control Signals or CS/Augmented CS or ACS are now obviated), HDF (which includes PSHF/PSCHF), and ITP (which likely involves MC2) is effectuated. By diminishing the likelihood of PSHF/ PSCHF, the probability of a BTW cascading effect is also decreased (thereby reducing the probability of a cascading failure/outage).

In terms of some quantitative metrics, some fairly stringent experimental parameters were utilized. While certain latencies can range up to 80ms (e.g., computational processing/algorithmic execution time along with CB time) for the first zone and 500ms for the second zone [45], a maximum reporting time of 8.3ms was utilized for the involved experimentation (some Ultra-High Speed or UHS protective relays can operate at 1.5ms [46]) [47]. For practical use, the involved PR/IPR must have an Operational Time Interval (OTI) (e.g., 1.5ms < OTI < 8.3ms) that is less than the CB Interruption time, any Breaker Failure Protection (BFP) time delay (e.g., 200ms), and the Critical Clearing Time (CCT). In accordance with international standards, the PR/IPR OTI should not be much "faster than a half-cycle of power-frequency (i.e., 10ms for 50 Hz and 8.3ms for 60 Hz)" [46]; if it were, the involved CBs might not be able to operate properly [48]. Hence, a high sampling frequency (>= 1 MHz) with 1.5ms < OTI < 3ms was not desired/considered (and clearly, UHS would not be as well), as this OTI range was too fast. On the flip side, low sampling frequency PR/IPR (e.g., <1kHz to <4 kHz) with 8.3ms < OTI < 20ms was not desired/considered, as this OTI range was too slow. Medium sampling frequency PR/IPR (4 kHz to 10 kHz) with 3ms < OTI < 8.3ms had the desired OTI range.

To achieve the desired OTI range, certain nonconvex MINLP solvers and convex solvers were examined (nonconvex MINLP problems were reformulated as convex MINLP) as part of the experimentation. Comparing the nonconvex and convex solvers together, although seemingly not an equitable comparison, highlighted the potential selection bias (even as general solvers), for the described environs described herein, towards nonconvex treatment; if so, these needed to be quickly eliminated, as OTI adherence is crucial. PAVER 2.0, an open-source environment for automated performance analysis of benchmarking data, was utilized. An Experimental Solver Set (ESS) A was winnowed, and certain solvers, such as Jump Nonlinear Integer Program Solver (Juniper) were removed from further consideration due to the algorithmic execution time per problem of approximately 36 milliseconds per problem (at a batch size of 25) and about 95 milliseconds per problem (at a batch size of 100); these results were consistent with those found by Kronqvist et al [49]. The solvers of resultant ESS B, which included Basic Open-source Nonlinear Mixed Integer Programming (Bonmin), Convex Over and Under ENvelopes for Nonlinear Estimation (Couenne), mbnb, mqg, mqgpar, mglob, and Supporting Hyperplane Optimization Toolkit (SHOT), were compared; mbnb, mqg, mqgpar, are mglob are solvers available as part of the Mixed-Integer Nonlinear Optimization (Minotaur) Toolkit. The results were quite similar with regards to algorithmic execution time per problem — approximately 4 milliseconds per problem (at a batch size of 25); however, at a batch size of 100, the performance was quite different. Bonmin was eliminated, as performance ranged from 14ms+. Couenne was eliminated, as performance was at about 80ms+. Interestingly, the solvers from Minotaur all achieved performances of about sub 5ms. Likewise, the performance of SHOT was at about 4 ms. To ensure a robust resultant ESS C, the experimentation was repeated in various increments. This allowed the various solvers to both return the optimal solution and to verify optimality within the desired OTI range. In addition, the settings used by [49], as pertains to gaptol, was also utilized herein. The resultant ESS C was then further compared for performance on the ET. Of the Minotaur solvers tested, mqg and mqgpar had the most consistent performance. Separately, SHOT also had consistent performance. This is shown in Figure 2 below. Hence, it seems that, for use with ET, the MILP decomposition-based solvers had better performance than Branch and Bound (BB)-based solvers; this was an interesting finding. Hence, the involved quantitative experimentation (which was partially inspired by [49]) atop ET, with the resultant ESS D, hints at the potential of certain MINLP solvers achieving near optimal solutions consistently.

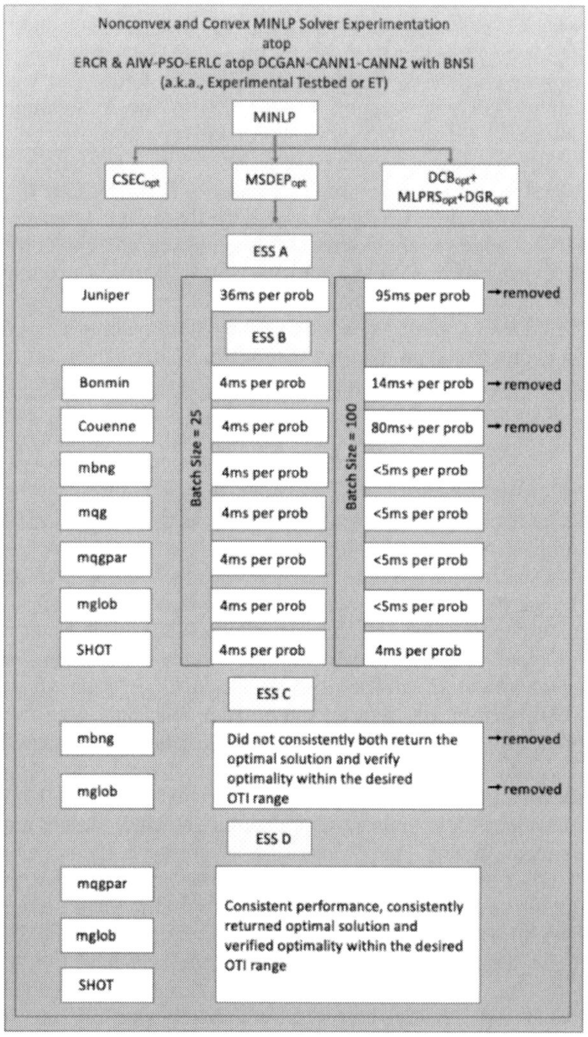

Figure 2. MINLP Experimentation atop ET

Taking the example of SHOT, it has the advantage of having robust performance for subclasses, such as Mixed Integer (MI) Nonlinear Programming (NLP) and Quadratically Constrained Quadratic Programming (QCQP). The significance of this centers upon the fact that an MINLP problem is often construed as convex when its continuous relaxation results in a convex NLP problem. Hence, SHOT's intrinsic subclass handling of the transformation from nonconvex to convex may, potentially, be more harmonious with ET, as both nicely handle those cases, wherein the involved transformations spawn yet other nonconvex optimization problems and the tightest possible relaxation is needed. Mqg and mqgpar are, likewise, quite robust.

IV. Conclusion and Future Work

The OT PSHF approximates the IT "0-Day," and should PSHF manifest, it is likely to induce a BTW cascading effect, serve as a key amplification factor, and segue to cascading failure (i.e., outage). Moreover, PSHF/PSCHF-induced STA have been shown to have higher impact and cause more pervasive failures than concurrent events. This seems to be counterintuitive for many, but this lesson learned is consistent with the previously referenced findings of Zhu et al., Yan et al., and others, who have noted that the STA has greater impact than a concurrent attack (which requires a higher CSEC and more concurrent resources to coordinate). A further lesson learned is that PSHF/PSCHF-related events are not necessarily HILF events. Indeed, they seem to more closely approximate VHIMF events; this particular lesson learned seems to be affirmed by NERC, which has noted that the distribution of cascading failures occurs more frequently than envisioned. Along this vein, it seems that PSHF/PSCHF are currently underprioritized and that efforts in this area are still nascent. This seems to beget the notion that the priorities within the OT domain are quite different from those within the IT domain. A yet further lesson learned is that for certain cyber thematics, such as ITP, the prioritization seems to be higher in the IT domain than that for the OT domain.

Among other obstacles in the OT domain, leveraging ML-based workstreams and incorporating higher-level cybersecurity paradigms, amidst the predilection for seeming reliability, seems to be a challenge. An example of a higher-level paradigm is that of an apriori architected mitigation paradigm to address the ITP-PSHF-STA triumvirate amalgam. However, this seems to be absent for current SGs. This paper posits that, among others, a prospective pragmatic mitigation approach — against PR2P STA, PSHF/PSCFH, and ITP — is to intercede in the successive event stream by effectuating the maximal optimum Control Signal Energy Cost ($CSEC_{opt}$) for reducing the diffusion of CS/ACS as well as other MC2. To best mitigate against PR2P ITP, deriving DCB_{opt}+$MLPRS_{opt}$+DGR_{opt} will contribute toward reducing the efficacy of MC2 (and the associated constituent CA/ACS). This same bespoke APS IPR schema with ET and ESS D well supports deriving $MSDEP_{opt}$ to mitigate against PR2P HDF (e.g., PSHF/ PSCHF). Central to this mitigation approach is not only the AIW-PSO support for ERLC (e.g., MARL, AAC, etc.), but the encompassing bespoke multi-CANN module. Finally, the ET and ESS D also nicely address $CSEC_{opt}$ for Non-ECP so as to mitigate against CS/ACS (i.e., STA). Overall, by endeavoring to reduce the fat tail, it is the hope that the involved incidence level will return to the currently anticipated/classified HILF or even better — Medium or even, ideally, Low-Impact, Low-Frequency (LILF). Future work will involve more quantitative experimentation in this area, particularly in the area of extrapolating upon the experimentation contained herein. First, further experimentation (inspired by Kronqvist et al.) involving the benchmarking of various MINLP solvers atop ET is needed. Second, further experimentation (inspired by Zhu et al., among others, which demonstrated that sequential failure of key elements causes a multiple factor greater power loss that that for simultaneous failures of the same key elements) involving the benchmarking of the STA multiple factor phenomenon is needed as well. Accordingly, mitigation approaches that satisfy the prevailing OTI constraint, such as explored herein by way of ET and ESS D, warrant further examination.

ACKNOWLEDGMENT

This research is supported by the Decision Engineering Analysis Laboratory (DEAL), an Underwatch initiative of VTIRL, VT. This is part of an ongoing VTIRL technical series, on behalf of the Quality Assurance/Quality Control (QA/QC) unit, to advance the involved TRLs.

REFERENCES

[1] S. Yankson and M. Ghamkhari, "Transactive Energy to Guard again a Zero-Day Load Altering Attack on Power Distribuion Systems," 2019 IEEE 7th International Conference on Smart Energy Grid Engineering (SEGE), 2019, pp. 171-177, doi: 10.1109/SEGE.2019.8859794.

[2] S. Chan, "Enhanced Robust Convex Relaxation Framework for Optimal Controllability of Certain Large Complex Networked Systems: An Accelerant Amalgam and Bespoke Numerical Stability Paradigm for a Decoupled and Sequenced Control Strategy on Dense and Homogeneous Temporal Networks," The 2022 IARIA Annual Congress on Frontiers in Science, Technology, Services, and Applications, ISBN: 978-1-68558-017-9.

[3] A. Guo, Y. Han, C. Guo, F. Lou, and Y. Wang, "Modeling and vulnerability analysis of cyber-physical power systems considering network topology and power flow properties," Energies, vol. 10, no. 1, p. 87, 2017, doi: 10.3390/en10010087.

[4] A. Dey, Y. Gel, and H. Poor, "What network motifs tell us about resilience and reliability of complex networks," Proc Natl Acad Sci, vol. 116, no. 39, pp. 19368-19373, doi: 10.1073/pnas.1819529116.

[5] M. Silveira, D. Dolezilek, S. Wenke, and J. Yellajousla, "Attack tree analysis of a digital secondary system in an electrical substation," 16th International Conference on Developments in Power System Protection (DPSP 2022), 2022, pp. 152-157, doi: 10.1049/icp.2022.0929.

[6] Y. Zhu, J. Yan, Y. Tang, Y. Sun, and H. He, "The Sequential Attack Against Power Grid Networks," 2014 IEEE International Conference on Communications (ICC), 2014, pp. 616-621, doi: 10.1109/ICC.2014.6883387.

[7] Y. Fang and E. Zio, "Optimizing the Resilience of Interdependent Infastructure Systems against Intentional Attacks," 2017 2nd International Conference on System Reliability and Safety (ICSRS), 2017, pp. 62-67, doi: 10.1109/ICSRS.2017.8272798.

[8] C. Cecati, G. Mokryani, A. Piccolo, and P. Siano, "An overview on the smart grid concept," IECON 2010 - 36th Annual Conference on IEEE Industrial Electronics Society, 2010, pp. 3322-3327, doi: 10.1109/IECON.2010.5675310.

[9] W. Wang, R. Wang, H. Zhang, Z. Zhou, and Y. He, "Matching Learning-Based Relay Selection for Substation Power Internet of Things," Wireless Communications and Mobile Computing, vol. 2022, Feb. 2022. https://doi.org/10.1155/2022/6795205.

[10] X. Fang, S. Misra, G. Xue, and D. Yang, "Smart Grid — The New and Improved Power Grid: A Survey," IEEE Communications Surveys & Tutorials, vol. 14, no. 4, pp. 944-980, Fourth Quarter 2012, doi: 10.1109/SURV.2011.101911.00087.

[11] A. Kawoosa and D. Prashar, "A Review of Cyber Securities in Smart Grid Technology," 2021 2nd International Conference on Computation, Automation and Knowledge Management (ICCAKM), 2021, pp. 151-156, doi: 10.1109/ICCAKM50778.2021.9357698.

[12] A. Barnes, "The Risk of Hidden Failures to the United States Electrical Grid and Potential for Mitigation," 2021 North American Power Symposium (NAPS), 2021, pp. 1-6, doi: 10.1109/NAPS52732.2021.9654709.

[13] Q. Chen and J. McCalley, "A cluster distribution as a model for estimating high-order event probabilities in power systems," 2004 International Conference on Probabilistic Methods Applied to Power Systems, 2004, pp. 622-628.

[14] N. Salim, et al., "Determination of available transfer capability with implication of cascading collapse uncertainty," IET Generation, Transmission & Distribtuion, vol 8, no. 4, pp. 705-715, Apr. 2014, doi: https://doi.org/10.1049/iet-gtd.2013.0395.

[15] J. Yan, H. He, X. Zhong, and Y. Tang, "Q-learning Based Vulnerability Analysis of Smart Grid against Sequential Topology Attacks," IEEE Transactions on Information Forensics and Security, vol. 12, no. 1, pp. 200-210, Jan. 2017, doi: 10.1109/TIFS.2016.2607701.

[16] P. Pourbeik, P. Kundur, and C. Taylor, "The anatomy of a power grid blackout – root causes and dynamics of reent major blackouts," IEEE Power and Energy Magazine, vol. 4, no. 5, pp. 22-29, Sept.-Oct. 2006, doi: 10.1109/MPAE.2006.1687814.

[17] J. Zhang, "Research on Hidden Failure Reliability Modeling of Electric Power System Protection," Energy and Power Engineering, vol. 5, 2013, doi: 10.4236/epe.2013.54B261.

[18] D. Elizondo, J. Ree, A. Phadke, and S. Horowitz, "Hidden failures in protection systems and their impact on wide-area disturbances," 2001 IEEE Power Engineering Society Winter Meeting, 2001, pp. 710-714, doi: 10.1109/PESW.2001.916941.

[19] J. Ree, Y. Liu, L. Mili, A. Phadke, and L. DaSilva, "Catastrophic Failures in Power Systems: Causes, Analyses, and Countermeasures," in Proceedings of the IEEE, vol. 93, no. 5, pp. 956-964, May 2005, doi: 10.1109/JPROC.2005.847246.

[20] K. Bae and J. Thorp, "A Stochastic Study of Hidden Failures in Power System Protection," J. Decis. Support. Syst., vol 24, no. 304, pp. 259-268, 1999, doi: https://doi.org/10.1016/S0167-9236(98)00069-4.

[21] P. Hines, H. Liao, D. Jia, and S. Talukdar, "Autonomous agents and cooperation for the control of cascading failures in electric grids," 2005 IEEE Networking, Sensing and Control, 2005., pp. 273-278, doi: 10.1109/ICNSC.2005.1461200.

[22] L. Zhao, et al., "Review and prospect of hidden failure: protection system and security and stability control system," J. Mod. Power Syst. Clean Energy, vol. 7, pp. 1735–1743, 2019. doi: 10.1007/s40565-015-0128-9.

[23] R. Sandoval, et al., "Using Fault Tree Analysis to Evaluate Protection Scheme Redundancy," 37th Annual Western

Protective Relay Conference, 2010, Accessed: Aug. 14, 2022. [Online]. Available from: https://www.semanticscholar.org/paper/Using-Fault-Tree-Analysis-to-Evaluate-Protection-Sandoval-Santana/584230d9f12239cae3e1d1b58b590138710980b7.

[24] H. Albinali et al. "A Centralized Substation Portection Scheme that Detects Hidden Failures," 2016 IEEE Power and Energy Society General Meeting (PESGM), 2016, pp. 1-5, doi: 10.1109/PESGM.2016.7741559.

[25] M. Khan, A. Haque, V. Kurukuru, and M. Saad, "Islanding detection techniques for grid-connected photovoltaic systems-A review," Renewable and Sustainable Energy Reviews, vol. 154, 2022, doi: 10.1016/j.rser.2021.111854.

[26] V. Telukunta, J. Pradham, A. Agrawal, M. Singh, and S. Srivani, "Protection Challenges Under Bulk Penetration of Renewable Energy Resources in Power Systems: A Review," CSEE Journal of Power and Energy Systems, vol. 3, no. 4, pp. 365-379, Dec. 2017, doi: 10.17775/CSEEJPES.2017.00030.

[27] V. Papspiliotopoulos, G. Korres, and N. Hatziargyriou, "An adaptive protection infrastructure for modern distribution grids with distributed generation," CIGRE Science & Engineering, February 2017, Accessed: Aug. 14, 2022. [Online]. Available from: https://e-cigre.org/share/publication/503/C6-108_2016.

[28] T. Patel and J. Hernandez-Alvidrez, "Adaptive Protection Scheme for a Real-World Microgrid with 100% Inverter-Based Resources," 2020 IEEE Kansas Power and Energy Conference (KPEC), 2020, pp. 1-6, doi: 10.1109/KPEC47870.2020.9167527.

[29] J. Zhang and Y. Dong, "Preventing False Trips of Zone 3 Protection Relays in Smart Grid," Tsinghua Scient and Technology International Journal on Information Science, vol 20, no. 2, pp. 142-154, 2015, doi: 10.1109/TST.2015.7085627.

[30] B. Liptak and H. Eren, "Instrument Engineers' Handbook: Process Software and Digital Networks," Research Triangle Park, NC, CRC Press, 2016.

[31] X. Gao, J. Thorp, and D. Hou, "Case Studies: Designing Protection Systems That Minimize Potential Hidden Failures," 2013 66th Annual Conference for Protective Relay Engineers, 2013, pp. 384-393, doi: 10.1109/CPRE.2013.6822053.

[32] F. Yang, A. P. S. Meliopoulos, G. J. Cokkinides, and Q. B. Dam, "Effects of Protection System Hidden Failures on Bulk Power System Reliability," 2006 38th North American Power Symposium, 2006, pp. 517-523, doi: 10.1109/NAPS.2006.359621.

[33] S. Tan, D. De, W. Song, J. Yang and S. Das, "Survey of Security Advances in Smart Grid: A Data Driven Approach," in IEEE Communications Surveys & Tutorials, vol. 19, no. 1, pp. 397-422, First quarter 2017, doi: 10.1109/COMST.2016.2616442.

[34] Y. Cheng, X. Chen, J. Ren, X. Xuan and X. Li, "Study on hidden failure of relay protection in power system," 2013 IEEE International Conference on Cyber Technology in Automation, Control and Intelligent Systems, 2013, pp. 434-439, doi: 10.1109/CYBER.2013.6705485.

[35] M. Moustafa and C. Chang, W. Song, J. Yang and S. Das, "Preventing cascading failure of electric power protection systems in nuclear power plant," Nuclear Engineering and Technology, vol. 53, no. 1, pp. 121-130, Jan. 2021, doi: https://doi.org/10.1016/j.net.2020.06.010.

[36] H. Liao, J. Apt, and S. Talukdar, "Phase Transitions in the Probability of Cascading Failures," Physics, 2004, Accessed: Aug. 14, 2022. [Online]. Available from: https://www.semanticscholar.org/paper/Phase-Transitions-in-the-Probability-of-Cascading-Liao-Apt/28a8ca494e5af264152c6191f6abf5b201582d39.

[37] S. Chan, M. Krunz and B. Griffin, "AI-based Robust Convex Relaxations for Supporting Diverse QoS in Next-Generation Wireless Systems," 2021 IEEE 41st International Conference on Distributed Computing Systems Workshops (ICDCSW), 2021, pp. 41-48, doi: 10.1109/ICDCSW53096.2021.00014.

[38] Chan, Steve, "Mitigation Factors for Multi-domain Resilient Networked Distributed Tessellation Communications," The Fifth International Conference on Cyber-Technologies and Cyber-Systems (CYBER 2020), 2020, p. 66-73, Accessed: Aug. 14, 2022. [Online]. Available from: https://ssrn.com/abstract=3789770.

[39] X. Liu, Q. Wang, H. Liu, and L. Li, "Particle swarm optimization with dynamic inertia weight and mutation," *2009 Third International Conference on Genetic and Evolutionary Computing*, Feb 2010, pp. 620–623, doi: 10.1109/WGEC.2009.99.

[40] C. Worasucheep, "A particle swarm optimization with stagnation detection and dispersion," *2008 IEEE Congress on Evolutionary Computation (IEEE World Congress on Computational Intelligence)*, Hong Kong, June 2008, pp. 424-429, doi: 10.1109/CEC.2008.4630832.

[41] E. Conti, V. Madhavan, F. Such, J. Lehman, K. Stanley, and J. Clune, "Improving exploration in evolution strategies for deep reinforcement learning via a population of novelty-seeking agents," Proceedings of the 32nd International Conference on Neural Information Processing Systems (NIPS), Dec. 2018, pp. 5032-5043, doi: https://dl.acm.org/doi/10.5555/3327345.3327410.

[42] K. Ly, K. Kwiat, C. Kamhoua, L. Njilla and Y. Jin, "Approximate Power Grid Protection Against False Data Injection Attacks," 2017 IEEE 15th Intl Conf on Dependable, Autonomic and Secure Computing, 15th Intl Conf on Pervasive Intelligence and Computing, 3rd Intl Conf on Big Data Intelligence and Computing and Cyber Science and Technology Congress (DASC/PiCom/DataCom/CyberSciTech), 2017, pp. 527-533, doi: 10.1109/DASC-PICom-DataCom-CyberSciTec.2017.97.

[43] M. Alhazmi, P. Dehghanian, S. Wang and B. Shinde, "Power Grid Optimal Topology Control Considering Correlations of System Uncertainties," in IEEE Transactions on Industry Applications, vol. 55, no. 6, pp. 5594-5604, Nov.-Dec. 2019, doi: 10.1109/TIA.2019.2934706.

[44] M. Nazemi, P. Dehghanian, and M. Lejeune, "A Mixed-Integer Distributionally Robust Chance-Constrained Model for Optimal Topology Control in Power Grids with Uncertain Renewables," 2019 IEEE Milan PowerTech, 2019, pp. 1-6, doi: 10.1109/PTC.2019.8810440.

[45] M. Eissa, "Resilient wide-area monitoring and protection scheme with IEEE Std. C37.118.1-2011 criteria for complex smart grid system using phase diagram," 2019 IET Smart Grid, vol 2, no. 2, pp. 309-317, 2019, doi: 10.1049/iet-stg.2018.0247.

[46] S. Zubic, Z. Gajic and D. Kralj, "Line Protection Operate Time: How Fast Shall It Be?," in IEEE Access, vol. 9, pp. 75608-75616, 2021, doi: 10.1109/ACCESS.2021.3081993.

[47] H. Wu, K. Tsakalis, and G. Heydt, "Evaluation of time delay effects to wide-area power system stabilizer design," IEEE Transactions on Power Systems, vol. 19, no. 4, pp. 1935-1941, Nov. 2004, doi: 10.1109/TPWRS.2004.836272.

[48] B. Kasztenny and J. Rostron, "Circuit breaker ratings—A primer for protection engineers," 2018 71st Annual Conference for Protective Relay Engineers (CPRE), 2018, pp. 1-13, doi: 10.1109/CPRE.2018.8349782.

[49] J. Kronqvist, D. Bernal, A. Lundell, and I. Grossman, "A review and comparison of solvers for convex MINLP," Optimization and Engineering, vol 20, pp. 397-455, 2019, doi: 10.1007/s11081-018-9411-8.

Dynamic Trust Evaluation of Evolving Cyber Physical Systems

Rainer Falk and Steffen Fries
Siemens AG
Technology
Munich, Germany
e-mail: {rainer.falk|steffen.fries}@siemens.com

Abstract—**The integrity of Cyber Physical Systems (CPS) as, e.g., industrial Internet of Things systems or automation and control systems for monitoring and controlling technical processes, has to be protected to ensure a reliable operation. This becomes increasingly challenging with systems that are flexibly updated and reconfigured to address evolving demands. This paper describes an approach for integrity monitoring for such dynamic systems. Instead of detecting changes to a CPS as integrity violation, the focus is on checking whether detected changes are in-line with a policy defining permitted changes. A key element is a reliable device lifecycle state attestation, so that a monitoring system can determine the current device configuration state and the way in which it was changed due to reconfigurations.**

Keywords–system integrity; trustworthiness; device integrity; attestation; lifecycle; resilience; cyber physical systems; Internet of Things; cyber security.

I. INTRODUCTION

The integrity and resilience of Cyber Physical Systems (CPS), e.g., technical automation and control systems, is an important security objective. Specifically, through the use of more and more Industrial Internet of Things (IIoT) devices in critical infrastructures, this security objective often becomes a regulative requirement, as seen in the EU Network Information Security (NIS) directive. An approach for enhanced integrity monitoring of overall industrial automation and control systems, combining integrity monitoring from physical processes up to control and support systems, has been described in [1]. Enhanced attack resilience allows a cyber physical system to stay operational, possibly with some limitations, during an attack [2]. Particularly challenging are dynamically changing CPS, that come with the IIoT and Industry 4.0. Cyber systems will become more open and dynamic to support flexible production down to lot size 1 by supporting plug-and-work reconfiguration of manufacturing equipment and flexible adaptation of production systems to changing needs. This implies that also security has to support such dynamically cyber physical systems that are evolving over time.

In the past, cyber physical systems and industrial automation systems have been often rather static. After being put into operation, changes to the configuration happen only rarely, e.g., to replace a defect component, or to install smaller upgrades during a planned maintenance window. To cope with increasing demands for flexible production and increased productivity, CPS will also become more dynamic, allowing for reconfiguration during regular operation. Such scenarios for adaptable, reconfigurable production have been described in the context of Industry 4.0 [3].

The flexibility starts at the device level, where smart devices allow for upgrading and enhancing device functionality by downloadable apps. But also the system of interconnected machines is reconfigured according to changing needs. Examples are Software Defined Networks (SDN) enabling a fast reconfiguration of the communication infrastructure to adapt flexibly to the communication needs. Another example relates to manufacturing systems (e.g., robots) in industrial automation systems, where smart tools are attached to a robot that in turn feature also a local communication network connecting to the robot's network.

The focus of cyber security is protection against cyber attacks, their detection, and the recovery from successful cyber attacks. An increasingly important further aspect is trustworthiness, where automated checks verify whether the overall systems and the used components meet the explicitly defined trustworthiness criteria. However, the concept of trustworthiness is subjective. The presented approach checks for changes within a CPS to determine whether the CPS is in a permitted, trustworthy state.

After summarizing related previous work in Section II on protecting integrity of cyber physical systems and their components, the monitoring of reliable device lifecycle information based on lifecycle state attestations is described in Sections III and IV as specific additional criteria for monitoring CPS integrity, and evaluated in Section V. Section VI concludes the paper.

II. CPS SYSTEM INTEGRITY PROTECTION

Information Technology (IT) security mechanisms have been known for many years and are applied in smart devices (Internet of Things, Cyber Physical Systems, industrial and energy automation systems, operation technology) [6]. Such mechanisms target source authentication, system and communication integrity, and confidentiality of data in transit or at rest. System integrity takes a broader approach where not only the integrity of individual components (device integrity) and of communication is addressed, but where integrity shall be ensured at the system level of multiple interconnected devices, e.g., a CPS.

A. Industrial Security

Protecting industrial automation and control systems against intentional attacks is increasingly demanded by operators to ensure a reliable operation, and also by regulation. The main relevant industrial security standard that describes security from a holistic view is IEC 62443 [6]. Security requirements defined by the industrial security standard IEC 62443 range from security processes, personal and physical security, device security, network security, and application security, addressing the device manufacturer, the integrator as well as the operator of the industrial automation and control system.

Industrial security is also called Operation Technology (OT) security, to distinguish it from general IT security. Industrial systems have different security requirements compared to general IT systems. Typically, availability and integrity of an automation system have higher priority than confidentiality.

Specific requirements and side conditions of industrial automation systems like high availability, planned configuration (engineering info), long life cycles, unattended operation, real-time operation, and communication, as well as safety requirements have to be considered when designing a security solution.

B. Device Integrity

The objective of device integrity is to ensure that a single device is not manipulated in an unauthorized way. This includes the integrity of the device firmware, of the device configuration, but also the physical integrity. The main technologies to protect device integrity are:

- Secure boot: A device loads at start-up only unmodified, authorized firmware.
- Measured boot: The loaded software modules are checked at the time they are loaded. Usually, a cryptographic hash value is recorded in a platform configuration register of a hardware of firmware Trusted Platform Module (TPM). The configuration information can be used to grant access to keys, or it can be attested towards third parties.
- Protected firmware update: When the firmware of a device is updated, the integrity and authenticity of the firmware update is checked. The firmware update image can be digitally signed.
- Application whitelisting: Only allowed, known applications can be started on a device. A whitelist defines which application binaries can be started.
- Runtime integrity checks: During operation, the device performs a self-test of security functionality and integrity checks to verify whether it is operating as expected. Integrity checks can verify the integrity of files, configuration data, software modules, and runtime data as the process list, i.e., the list of currently executed processes.
- Process isolation, kernel-based Mandatory Access Control (MAC): Hypervisors or kernel-based MAC systems can be used to isolate different classes of software (security domains). An attack or malfunction of one security domain does not affect other security domains on the same device.
- Tamper evidence, tamper protection: The physical integrity of a device can be protected, e.g., by security seals or by tamper sensors that detect opening or manipulation of the housing.
- Device integrity self-test: A device performs a self-test to detect failures. The self-test is performed typically during startup and is repeated regularly during operation.
- Operation integrity checks: measurements on the device can be compared with the expected behavior in the operative environment. An example is the measurement of connection attempts to/from the device, based on parameters of a Management Information Base (MIB).

The known approaches to protect device integrity focus on the IT-related functionality of a device (with the exception of tamper protection). Also, a strong tamper protection is not common at device level. The main protection objective for device integrity shall ensure that the device's control functionality operates as designed. However, the integrity of input/output interfaces, sensors, and actuators are typically out of scope. In typical industrial environments, applying a strong tamper protection to each control device, sensor, and actuator would not be economically feasible. Therefore, protecting device integrity of used devices alone would be too limited to achieve the goal of protection the integrity of an overall CPS.

C. Cyber Physical System Integrity Monitoring

Classical approaches for protecting device and system integrity target at preventing any changes and compare the current configuration to a fixed reference policy. More flexible approaches are needed to protect integrity for flexibly reconfigurable and self-adapting CPSs. In previous work [1], we described an integrated, holistic approach for ensuring CPS integrity that is an extensible framework to include integrity information from IT-based functions and the physical world of a CPS. This allows integrating integrity information from the digital and the physical world. Trusted physical integrity sensors can be installed as add-on to existing automation and control systems. One-way gateways can be used to extract integrity monitoring information from closed control networks, while ensuring freedom from interference.

Integrity does not only affect single devices, but also the overall system level comprising a set of interconnected devices. The main approaches to protect system integrity are collecting and analyzing information at system level [1]:

- Device inventory: Complete and up-to-date list of installed devices (including manufacturer, model, serial number version, firmware version, current configuration, installed software components, location)

- Centralized Logging: Devices provide log data, e.g., using Open Platform Communication Unified Architecture (OPC UA) protocol, Simple Network Management Protocol (SNMP), or syslog protocol, to a centralized logging system.
- Runtime device integrity measurements: A device integrity agent provides information gathered during the operation of the device (see also point B above). It collects integrity information on the device and provides it for further analysis. Basic integrity information includes the results of a device self-test, and information on the current device configuration (firmware version, patches, installed applications, configuration). Furthermore, runtime information can be gathered and provided for analysis (e.g., process list, file system integrity check values, partial copy of memory).
- Network monitoring: The network communication is intercepted, e.g., using a network tap or a mirror port of a network switch. A challenge is the fact that network communication is increasingly encrypted.
- Physical Automation process monitoring: Trusted sensors provide information on the physical world that can be used to cross-check the view of the control system on the physical world. Adding trusted sensors to existing installation allows for a smooth migration from legacy systems to systems providing integrated sensors.
- Physical world integrity: Trusted sensors (of physical world), integrated monitoring of embedded devices and IT-based control systems, and of the technical process allow now quality of integrity monitoring as physical world and IT world are checked together.

The captured integrity information can be used for system runtime integrity monitoring to detect integrity violations in real-time. Operators can be informed, or actions can be triggered automatically. Furthermore, the information is archived for later investigations. This allows that integrity violations can be detected also later with a high probability, so that corresponding countermeasures can be initiated (e.g., plan for an additional quality check of produced goods). The integrity information can be integrated in or linked to data of a production management system, so that it can be investigated under which integrity conditions certain production steps have been performed. Product data is enhanced with integrity monitoring data related to the production of the product.

An intelligent analysis platform performs data analysis (e.g., statistical analysis, big data analysis, artificial intelligence) and triggers suitable respondence actions (e.g., alarm, remote wipe of a device, revocation of a device, stop of a production site, planning for additional test of manufactured goods).

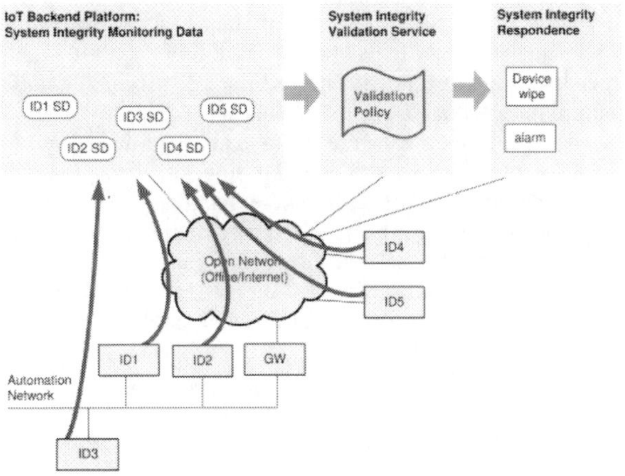

Figure 1. CPS Integrity Monitoring System [1]

Figure 1 shows an example for an IoT system with IoT devices (ID1, ID2, etc.) that communicate with an IoT backend platform. The devices provide current integrity monitoring information to the backend platform. The devices can be automation devices that include integrity measurement functionality, or dedicated integrity sensor devices. The device monitoring system itself has to be protected against attacks, following the industrial security standard IEC 62443.

An integrity data validation service checks the obtained integrity measurement data for validity using a configurable validation policy. If a policy violation is detected, a corrective action is triggered. For example, an alarm message can be displayed on a dashboard. Furthermore, an alarm message can be sent to the IoT backend platform to terminate the communication session of the affected IoT device. Moreover, the device security service can be informed so that it can revoke the devices access permissions, or revoke the device authentication credential.

The integrity monitoring events are analyzed using known data analysis tools. As stated before, in industrial environments, it is also important to have reliable information about the system integrity of a production system for the time period during which a certain production batch was performed. This allows performing the verification also afterwards to check whether during a past production batch integrity-violations occurred.

The final decision whether a certain configuration is accepted as correct is up to human operators. After reconfiguration, or for a production step, the configuration is to be approved. The approval decision can be automated according to previously accepted decisions, or preconfigured good configurations.

D. Resilience Under Attack

Being resilient means to be able to withstand or recover quickly from difficult conditions [4]. It shifts the focus of "classical" IT and OT security, which put the focus on preventing, detecting, and reacting to cyber-security attacks, to the aspect to continue to deliver an intended outcome despite an adverse cyber attack taking place, and to recover quickly to regular operation. More specifically, resilience of a system is the property to be resistant to a range of threats and withstand the effects of a partial loss of capability, and to recover and resume its provision of service with the minimum reasonable loss of performance [5].

Risk management, the "classical" approach to cyber security, identifies threats and determines the risk depending on probability and impact of a potential attack. The objective is to put the focus of defined security measures on the most relevant risks. Resilience, however, puts the focus on a reduction of the impact, so that the system stays operational with a degraded performance or functionality even when it has been attacked successfully, and to recover quickly from a successful attack. Robustness is a further related approach that tries to keep the system operational *without* a reduction of the system performance, i.e., to withstand attacks.

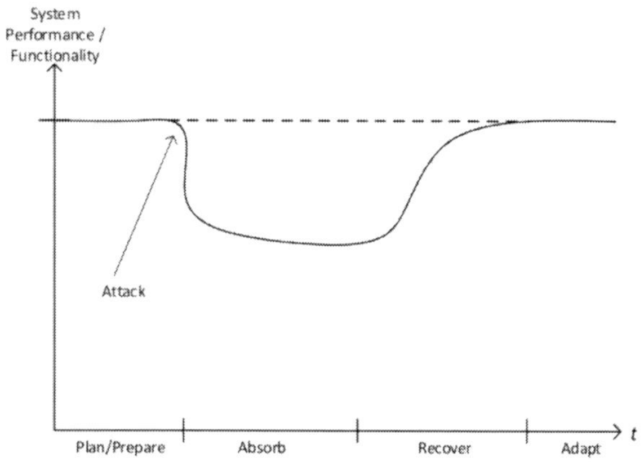

Figure 2. Concept of Cyber Resilience [2]

Figure 2 illustrates the concept of cyber resilience: Even if an attack is carried out, the impact on the system operation, i.e., the performance or functionality of the system, is limited [2]. The effects of an attack are "absorbed", so that the system stays operational, but with limited performance or functionality. A recovery takes place to bring the system up to the regular operation. In adaptation of resilience, the system might be enhanced to better prepare for future attacks leading to a sort of self-healing functionality. In a cyber physical environment, a main objective is that the CPS stays operational and that its integrity is ensured. In the context of an industrial automation and control system, that means that (only) intended actions of the system in the physical world continue to take place even when the automation and control system of the CPS should be attacked.

III. Lifecycle Configuration Change Monitoring

A main concept presented in this paper is an enhancement to the system-level integrity monitoring system, described in Section II.C. Instead of comparing integrity measurements to a fixed reference policy, the observed changes to device configuration along their lifecycle is validated. An integrity violation is detected if changes are detected that are not in-line with a policy on what and how changes are applied.

Lifecycle state agents on the system components act as integrity sensors that collect lifecycle state information of a device and provide it in the form of a lifecycle state attestation to the system integrity monitoring system. The policy defining permitted changes of lifecycle states can be preconfigured. However, this would require significant effort. Therefore, an automated learning system, based on artificial intelligence, is proposed that learns from good examples of permitted changes. In an initial introduction phase, good changes (allowed changes from a system operation level) have to be marked by the OT personnel. Over time, the system learns from these good examples. This approach is similar to a network firewall for which the filter policy is determined automatically during a learning phase.

Such a self-learning of permitted changes leads to an automated learning of what changes lead to a trustworthy CPS. It is in real-world practice often not easy to determine explicit rules on which specific properties make a component or a change being considered as trustworthy. By learning from good and bad examples, the attributes that are relevant for the trustworthiness evaluation can also be determined over time automatically. The system learns which attributes of a lifecycle state attestation are relevant for determining which changes are permitted. This self-learning approach allows also for subjective trust policies: Different users, i.e., operators of a CPS, can give examples of what they consider to be trustworthy or not so trustworthy. Depending on these examples, a trustworthiness evaluation policy is derived. The idea of this self-learning trust policy is conceptually similar to areas, e.g., firewalls with a learning mode. However, it is a more open approach where even the attributes (criteria) that are relevant for making trust decisions do not have to be predefined.

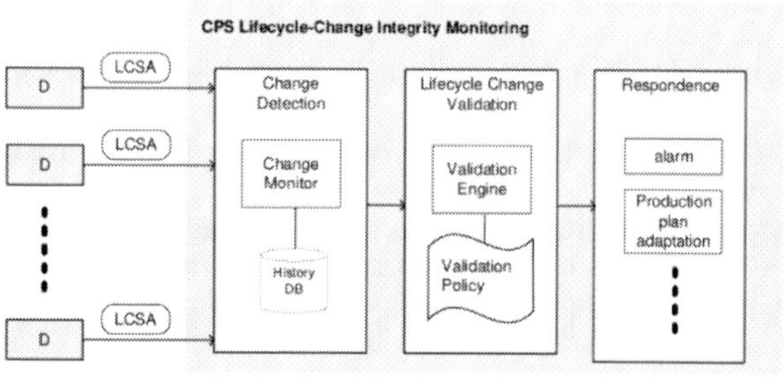

Figure 3. CPS Lifecycle Change Monitoring

Figure 3 shows devices (D) that provide Life Cycle State Attestations (LCSA) to a CPS Lifecycle-change Integrity Monitoring system. It determines changes on device lifecycle states based on the provided attestations, and validates whether changes are in-line with a lifecycle change validation policy. If the policy is violated, e.g., an alarm can be generated, or the production plan can be adapted accordingly.

IV. Device Lifecycle State Attestation

Different lifecycle states of industrial IoT devices can be distinguished, including factory default state, commissioned, operational, failure, network connected, provisioned, repair, service, or being put out of service. The current lifecycle state of a device can be determined based on its current configuration data. Some security standards, e.g., ETSI EN 303645 on Consumer IoT Security includes an example of a device life cycle model [10]. Besides the life cycle phase information, also the parts of the specific configuration can be provided as part of the life cycle attestation and analyzed. It is not assumed that a common life-cycle model is explicitly supported by the devices, as in a real-world CPS, different device types originating from various manufacturers are used. Instead, the available information of the device configuration is taken as basis to derive/estimate the related life-cycle phase, at least if it is not provided explicitly.

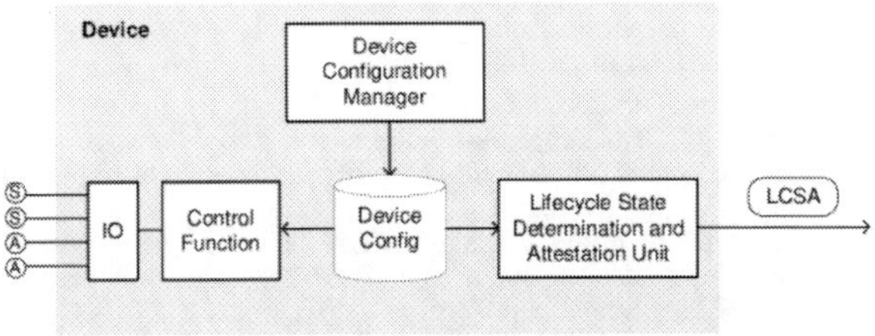

Figure 4. Control Device with Lifecycle State Attestation

A device can determine its own lifecycle state and confirm it externally by a device lifecycle state attestation. Figure 4 shows a device, e.g., a control device for monitoring and controlling a technical process via sensors (S) and actuators (A) by a control function that interacts via an input-output unit (IO) with the sensors and actuators, according to the device configuration established by a device configuration manager. The lifecycle state attestation unit determines the device lifecycle state based on the current device configuration and creates a cryptographically protected LCSA. Besides the current lifecycle state, also previous lifecycle states can be kept and attested, providing a more comprehensive information on the device lifecycle history. Alternatively, the lifecycle state may be determined and attested by an external add-on component, allowing that a LCSA can be provided also for legacy devices that do not have an integrated functionality for determining and attesting the device lifecycle state.

The LCSA can be provided in a dedicated attestation data structure, i.e., a data structure that describes the current lifecycle state of the device, and that is protected by a cryptographic checksum, i.e., a digital signature or a message authentication code. However, it is also possible to encode the life cycle information in a device credential, e.g., a device authentication certificate, a device attribute certificate, a device authentication token, or a verifiable credential.

V. Evaluation

From the perspective of a real-world CPS, the approach presented in Sections III and IV is not self-contained, but is an extension to other, well-established security measures to protect a CPS. The main advantage comes by the support for increasingly dynamic, evolving CPS. To ensure that a CPS and its components are in a trustworthy state, it is not ensured that the configuration corresponds to a fixed reference, but to check whether the detected changes are acceptable. This approach can compensate when classical, rather strict security controls preventing heavy changes to a CPS cannot be applied anymore in the same way as for static CPS deployments.

The security of a cyber system can be evaluated in practice in various approaches and stages of the system's lifecycle:

- Threat and Risk Analysis (TRA) of cyber system
- Checks during operation to determine key performance indicators (e.g., check for compliance of device configurations).
- Security testing (penetration testing)

During the design phase of a cyber system, the security demand is determined, and the appropriateness of a security design is validated using a TRA. Assets to be protected and possible threats are identified, and the risk is evaluated in a qualitative way depending on probability and impact of threats. The effectiveness of the proposed enhanced device authentication means can be reflected in a system TRA.

The main evaluation using security tools is performed during secure operation, when as part of an overall operational security management appropriate technologies are deployed that, in combination, reduce the risk to an acceptable level. The new approach presented in this paper provides an additional element, integrated into the overall system security architecture that is used to reduce the risk of integrity violations, despite a dynamically changing CPS configuration.

For the applicability to real-world CPS environments, the approach allows for:

- Flexibility for updates: The device life cycle integrity monitoring system can be updated independently from the actual CPS.
- It can be installed as add-on to existing automation systems (brownfield). It can be introduced stepwise, starting with lifecycle monitoring for most relevant devices.
- It can be installed as an add-on system that does not endanger the reliable operation of a CPS or invalidate its certifications.

Such non-technical properties simplify the adoption in real-world CPS, and they are often important factors for acceptance by OT operators.

VI. Conclusion

Ensuring device and system integrity is an essential security feature for cyber physical systems and the (industrial) Internet of Things. This must be ensured from the beginning using the security design principle of "defense in depth". It allows to support system integrity based on the information provided from single components or devices that build the CPS.

This paper proposed a framework for ensuring system integrity in flexibly adaptable cyber physical systems. With new concepts for flexible automation systems coming with Industrial IoT / Industry 4.0, the focus of system integrity has to move from preventing changes to device and system configuration to having transparency on the device and system configuration and checking it for compliance.

The approaches for integrity monitoring in industrial automation and control systems described in this paper focus on the operation phase by relying on lifecycle attestations for single components building a CPS. This approach enhances the existing systems, with an attestation about a specific state in the lifecycle, which allows an industrial monitoring system to evaluate the current life cycle state with the expected one. This can be done in addition to classical system monitoring, which verifies configuration and system behavior against expected patterns.

Integrity in a broader sense has to cover the whole life cycle, from development, secure procurement, secure manufacturing, and supply chain security up to the commissioning phase in the operational environment. This lifecycle information can then be used to enhance the current system state information. Due to the life cycle information available on the device or its associated management system, feedback to manufacturer can be provided in case of failure, in which the problem may be traced back to a specific production step. This also allows the manufacturer to better react in future versions of a device.

Security-critical operations of a device, e.g., using for control operations, provisioning operational keys, or providing sensitive commissioning data is performed only for devices being in an expected state. A device can be used for regular operational purposes only if, according to its lifecycle, it is in a valid lifecycle state, and if this lifecycle state has been established in a permitted way.

References

[1] R. Falk and S. Fries, "System Integrity Monitoring for Industrial Cyber Physical Systems", International Journal On Advances in Security, volume 11, numbers 1&2, pp. 170-179, 2018, [Online]. Available from https://www.thinkmind.org/index.php?view=article&articleid=sec_v11_n12_2018_14 [retrieved August, 2022]

[2] R. Falk and S. Fries, "Enhancing the Resilience of Cyber-Physical Systems by Protecting the Physical-World Interface", International Journal On Advances in Security, volume 13, numbers 1 and 2, pp. 54-65, 2020, [Online]. Available from: http://www.thinkmind.org/index.php?view=article&articleid=sec_v13_n12_2020_5 [retrieved August, 2022]

[3] Plattform Industrie 4.0, "Industrie 4.0 Plug-and-produce for adaptable factories: example use case definition, models, and implementation", Plattform Industrie 4.0 working paper, June 2017, [Online]. Available from: https://www.plattform-i40.de/PI40/Redaktion/DE/Downloads/Publikation/Industrie-40-Plug-and-Produce.pdf [retrieved August, 2022]

[4] P. England, R. Aigner, A. Marochko, D. Mattoon, R. Spiger, and S. Thom, "Cyber resilient platforms", Microsoft Technical Report MSR-TR-2017-40, Sep. 2017, [Online]. Available from: https://www.microsoft.com/en-us/research/publication/cyber-resilient-platforms-overview/ [retrieved August, 2022]

[5] Electronic Communications Resilience&Response Group, "EC-RRG resilience guidelines for providers of critical national telecommunications infrastructure", version 0.7, March 2008, available from: https://assets.publishing.service.gov.uk/government/uploads/system/uploads/attachment_data/file/62281/telecoms-ecrrg-resilience-guidelines.pdf [retrieved August, 2022]

[6] IEC 62443, "Industrial Automation and Control System Security" (formerly ISA99), available from: http://isa99.isa.org/Documents/Forms/AllItems.aspx [retrieved August, 2022]

[7] ISO/IEC 27001, "Information technology – Security techniques – Information security management systems – Requirements", October 2013, available from: https://www.iso.org/standard/54534.html [retrieved August, 2022]

[8] IEC 62443-3-3:2013, "Industrial communication networks – Network and system security – Part 3-3: System security requirements and security levels", Edition 1.0, August 2013

[9] IEC 62554-4.2, "Industrial communication networks - Security for industrial automation and control systems - Part 4-2: Technical security requirements for IACS components", CDV:2017-05, May 2017

[10] EN 303 645, "Cyber Security for Consumer Internet of Things: Baseline Requirements", ETSI, V2.1.1 (2020-06), June 2020, [Online]. Available from: https://www.etsi.org/deliver/etsi_en/303600_303699/303645/02.01.01_60/en_303645v020101p.pdf [retrieved August, 2022]

How Good is Openly Available Code Snippets Containing Software Vulnerabilities to Train Machine Learning Algorithms?

Kaan Oguzhan
T RDA CST SEL-DE
Siemens AG
Munich, Germany
email: kaan.oguzhan@siemens.com

Tiago Espinha Gasiba
T RDA CST SEL-DE
Siemens AG
Munich, Germany
email: tiago.gasiba@siemens.com

Akram Louati
T RDA CST SEL-DE
Siemens AG
Munich, Germany
email: akram.louati@siemens.com

***Abstract*—Machine learning has been gaining more and more attention over the last years. One of the recent areas where machine learning has been applied is secure software development to identify software vulnerabilities. The algorithms depend on the amount and quality of data used for training. Although many studies are emerging on machine learning algorithms, one must enquire about the data used to train these algorithms. This paper addresses this question by investigating and analyzing freely available vulnerable code snippets. We investigate their quantity and quality in terms of the existing categorization of security vulnerabilities used in industrial environments. Furthermore, we investigate these aspects in dependency on several different programming languages. In addition, we provide the database containing the collected vulnerable code snippets for further research. Our results show that, while a large number of training data is available for some programming languages, this is not the case for every language. Our results can be used by researchers and industry practitioners working on machine learning and applying these algorithms to improve software security.**

Keywords–machine learning; deep learning; industry; software; vulnerabilities.

I. INTRODUCTION

The rapid increase of digitalization and the fast-changing technology landscape are continuously increasing the potential attack surfaces for organizations [1]. According to AV-TEST [2], the number of cybersecurity incidents has been steadily increasing swiftly. One possible root cause of these incidents is poor software development that results in vulnerable code. A cybersecurity incident occurs when vulnerable code is attacked by malware. In 2013, the total number of known malware was about 182 million, whereas, in 2021, this number increased to 1313 million - an increase by more than sixfold compared to preceding years.

One way to address vulnerabilities in software, which is widely used in the industry, is by detecting vulnerabilities during the software development lifecycle through static code analysis. The traditional method of developing a new vulnerability detection algorithm starts from mathematical formulas or known vulnerable patterns and turns them into computer code that follows the exact mathematical formula or matches the exact pattern [3]–[7]. There are already many examples of static code analysis tools as both open source, such as [8] and commercial, such as [9]. The biggest drawback in developing such tools is the need for handcrafting new formulas or patterns for every type of vulnerability or, in the best case, adapting the old patterns to capture the new vulnerabilities. This process is time-consuming and requires much expertise in cybersecurity, which is not always available and can incur high costs.

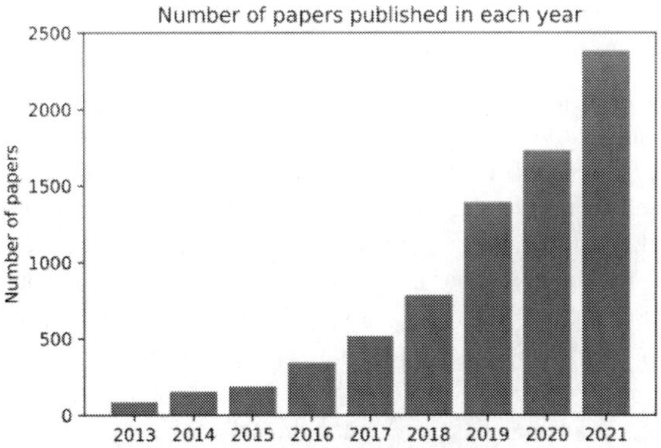

Figure 1. Appearance of both keywords "Cybersecurity" and "Machine Learning" in Academic Papers according to Scopus

It is not surprising that the traditional methods have started failing to keep up with the pace of new vulnerabilities, which are being introduced at an ever-increasing rate. It is beneficial to introduce new vulnerability detection methods to keep pace with the increasing number of vulnerabilities.

Machine learning is a sub-field of artificial intelligence; in contrast to the traditional methods, it does not require handcrafted formulas by experts. It is based on the idea that a neural network, which is essentially a vastly complex model designed after the human brain, can learn to make accurate decisions from large amounts of data through optimization processes like Gradient Descent [10] with minimal human intervention.

Although relatively new, the field of machine learning is expanding at an accelerating pace. Its expansion is driven by the explosion of Big Data [11], [12] and the ever-increasing pace of growth in accelerator computing power [13]. The implementation of these algorithms can be very efficient through the usage of highly optimized computations, such as Coppersmith–Winograd algorithms [14] and the use of specialized primitives [15].

Machine learning and deep learning algorithms can potentially significantly transform the cybersecurity field, e.g., by

Figure 2. Word Cloud generated from 2-gram's over all the snippet titles

allowing adaptation to changes at a much faster pace and detecting very complex patterns in the data. Through the literature, we observe a significant uptrend in the number of work-related to deep learning applications in cybersecurity over the last decade (see Figure 1). We expect to see a growth in the number of static code analysis tools both open source and commercial following the trend by harnessing the power of machine learning for source-code [16] or byte-code analysis [17]–[19].

Deep learning has the potential to make cybersecurity simpler and more effective. However, it can only do so if the underlying data has enough samples and contain a distinct variety of information. In other words, deep learning models can only be as good as the data in which it has been trained. Unfortunately, when it comes to cybersecurity, that data is often lacking.

Secure coding is vital in the industry because it helps to ensure that software is free from vulnerabilities that attackers could exploit to gain access to systems and data. By ensuring that the code is secure, organizations can reduce the risk of data breaches and other cybersecurity incidents and improve their compliance with regulations, such as the General Data Protection Regulation (GDPR) [20], Payment Card Industry Data Security Standard (PCI-DSS) [21] and IEC 62.443 from the International Electrotechnical Commission.

There are several ways to improve code security, e.g., through following secure coding guidelines, conducting code reviews, and using static analysis tools. Until recently, commercial and open-sourced static code analysis tools existed using non machine learning techniques. These tools are built by handcrafting rules and using pattern matching techniques to detect vulnerabilities [3]–[7] However, following the recent trend in deep learning getting into many areas of Information Technologies, we expect to see the same up trend in cybersecurity applications, such as [22]–[24] and more specifically, into the field of static code analysis tools, such as [25].

The large amounts of data required to train deep learning algorithms are difficult to acquire. A possible way to obtain such a large amount of training data is to inspect existing open-source projects and secure programming language standards. After vulnerabilities in open-source projects are publicly disclosed, it is generally followed by the project maintainers providing a fix. Therefore, the code before and after the fix would be one way to train deep learning algorithms, as many such code examples are available. According to GitHub-2020-Digital-Insight-Report [26], as of 2020, there are over 1.05 million open-source projects across all of GitHub. This number should be more than enough for most machine learning tasks. However, most open-source projects do not use standardized vulnerability classifications, such as Common Weakness Enumeration (CWE), for their code fixes. As such, the task of collecting vulnerable code snippets directly from GitHub repositories remains very challenging.

Our work focuses on known vulnerabilities with a standardized classification that aligns with industrial security standards. We explore existing and openly available sources that contain vulnerable codes. In addition, we look at the possibility of using these sources to create static code analysis tools using machine learning techniques, thus improving overall security. Our work contributes by analyzing the quality of openly available data sources and the amount of data they can provide. Our work also assists further research in this young discipline by pointing to these data sources and also unveils possible obstacles that further work in this field can experience - both by researchers and practitioners alike. Furthermore, our work presents an overview of the state of secure coding knowledge of individual programming languages. Industry practitioners can use our results to motivate their choice of a programming language so that they can fulfill the requirements of industrial security standards.

Our work is structured as follows. In Section II, we discuss previous and related work. In Section III, we describe our methodology and experiment. In Section IV, we provide the significant contribution of the present work through a critical discussion of the results obtained in the experiment. Finally, in Section V, we finalize the paper through a brief overview and consideration of further work.

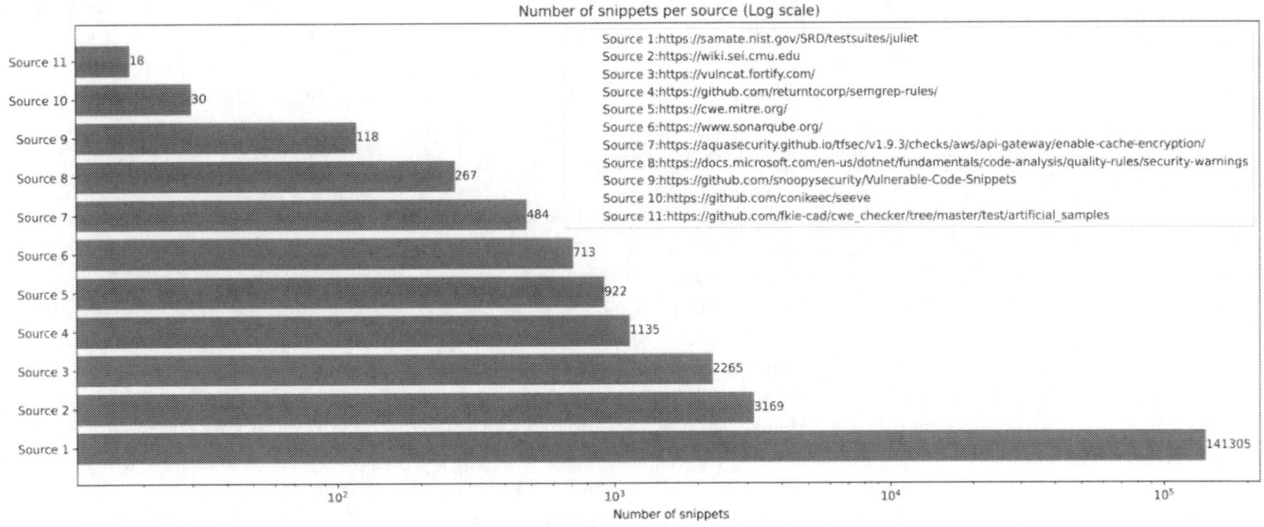

Figure 3. Number of snippets taken from their respective sources

II. RELATED WORK

As the quantity and quality of Big Data increases, many organizations have inevitably more and more demand for secure software that can protect the data of their customers and themselves. Due to the ever-increasing complexity of developing standardization, we can see more and more standardization and categorization being done by organizations such as, the PCI-DSS [21], International Standard Organization ISO/IEC 27000 series [27], Computer Emergency Response Team CERT [28], CWE [29], and Open Web Application Security Project OWASP Top 10 [30].

Producers such as, the International Organization for Standardization (ISO) [31] and the International Electrotechnical Commission (IEC) [32] have created a whole new standard for data security, ISO/IEC 27000 family, due to the need for a new standard ensuring the security of Big Data.

The ISO/IEC 27000 is a family of standards for Information Security Management Systems (ISMS) used by organizations of all sizes and industry sectors to protect their data. The standard is based on a risk management approach and provides a framework for organizations to identify, assess and manage the risks to their Information security. The standards cover various topics, including security policy, risk assessment, security controls, incident management, and business continuity.

IEC 62.443 is a family of standards for industrial automation and control systems security. The standards cover various topics, including risk assessment, security controls, incident management, and business continuity.

The ISO/IEC 27000 family of standards and the IEC 62.443 family of standards are complementary to each other. The ISO/IEC 27000 family of standards provides a general framework for Information security management, while the IEC 62.443 family of standards provides specific guidance for industrial automation and control systems.

Static code analysis is a process where the source code of a software application is analyzed without executing it. Static code analysis aims to find errors and vulnerabilities in the code that attackers can exploit. By finding these vulnerabilities, software developers can fix them before the application reaches end customers. Static code analysis tools can be used to find a wide range of security vulnerabilities in software. The classical static code analysis tools use a set of rules and patterns to find vulnerabilities in the code; however, they require much manual work to create those rules and patterns. Another disadvantage of static code analysis is that it can be time-consuming to run on large codebases. In addition, those classic static code analysis tools can produce many false positives and negatives, making it difficult to identify real security issues while highlighting the fact that additional processes must be used to write secure code.

With the rise of Big Data and machine learning, it is inevitable to think about other potentially promising and attractive solutions to the problem of finding security vulnerabilities in software. By applying machine learning techniques, we can accelerate the process of static code analysis and potentially even reduce the number of false positives. These methods require data to train the algorithms.

In our work, we look at vulnerable code snippets from those that are openly available, e.g., the Juliet Test Suite from the National Institute for Standards and Technology, the Common Weakness Enumeration [29] from the MITRE foundation, the Software Engineering Institute of the Computer Emergency Response Team (SEI CERT) [28] from Carnegie Mellon, and openly available data sets from commercial providers such as, SonarQube [9] and Fortify [33].

The CWE list from the MITRE foundation constitutes a standardized means to classify software vulnerabilities. In the documentation of each vulnerability are vulnerable code snippets for several programming languages.

The Juliet Test Suite contains a large and well-known collection of vulnerable snippets for the C, C#, C++, and Java programming languages. Although this data set is extensive, it exists for only a few programming languages. Many providers of static code analysis use this data set as a means of benchmarking their tool.

SEI CERT provides a secure coding standard for C, C++, Perl, Java, and Android. The standard contains code snippets as examples for each described vulnerability.

Fortify is a commercial company that does not focus on categorizing vulnerabilities; nevertheless, they provide snippet examples for each vulnerability they document. SonarQube is a commercial company selling a static code analysis tool; their openly available documentation provides several examples of code vulnerabilities and their corresponding CWE number.

Despite deep learning being still in its infancy in terms of popularity, it has already performed well in solving several problems in the cybersecurity field. It is worth noting that although there are many examples in academia such as, [34] most of these applications are not yet made into fully functional and production-grade software.

Deep learning models optimize to predict certain outputs given an input and is only as good as the data it has been trained on. Thus dumping sheer amounts of data might not always produce good results, after all the data quality is of importance. Withing a dataset there is always some variance, which can be minimized by increasing the number of samples, but the noise in the data might never go away. Another form of noise is the bias, which is a more structural problem and it represents the difference between an algorithm's expected output on a dataset and its actual output. When not dealt with properly, both of the problems would cripple the models performance. This concept is called the Bias-Variance trade-off.

III. EXPERIMENT

This section briefly discusses the methodology used to collect openly available vulnerable code snippets. We also present the results of the experiment together with an analysis thereof.

A. METHODOLOGY

To collect data for our experiment, we considered the following types of sources: (1) secure coding standards used in the industry, (2) official databases, (3) open documentation of available static code analysis tools, and (4) miscellaneous.

The following methods were employed in our work for each source type to obtain vulnerable code snippets :

- **(1) Standards**, and **(3) Documentation** - the web page where the standard or documentation is hosted was parsed, and the code snippets were extracted employing web crawling,
- **(2) Official Databases** - in this case, the code snippets were already provided in individual files,
- **(3) Miscellaneous** - depending on the repository, web crawling was used, or the code snippets were copied from individual files.

One crucial aspect that was also carried out was the creation of an SQL database, which contains one entry for each of the vulnerable code snippets, with a corresponding classification on the programming language and the standard secure coding rule number.

Figure 4 shows the number of code snippets gathered from each source. In [35], we provide the entire database to assist further researchers and practitioners.

B. RESULTS

For our analysis, we have gathered data from the online websites that provide vulnerable code snippets and their standardized categories. We analyzed snippets from 11 sources and then sorted these by programming language and vulnerability types. In Figure 3, we have listed all the external sources we have used and how many snippet examples they have publicly provided, as discussed in the methodology sub-section.

When categorized by the programming language Figure 4, we have found that four languages dominate the number of snippets by a considerable margin. We have found more than 45.000 code snippets for the C programming language, about 37.000 for Java, about 34.000 for C#, and 29.000 for C++. This large number is primarily due to the Julie Set. The number of available code snippets sees a sudden drop starting with 437 for Python. These results indicate that the number of vulnerable code snippets openly found on the internet is very language-specific and thus raises concerns about the performance of machine learning models trained with minimal data for these programming languages. Moreover, we have 355 standard vulnerability categories for Python, with an average of around six code snippets per category. We note that some categories overlap between different standards. To our knowledge, it is almost impossible to train a machine learning model with such limited data. Nevertheless, we expect to see models trained solely on the publicly available data for languages C, C#, C++, and Java as an extensive data set exists to train the respective algorithms.

In our experiment, we have also analysed the standardised vulnerability categories. Our main focus are on two categories, namely *OWASP TOP 10* (see Figure 5) and *PCI-DSS* (see Figure 6).

For the OWASP TOP 10, we found and collected openly available code snippets from 2004 to 2021. We have observed that the number of publicly available snippets has increased steadily over the years from approx. 1500 to approx. 2000 (see Figure 5). However, when investigating their categories, it is clear that the snippets are not equally distributed among all the ten categories (see Figure 5). To emphasize the difference, the category with the highest snippet count, "2017-A03 Sensitive Data Exposure," has 721 snippets, whereas "2017-A04 Server-Side Request Forgery" has only eight snippets. It is also important to note that the number of publicly available snippets is not necessarily representative of the number of vulnerabilities that exist in the real world. There may be more real-world vulnerabilities in category 2012:A10 than in category 2017:A3.

These results highlight the importance of analyzing the sub-dimension of a data set before deciding on a machine learning

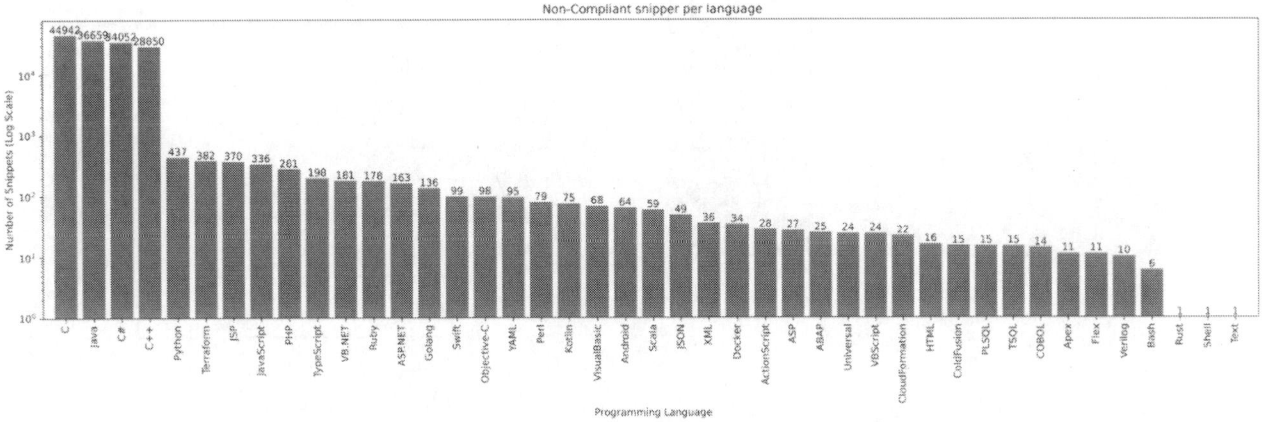

Figure 4. Number of non-compliant snippets per language

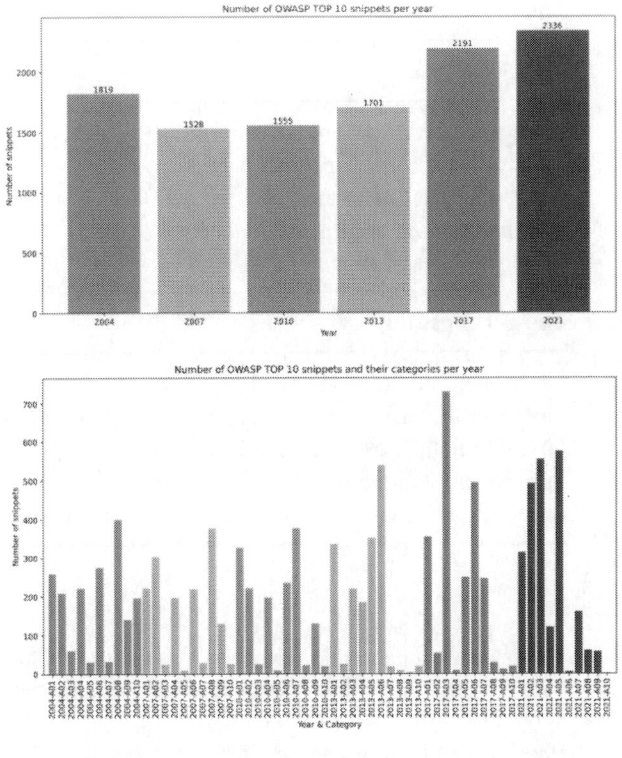

Figure 5. OWASP TOP-10 Snippet count for each Year as well as snippet count for sub-categories for each year

model. In the case of OWASP TOP 10, it is clear that if one looks at the uniformity amongst years and directly trains a machine learning model on them, the trained model will not be able to generalize well for all categories. The reason is that the model will be over-fitted on the categories with many snippets and will not work for categories with only a few snippets. In order to avoid such problems, one has to investigate the sub-categories further and explore possible sub-dimensions of the data to ensure that they are uniform.

For the case of PCI-DSS, we have snippets from main categories (V X) V1, V2, and V3 from the years 2005, 2010, and 2015. We did not observe an uptrend in the number of available snippets between versions, as was the case for OWASP TOP 10 (see Figure 5). However, by looking into categories (V X.X), we can observe that the number of snippets is uniformly distributed among them. It already looks much better for a machine learning model to train on than OWASP TOP 10. On the other hand if we go more finer into sub-categories(V X.X-X), see Figure 6. We again see an uneven distribution of snippets. For example, "V1.2-02" has only one snippet compared to "V1.2-06," which has 2782 snippets.

Again, the number of snippets is not equally distributed among the PCI-DSS sub-categories. To the best of our knowledge, if one trains a machine learning model based solely on categories, where the numbers look uniformly distributed, one will end up with a model trained only on a few sub-categories without realizing it. In the best case, the model will be accurate for those categories with abundant snippets, but it will surely be heavily biased towards detecting them and will detect categories with a very sparse number of snippets, see Figure 6.

For our subsequent analysis, we wanted to understand the most commonly used wordings among the vulnerabilities to see if we could observe some patterns. For the analysis, we have gathered all titles given to snippets by their respective source. In the case of no title, we refer to their standard category and get the name given to the category. If the snippet has no title but has a standard category "OWASP TOP 10 2017-A03," then we assume it has the title "Sensitive Data Exposure" and add it to our corpus. After we had gathered all the titles and then calculated 2,3,4-grams as well as made a word cloud out of the 2-grams, the word cloud can be seen in Figure 2. The Top-5 n-gram can be seen for each category in Table. Table I. It is important to note that the stop-words are only removed for the 2-gram and the word cloud, but for the 3-gram and 4-gram, they are kept as they are important to keep the semantics of the word groups intact. However, after the n-gram calculations, we made an elimination for selecting the Top-5; in case the n-gram starts or ends with a stop-word, we ignore it.

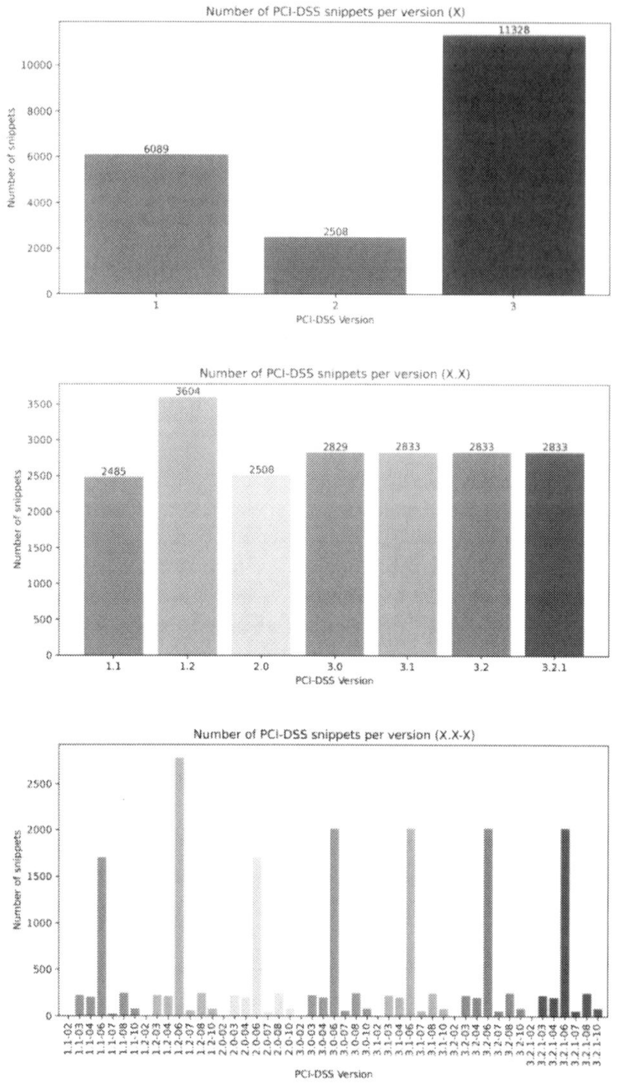

Figure 6. Number of snippets per PCI-DSS Version, going into finer categories from top to bottom

TABLE I
TOP-5 N-GRAMS

Top-5 | 2-gram
(improper, neutralization)
(integer, overflow)
(buffer, overflow)
(special, elements)
(integer, underflow)
Top-5 | 3-gram
(overflow, or, wraparound)
(neutralization, of, special)
(special, elements, used)
(integer, underflow, wrap)
(numeric, truncation, error)
Top-5 | 4-gram
(integer, overflow, or, wraparound)
(neutralization, of, special, elements)
(improper, neutralization, of, special)
(command, os, command, injection)
(improper, validation, of, array)
Top-5 | 5-gram
(improper, neutralization, of, special, elements)
(integer, underflow, wrap, or, wraparound)
(os, command, os, command, injection)
(improper, validation, of, array, index)
(use, of, externally-controlled, format, string)

For the last analysis, we wanted to see if we could observe some uniform patterns or detect unevenness for one of the most common and comprehensive data sets, the Juliet Test Suite. Many static code analysis tools use the Juliet Test Suite to benchmark their software as well as due to the sheer number of vulnerable snippets it includes, it is a tempting target for training deep learning models. This data set has been used in several previous studies [36]–[38]. We have used the same techniques as in the previous analysis and focused on the standardized vulnerability categorization CWE.

We again observed that the number of snippets is very unevenly distributed among the CWE categories. Some categories have a whooping number of snippets compared to others. For example, "CWE-121" has 5906 snippets compared to "CWE-561," which has only two snippets, see Table II. The difference is again significant, and if one were to train a machine learning model directly on the Juliet Test Suite as the data set, one would end up with a model that is heavily biased towards detecting top categories such as, "CWE-121", "CWE-78", "CWE-190". Meanwhile, detecting other categories such as, "CWE-561" would be very unlikely.

Before concluding our analysis, albeit not directly related to vulnerability categories or classes, it is worth mentioning that Juliet Test Suite snippets are usually very long. This fact contrasts with our previous sources, where snippets were relatively short and contained only a few lines of code. Such a difference can potentially significantly impact the performance of deep learning models. The Juliet Test Suite can test and benchmark static code analysis tools. Therefore, it contains many snippets that are very similar but have slight variations that make them unique. Those minor differences allow the Juliet Test Suite to cover the vulnerabilities from many angles. An oversimplified example would be "if(True)..." vs "if(1==1)..." vs "if(varTrue)...".

Due to the Juliet Test Suite's previously mentioned goal

TABLE II
JULIET DATA SET SNIPPET COUNT PER CWE ID

C		Java		C#		C++	
ID	*Snippet count*	*ID*	*Snippet count*	*ID*	*Snippet count*	*ID*	*Snippet count*
CWE 121	5906	CWE 190	6555	CWE 197	7695	CWE 762	5180
CWE 78	5600	CWE 191	5244	CWE 190	5643	CWE 122	4948
CWE 190	5040	CWE 129	4104	CWE 191	3762	CWE 36	3500
...		...		...		...	
CWE 674	2	CWE 499	1	CWE 397	1	CWE 562	1
CWE 562	2	CWE 248	1	CWE 366	1	CWE 468	1
CWE 561	2	CWE 111	1	CWE 248	1	CWE 440	1

of coverage completeness, it is easy to find snippets designed to reproduce the same vulnerability from 50 different approaches, where the difference between each approach is very tiny such as, 15 lines in a 450-line of code. (CWE122_Heap_Based_Buffer_Overflow snippets). In this case, the common acceptance of "the more data, the better" for machine learning is misleading. Having such a high similarity between the data means no good; if not handled correctly, those similarities can easily lead to overfitting, or worse, the model will learn the similarities and ignore the difference where the actual vulnerability is. Another likely pitfall is that if Juliet Test Suite alone is used for training, validation, and testing, the validation-split and test-split will be very similar to the training-split as they would share the same "common" parts of the vulnerable snippets. Therefore, using Juliet Test Suite alone for training the model and evaluating its performance will not be a good representation of real-world vulnerabilities, thus leading to a poor representation of the model's generalization capabilities.

IV. DISCUSSION

Throughout our experiment, we have tried to analyze publicly available vulnerable code snippets across programming languages and tried to understand their fitness for training popular deep learning models. As our first finding, we have seen a big difference in the number of publicly available vulnerable code snippets across programming languages, which to the best of our knowledge, has not been addressed in the literature. There are so few snippets available for some languages that it is impossible to train a model to detect vulnerabilities in that language, see Figure 4. For others, we have found that the sheer number of available snippets seems sufficient for training a model, but just the number of snippets is not enough to justify that a deep learning model trained directly on the publicly available code snippets would generalize well.

For a deep learning model to generalize well, there needs to be a certain amount of diversity in the snippets to make sure that the model is not just memorizing the available code snippets, as well as a uniformity among different vulnerabilities to make sure that the model will not be biased towards some specific vulnerabilities. A model lacking these two properties cannot perform well enough to be deployed in production environments.

We also looked at the distribution of snippets vs. standardized vulnerability categories and tried to draw some patterns to pin down possible pitfalls. We have found that one needs to be very careful during inspection of the data as the distribution of snippets might look uniform from a higher perspective, like the year for OWASP TOP 10 (e.g., 2007 vs. 2010 vs. 2013 (see Figure 5, Graph-1), but there could be a significant underlying bias in the sub-categorizations, like the case of OWASP-2017-A03 vs. OWASP-2017-A04 (see Figure 5, Graph-2). Such a bias will ultimately make the model biased towards specific vulnerabilities and lead to a bad performance. Depending on the severity of the bias, the model might not learn to detect some sub-categories.

We acknowledge that during the generation of our data set, although we tried our best not to miss anything, we could not have included some sources. The results of our analysis are solely based on the snippets we have collected. However, we believe that our data set is large enough and includes the most common public sources to give some insight into the distribution of vulnerable code snippets that are publicly available. Moreover, the results of our analysis can be used to evaluate machine learning models that are trained on publicly available vulnerable code snippets to see if they are indeed biased towards some vulnerabilities or vulnerability categories.

We also acknowledge that the static code analysis can either be done on source code or the byte/machine code; throughout our analysis, we have not delved into the task of analyzing the available byte code examples as we limited ourselves only to the publicly available and reviewed code snippets.

Practitioners and researchers can use our work as a source of information on where to find openly available data to perform machine learning experiments. We also highlight the limitations of the currently existing data. In particular, we observe that many vulnerable code snippets exist for the C, C++, Java, and C# programming language, while other programming languages, e.g., Python and Rust lack a good number of vulnerable samples to carry out meaningful experiments.

V. CONCLUSION AND FUTURE WORK

In cybersecurity and secure software development, novel methods that improve the security of applications are highly desirable. Securing software development is an essential topic for the industry as several cybersecurity standards require it. One possible way to achieve such compliance is using machine learning algorithms to identify vulnerabilities in software, as academia has demonstrated.

We expect that static code analysis using machine learning will become an essential part of future software development, in particular, using deep learning algorithms. We foresee that the developed tools will be integrated into existing Continuous Integration / Continuous Deliver (CI/CD) pipelines.

In this work, we explore freely available only databases containing vulnerable code snippets for different programming languages, as a means to train our machine learning algorithm. In particular, we focus on databases where the code snippets are categorized by a standard vulnerability classification - the common weakness enumeration from MITRE.

It is known that a large amount of high-quality data is needed to train these algorithms, in order to achieve a good detection rate. Our work shows that the number of freely available code snippets that can be used to train machine learning algorithms strongly depends on the programming language. Even for programming languages for which a large amount of snippets exist, these are not evenly distributed depending on the type of vulnerability classification. This presents a huge challenge to the field, as a non-uniform distribution certainly causes a bias in the trained model. Our results are in line with the authors' expectation and experience in secure coding field, and with standardized secure coding guidelines.

Furthermore, we observed that exploring a data set from different perspectives is essential, particularly in understanding the amount of existing data and its quality. Exploring the data set allows understanding it from different angles and avoiding possible pitfalls when training machine learning algorithms.

In further work, we will intend to implement a machine learning algorithm to detect vulnerabilities in C# code. We will aim to study the performance of such algorithm in relation to existing open-source static application security testing tools. The authors would also like to explore more simple criteria than the vulnerability type, in particular on whether the algorithm is simply vulnerable or not.

References

[1] The MITRE Corporation, "Common Vulnerabilities and Enumeration Security Vulnerability Database." https://www.cvedetails.com. [retrieved July, 2022].

[2] AV-TEST, "Malware statistics and trends report: AV-TEST." https://www.av-test.org/en/statistics/malware/. [retrieved July, 2022].

[3] C. Flanagan *et al.*, "Extended static checking for java," in ACM SIGPLAN Notices, vol. 37, 05 2002.

[4] Y. Xie and A. Aiken, "Context- and path-sensitive memory leak detection," in ACM Sigsoft Software Engineering Notes, vol. 30, pp. 115–125, Association for Computing Machinery, 09 2005.

[5] K. Karakaya and E. Bodden, "Sootfx: A static code feature extraction tool for java and android," in 2021 IEEE 21st International Working Conference on Source Code Analysis and Manipulation (SCAM), pp. 181–186, 2021.

[6] E. Ersoy and H. Sözer, "Extending static code analysis with application-specific rules by analyzing runtime execution traces," in Computer and Information Sciences (T. Czachórski, E. Gelenbe, K. Grochla, and R. Lent, eds.), pp. 30–38, Springer International Publishing, 2016.

[7] J. Vanegue, S. Heelan, and R. Rolles, "SMT solvers in software security," in 6th USENIX Workshop on Offensive Technologies (WOOT 12), USENIX Association, 08 2012.

[8] AquaSecurity, "tfsec." https://github.com/aquasecurity/tfsec. [retrieved July, 2022].

[9] SonarSource, "Sonarqube." https://www.sonarqube.org. [retrieved March, 2022].

[10] H. Robbins and S. Monro, "A stochastic approximation method," The Annals of Mathematical Statistics, vol. 22, no. 3, pp. 400–407, 1951.

[11] D. Fasel and A. Meier, *Big Data: Grundlagen, Systeme und Nutzungspotenziale, in English: Big Data: Fundamentals, Systems and Potential Uses*. Springer-Verlag, 01 2016.

[12] J. Tang, T. Ma, and Q. Luo, "Trends prediction of big data: A case study based on fusion data," Procedia Computer Science, vol. 174, pp. 181–190, 2020. 2019 International Conference on Identification, Information and Knowledge in the Internet of Things.

[13] Y. Sun, N. B. Agostini, S. Dong, and D. R. Kaeli, "Summarizing CPU and GPU design trends with product data," CoRR, vol. abs/1911.11313, 2019.

[14] D. Coppersmith and S. Winograd, "Matrix multiplication via arithmetic progressions," Journal of Symbolic Computation, vol. 9, no. 3, pp. 251–280, 1990.

[15] S. Chetlur *et al.*, "cudnn: Efficient primitives for deep learning," 2014.

[16] F. Yamaguchi, F. Lindner, and K. Rieck, "Vulnerability extrapolation: Assisted discovery of vulnerabilities using machine learning," in 5th USENIX Workshop on Offensive Technologies (WOOT 11), USENIX Association, 08 2011.

[17] H. Xue, S. Sun, G. Venkataramani, and T. Lan, "Machine learning-based analysis of program binaries: A comprehensive study," IEEE Access, vol. 7, pp. 65889–65912, 2019.

[18] W. Niu *et al.*, "Opcode-level function call graph based android malware classification using deep learning," Sensors, vol. 20, no. 13, p. 3645, 2020.

[19] A. Drewek-Ossowicka, M. Pietrołaj, and J. Rumiński, "A survey of neural networks usage for intrusion detection systems," Journal of Ambient Intelligence and Humanized Computing, vol. 12, pp. 497–514, 2020.

[20] Intersoft Consulting, "General data protection regulation GDPR." https://gdpr-info.eu. [retrieved July, 2022].

[21] Payment Card Industry, "Payment Card Industry Data Security Standard PCI-DSS." https://listings.pcisecuritystandards.org/documents/PCI-DSS-v4_0.pdf. [retrieved July, 2022].

[22] T. Guzella and W. Caminhas, "A review of machine learning approaches to spam filtering," Expert Systems with Applications, vol. 36, pp. 10206–10222, 09 2009.

[23] J. Z. Kolter and M. A. Maloof, "Learning to detect and classify malicious executables in the wild," Journal of Machine Learning Research, vol. 7, pp. 2721–2744, dec 2006.

[24] X.-S. Gan, J.-S. Duanmu, J.-F. Wang, and W. Cong, "Anomaly intrusion detection based on PLS feature extraction and core vector machine," Knowledge-Based Systems, vol. 40, pp. 1–6, 2013.

[25] G. Tang *et al.*, "A Comparative Study of Neural Network Techniques for Automatic Software Vulnerability Detection," CoRR, vol. abs/2104.14978, 2021.

[26] GitHub Inc., "Github 2020 digital insight report." [retrieved July, 2022].

[27] G. Disterer, "ISO/IEC 27000, 27001 and 27002 for information security management," Journal of Information Security, vol. 04 No.02, p. 9, 2013.

[28] Carnegie Mellon University, "SEI external Wiki." https://wiki.sei.cmu.edu. [retrieved July, 2022].

[29] MITRE, "Common weakness enumeration CWE." https://cwe.mitre.org. [retrieved July, 2022].

[30] Open Web Application Security Project, "OWASP Top Ten." https://owasp.org/www-project-top-ten. [retrieved July, 2022].

[31] International Organization for Standardization. https://www.iso.org. [retrieved July, 2022].

[32] International Electrotechnical Commission. https://iec.ch. [retrieved July, 2022].
[33] Micro Focus, "Fortify Taxonomy: Software Security Errors." https://vulncat.fortify.com. [retrieved March, 2022].
[34] R. Jusoh *et al.*, "Malware detection using static analysis in android: a review of feco (features, classification, and obfuscation)," PeerJ Computer Science, vol. 7, p. 522, 2021.
[35] K. Oguzhan, T. Gasiba, and A. Louati, "List Vulnerable Code Snippets." https://zenodo.org/record/7019175. Online, Accessed 24 August 2022.
[36] F. Wu, J. Wang, J. Liu, and W. Wang, "Vulnerability Detection with Deep Learning," in 2017 3rd IEEE International Conference on Computer and Communications (ICCC), pp. 1298–1302, 2017.
[37] N. Ziems and S. Wu, "Security Vulnerability Detection Using Deep Learning Natural Language Processing," CoRR, vol. abs/2105.02388, 2021.
[38] Z. Li *et al.*, "Vuldeepecker: A deep learning-based system for vulnerability detection," CoRR, vol. abs/1801.01681, 2018.

Towards Secure Content Sharing in Social Networks

Clara Bertolissi
Aix-Marseille Univ., CNRS
Marseille, France
clara.bertolissi@lis-lab.fr

Alba Martinez Anton
Aix-Marseille Univ., CNRS
Marseille, France
alba.martinez-anton@lis-lab.fr

Romain Testud
Aix-Marseille Univ., CNRS
Marseille, France
romain.testud@lis-lab.fr

Nicola Zannone
Eindhoven Univ. of Technology
Eindhoven, The Netherlands
n.zannone@tue.nl

***Abstract*—We propose a solution for securing access to data shared on a community-centered collaborative platform, such as a Facebook style social network. Our solution leverages provenance information and social relationships between users to define a fine-grained access control model capturing users privacy preferences. We present a prototype implementation of our model and its validation on a case study.**

Keywords-Security; Privacy; Access control.

I. Introduction

In recent years, we have seen an increasing interest in community-centered collaborative systems, where users interact and provide access to a variety of information and personal data with different degrees of sensitivity [4]. In this context, balancing data sharing and security is a difficult problem. Traditional access control policies are insufficient for dealing with jointly-owned and jointly-managed content in such collaborative environments. In this work, we address the problem of secure sharing of information in social networks and discuss to what extent the access control mechanism provided by social networks allow users to control the permissions over the content they share.

Social networks, such as Facebook, offer their users an environment and functionalities to share contents with other users. These functionalities, however, can introduce privacy concerns for users, for instance when a user is tagged [2]. In this situation, the tag target has permissions to remove the tag from the content, but cannot modify the visibility of the tag. Methods for providing a fine-grained access control at the tag level are missing. The idea that inspired our approach is that the access control model should allow the tag target to specify its privacy preferences for tags and these preferences should be taken into account when displaying the photo to a requesting user.

Our framework considers a shared content as a compound object, possibly containing other objects as subcomponents. For instance, a photo may contain a list of comments and tags associated to it. Access requests are then evaluated considering the privacy settings not only of the requested object, but those of all its components. Moreover, we consider that the privacy settings, not only of the object owner, but also of other users involved in the creation of an object should be taken into account. Our solution uses a provenance data model inspired from the Open Provenance Model [3]. Using provenance information in the evaluation allows us to identify dependencies between objects (e.g., a comment associated to a photo in a post) and retrieve all users that are related to an object, either because they have triggered the process for creating the object or because they are involved in it with some specific role (e.g., host or tag

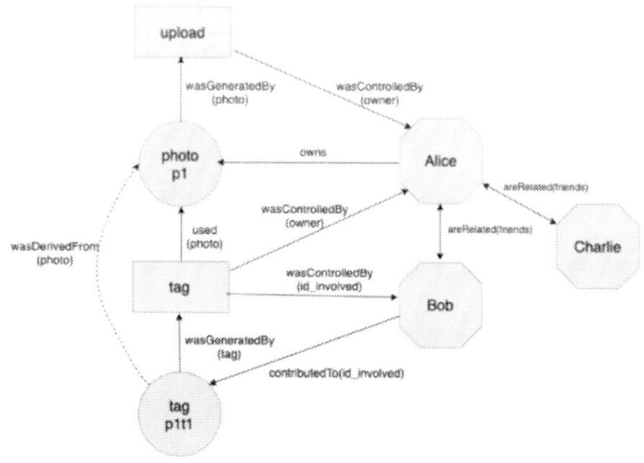

Fig. 1. Sample of the implemented evaluation graph

target). We briefly describe our model in Section II, present a proof-of-concept prototype in Section III and apply it on a social case scenario in Section IV. We conclude in Section V.

II. Extension of the Provenance model with user interaction dependencies

In this work, we leverage the Open Provenance (OP) Model [3] to capture causality dependencies between provenance entities within the social network, namely artefacts, agents and processes. Five main dependencies between two entities are defined: used (process on artifact), wasGeneratedBy (artifact on process), wasControlledBy (process on agent), wasDerivedFrom (artifact on artifact), and wasTriggeredBy (process on process). Altogether entities and dependencies form the nodes and the edges, respectively, of a directed acyclic graph. We apply the OP model to the setting of social networks, where artifacts are used to capture data objects (e.g., posts or comments); processes are used to capture the functional actions such as upload, comment, tag, etc.; agents correspond to the members of the social network. An example of provenance graph is presented in Fig. 1.

To reason about access constraints in a social network, we have extended the OP model by introducing new direct dependencies, such as owns (agent on artefact), and contributedTo (agent on process). Note that the OP model provides a notion of role that may be used to further specify dependencies. For example, an agent may have a dependency contributedTo(*id_involved*) with a tag artefact, meaning that the agent identifier has been used as tag target. We also introduce a NotAvaliable dependency which adds a cyclic dependency in

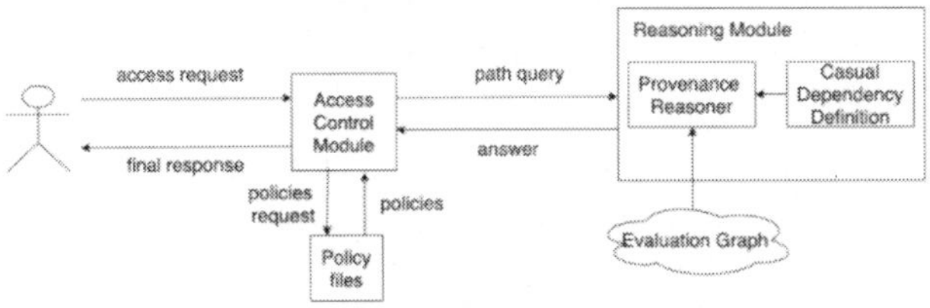

Fig. 2. Prototype Architecture

the provenance graph when an artefact has been deleted and is no longer visible.

In addition to provenance information, we also consider interpersonal social relationships between users, denoted by a dependency isRelated (and its symmetric closure areRelated) and characterized by a role such as *friend* or *family* specifying the nature of the relationship. Unlike provenance information, which represents the evolving of provenance data in the system, the social information shows a snapshot of the current relationships between users at a particular moment in time. Due to space limits, we depict the provenance and interpersonal dependencies as part of the same graph in Fig. 1.

III. Prototype: Architecture and Implementation

We describe the main components of our prototype, which are depicted in Fig. 2.

a) Access Control Module: The access control module intercepts access requests and computes the final access decision that is returned to the user. It uses auxiliary functions to retrieve user policies, to evaluate an access request and to pass path queries to the reasoning module.

b) User Policies: Each member of the social network can specify his privacy settings which are registered in a policy file. Following the Attribute-Based Access Control model, we define policies and access requests in terms of attribute name-value pairs, with the addition of path conditions (see [1]). User policies are defined in a simple language which provides an abstraction of the XACML policy specification language. For example, Alice can define her policy for objects of type *photo* as follows:

$$(\texttt{resource\_type} = \mathit{photo} \wedge \texttt{resource\_owner} = \mathit{Alice}$$
$$(\texttt{action} = \mathit{comment} \vee \texttt{action} = \mathit{view}))\wedge$$
$$(\texttt{areRelated}(\mathit{Alice}, \texttt{user\_id}, \mathit{friend})), \texttt{Permit})$$

meaning that a user can see and comment a photo owned by Alice if and only if he/she is a friend of Alice.

c) Reasoning Module: The Reasoner is implemented as a python program using the pyDatalog library. This allows us to benefit from the efficient reasoning capabilities provided by Datalog solvers for path condition resolution. In particular, we implemented rules both for constructing the evaluation graph from a given access log and for resolving path queries based on the obtained graph and the casual dependency definition.

d) Evaluation graph: The evaluation graph is built from the provenance information retrieved from the logs of the system together with the information about user relationships, which is updated at the moment of the access control request.

IV. Demonstration

Consider the social network represented by the OP model in Fig. 1 and assume an access request made by *Bob* to add a comment on Alice's photo $p1$. First, the request is received by the access control module. The object *owner* and *host*'s access policies are retrieved from the policy repository (they may be the same, say Alice policy, presented in the previous section). To evaluate the policy, the engine retrieves the regular path query from the policy $\texttt{areRelated}(\mathit{Alice}, \mathrm{Bob}, \mathit{friend}))$ and pass it to the reasoning module to resolve it. If the answer is positive, the access control module returns a positive response to Bob: $[p1, \mathit{permit}]$. When necessary (e.g., host and owner are different users), a rule combining algorithm (we implemented, e.g., grant and deny override) is applied to combine multiple response into a final decision.

Consider now a request made by *Charlie* to view Alice's photo $p1$. The request is received by the access control module and treated as before. If the permission for viewing the photo is granted, the privacy settings associated to the comments and the tags attached to the photo are considered. In this case, the access control module interacts with the reasoning engine for retrieving all the users that contributed to the comments and tags of $p1$ (i.e., Bob for the tag $p1t1$ in Fig. 1) and gather the corresponding user policies. The request is thus decomposed in a list of access requests, each returning an access response for the associated object. The access control module gathers all the responses and compose them in the form of a list. Supposing Bob let only his friends view the tags where he is targeted, we obtain for our example $[[p1, \mathit{permit}], [p0c1, \mathit{deny}]]$, that is Charlie is granted access to view the photo but not the associated tag.

V. Conclusion

We have presented an approach that uses provenance data extended with social information for enabling a fine-grained access control mechanism implementing users privacy preferences. A proof-of-concept prototype is provided to demonstrate the feasibility of our approach. The integration of our work into an XACML architecture is left for future work. Path conditions can be specified in XACML policies using the element <PolicyIdReference> or they can be they can be encoded as user-defined functions.

Acknowledgment

The project leading to this publication has received funding from Excellence Initiative of Aix-Marseille - A*MIDEX (Archimedes Institute AMX-19-IET-009).

References

[1] C. Bertolissi, J. den Hartog, and N. Zannone, "Using provenance for secure data fusion in cooperative systems", In Proc. of SACMAT 2019, pp. 185-194. ACM, 2019.
[2] S. Damen and N. Zannone, "Privacy implications of privacy settings and tagging in Facebook", In Secure Data Management 2013, pp. 121-138.
[3] L. Moreau, et al., "The Open Provenance Model core specification," in Future Generation Computer Systems, 27(6), pp. 743–756, 2011.
[4] F. Paci, A. C. Squicciarini, N. Zannone, "Survey on Access Control for Community-Centered Collaborative Systems", ACM Comput. Surv. 51(1), pp. 6:1-6:38, 2018.

Attack Path Generation Based on Attack and Penetration Testing Knowledge

Florian Sommer
Institute of Energy Efficient Mobility
Karlsruhe University of Applied Sciences
Karlsruhe, Germany
e-mail: florian.sommer@h-ka.de

Reiner Kriesten
Institute of Energy Efficient Mobility
Karlsruhe University of Applied Sciences
Karlsruhe, Germany
e-mail: reiner.kriesten@h-ka.de

***Abstract*—To protect modern vehicles against security attacks, new standards, such as ISO/SAE 21434, and regulations, such as UN R155, require security testing activities during development. For this purpose, penetration testing is often used, which is a manually performed, experience-based, and explorative test method. Due to the high complexity of modern vehicles, manual penetration testing methods reach their limits. As a result, potential vulnerabilities could be overlooked and thus remain in the vehicle. In case of a security attack, this can endanger passengers and road traffic participants. So far, penetration testing has been considered as difficult to automate, since it is an experience-based method. This paper presents a model-based approach which aims close that gap. Our approach uses knowledge of existing security attacks on vehicles to automate the security testing process. We apply our attack database (361 attacks, consisting of 621 attack steps) to a formal security model to automatically derive attack paths for testing. We also present a proposal of how this method can be transferred to derive attack paths based on knowledge and experience of penetration testers.**

Keywords*—*security testing; automation; tester experience.

I. Introduction

The increasing complexity of modern vehicles and the growing number of automotive security attacks [1] in recent years have led to automotive security becoming a high priority in industry and research. As a result of this trend, the ISO/SAE 21434 [2] and UN R155 [3] were published. Both documents require vehicle manufacturers to comply with a specific security process during the development and life cycle of vehicles. In addition to performing a Threat Analysis and Risk Assessment (TARA) [2], as well as the derivation of security requirements and measures, a focus is also on the verification and validation of security. The latter usually takes place within a security test process. For this purpose, ISO/SAE 21434 proposes in particular an execution of penetration tests.

Problem: Penetration testing is an experience-based and explorative method, which is carried out late in development. Thus, the vehicle and its components have already been developed at that point. As a result, potential vulnerabilities can only be identified at a late stage. This type of testing is often carried out by third parties as manual black-box or grey-box tests. Modern vehicles are highly complex systems and there is usually a limited time frame available for testing. Thus, Marksteiner et al. [4] see a risk that manual penetration testing reaches its limits regarding comprehensive testing. This implies that vulnerabilities could be overlooked or not captured by testing and thus remain in the vehicle.

Solution: To face these challenges, we propose a model-based approach using knowledge and experience from past security attacks and penetration tests of vehicles. For this purpose, attack paths are automatically generated and used in security testing. This allows an early execution of testing activities in vehicle development. Our approach can be used in the context of penetration testing to systematically support testers by providing attack paths based on successful real-world attacks. This allows the security test process to be partially automated by using knowledge and experience of attacks and penetration tests. Our method can further be used to estimate the effort of test activities.

Contribution: In this publication, we present a model-based security testing method. For this purpose, a security model of a vehicle E/E architecture is created based on our past work [5] [6]. Our model can be examined for possible attack paths based on real-world attacks by applying our automotive attack database [7], which currently includes 361 attacks (consisting of 621 attack steps). Further, this approach enables us to find new attack paths by permutation of existing attack steps from the database. We also present a proposal of how this approach can be used to capture and reuse experience of penetration testers to achieve partial automation of the security test process.

This paper is structured as follows: In Section II, we describe fundamentals of security testing and model-based security testing. In Section III, the approach of this work and the creation of a security model is presented. Section IV shows how our attack database can be used to automatically derive attack paths from the security model. Section V presents a proposal how the experience of penetration testers can be captured and reused for automatic attack path generation. A discussion about the feasibility of this method and challenges is given in Section VI. In Section VII, we draw a conclusion and give an outlook on future work.

II. Background and Related Work

In this section, we provide a brief overview of security testing and model-based security testing and their application in the automotive context.

A. Security Testing

Security testing examines a system for security weaknesses [8]. This is generally done in two ways. The first way concerns functional or positive security testing [9]. This typically involves testing functional security mechanisms (for example, encryption and authentication of messages) for correct functionality. This can be done as part of the traditional testing process based on requirements of security mechanisms. The second way concerns non-functional and negative security testing [9]. This type of testing is also called security vulnerability testing and is often performed through penetration tests. The tester takes the role of an attacker and attempts to find vulnerabilities in a system by carrying out security attacks [8]. Penetration testing represents an experience-based and exploratory testing method. Tests are usually performed as black-box (without system knowledge) or grey-box (partial system knowledge) tests. Several penetration testing standards exist to support testers in a structured way. Examples are Penetration Testing Execution Standard (PTES) [10] and Open Web Application Security Project (OWASP) [11] Testing Guide. For the automotive sector, the Automotive Security Testing Methodology (ASTM) [12] can be applied.

B. Security Testing in the Automotive Domain

In 2021, ISO/SAE 21434 [2] and UN R155 [3] were published for the automotive sector. These documents demand that security should be addressed throughout the development and life cycle of a vehicle. With regard to security testing, ISO/SAE 21434 in particular proposes an execution of functional testing, vulnerability scanning, fuzz testing, and penetration testing. The application of these testing techniques to automotive systems has been a subject of several recent publications. Bayer et al. [13] analyze the mentioned test methods and show potential use cases based on specific automotive technologies, such as Controller Area Network (CAN) [14], or protocols, such as Unified Diagnostic Services (UDS) [15]. Smith [16] provides a complete guide on penetration testing in vehicles. Various attack techniques on bus and diagnostic protocols, wireless communication systems, Electronic Control Units (ECUs), etc. are explained in detail. Further standards and publications propose the consideration of threat modeling for penetration testing. In this context, Dürrwang et al. [17] were able to uncover a critical vulnerability in an airbag ECU, which could lead to an unauthorized airbag deployment.

C. Model-Based Security Testing in the Automotive Domain

Model-based testing enables early testing and automation of the test process [18]. For this purpose, a System Under Test (SUT) is defined, which is commonly represented as a formal model (e.g., as a state machine). By applying test selection criteria, such as coverage criteria, test cases are derived and executed on the system. With appropriate tooling, many parts of this process can be automated. Model-based security testing combines this process with traditional security testing. The models of the SUT are extended by security-specific aspects, such as security properties, risk values, vulnerabilities, or security mechanisms. Resulting models are used to derive security test cases or attack paths. An example of a model-based security test method in the automotive domain is presented by Cheah et al. [19]. Here, attack trees, which emerge as part of a threat modeling process, are formally described by Communicating Sequential Processes (CSP) [20]. From the resulting model, a refinement checking tool is used to derive test cases to test a Bluetooth [21] device. Further, Oruganti et al. [22] and Appel et al. [23] present approaches based on Matlab/Simulink models for hardware-in-the-loop testing. Volkersdorfer et al. [24] present a model-based security approach using attack and adversary models to simulate attacks on a specific attack target. This approach is demonstrated using two application scenarios: attacks on a user's access data to a web application and the manipulation of an automotive ECU.

The presented related work focuses on finding attacks or test cases which reveal vulnerabilities in a system. This is done in an exploratory, but also in a systematic, guided, and model-based way. The authors use information about the system and its functionality and analyze how these systems can be attacked/tested. In comparison, our approach is based on a formal vehicle network model, which is specified in a generic way. This allows an application of a wide range of different attacks. For this purpose, we combine collected knowledge of attackers or security testers within a database containing successful real-world attacks. These serve as a basis for analyzing and generating attack paths as part of the security testing process.

III. Approach and Modeling Process

Penetration testing is an experience-based testing method which leverages an attacker's perspective to compromise and test systems. Therefore, knowledge about security attacks and how they are executed is an important source of information for a tester. In this section, a model-based approach is presented using knowledge and experience of attackers and penetration testers to automatically generate attack paths for security testing. Our approach and its overall process is illustrated in Figure 1. First, a security model is generated based on an Electrical/Electronic (E/E) architecture. Since we cover security testing in our approach, we need to consider all entities of the E/E architecture which have an impact on the cyber security of a vehicle. This especially involves ECUs, sensors, actuators, software applications, communication systems, and interfaces. These elements and their interactions are enhanced with security-specific aspects to create a security model. By applying our attack database [7], the model can be analyzed for possible attack paths based on successful real-world attacks. Furthermore, attack paths can be derived and adapted to the vehicle under test. In the following sections, we explain that process and further introduce details on how this approach can be implemented based on experience of penetration testers. In the first step, we build a model which represents both the network architecture of a vehicle and security-specific properties. Therefore, we build on our previous work [5], in which we introduced our concept of *Attacker Privileges*. These privileges represent abstract states an attacker can achieve in a system by exploiting vulnerabilities. Thus, we are able to introduce attack paths in our model.

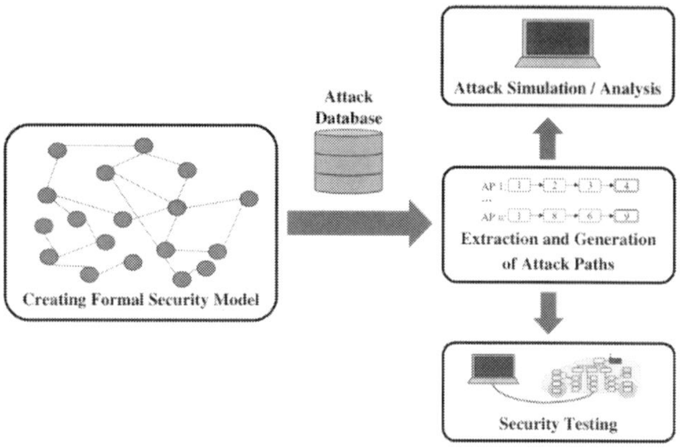

Figure 1. Model-based approach for security testing. A security model is created which is used to derive attack paths for the SUT. These paths can be used for attack simulation/analysis and security testing.

We distinguish five privileges as illustrated in Figure 2. The *Read/Write* privilege describes an attackers ability to read and write data or messages on a communication channel. By acquiring the *Execute* privilege an attacker is able to trigger implemented functions on a component (e.g., controlling an actuator via diagnostic functions). The *Read* privilege enables an attacker to extract data or information from a component (e.g., extracting secret keys). The *Write* privilege describes an ability to write or change data on a component (e.g., deleting error logs). By acquiring the *Full Control* privilege an attacker has total control over a component (e.g., by updating an ECU with malicious software). All five privileges can be assigned to elements of a vehicle network as shown in Figure 2. The *Read/Write* privilege can only be assigned to communication systems (e.g., CAN or Bluetooth). The other four privileges are assigned to components (e.g., ECUs or sensors). If an attacker reaches the *Read/Write* privilege (PL1, Figure 2 left), any other privilege (PL2 - PL5) on a component can be acquired from there if corresponding vulnerabilities are exploited. On the component, the attacker is able to switch between privileges PL2 - PL5 when exploiting vulnerabilities. We also assume that it is possible for an attacker to access communication interfaces of a component once PL4 or PL5 has been reached. This would allow access to further connected communication systems (PL1, Figure 2 right). Applying the *Attacker Privileges* to an entire E/E architecture of a vehicle thus allows to compose chains of privileges an attacker can reach. Since the successful exploitation of a vulnerability is necessary to achieve a privilege, attack paths within a vehicle network can be modeled. In [5], we used this approach to create a formal transition system based on a vehicle network. This model was used to automatically generate attack trees by applying model checking techniques in the context of threat modeling. The resulting attack tree contained a critical real-world airbag vulnerability. Thus, we could show that our *Attacker Privileges* are able to represent critical attack paths in vehicle networks. In this paper, we apply this approach in the context of a model-based security test method we introduced in [6]. For this purpose, we assume a simple E/E architecture example.

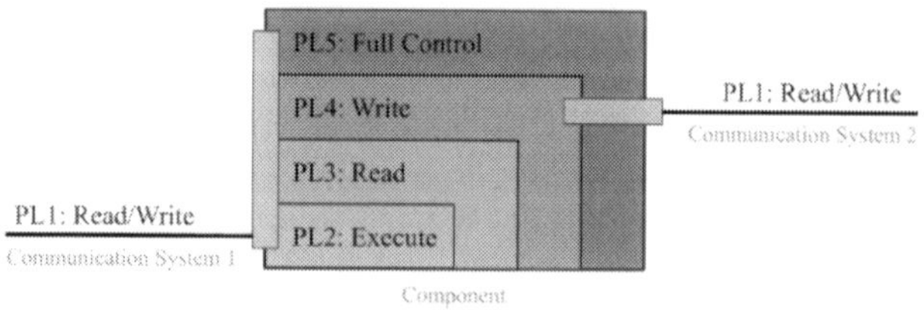

Figure 2. Distribution of *Attacker Privileges* to elements of a vehicular network [5].

In this example, an On-Board Diagnostics (OBD) interface is connected to a Central Gateway (CGW) via a CAN bus (CAN 1). The CGW is also connected to another CAN bus (CAN 2). Applying the *Attacker Privileges* to that network results in a security model shown in Figure 3. The illustrated security model corresponds to the graphical representation of an Extended Finite State Machine (EFSM) [25] we use for formalization. For the two CAN buses and the OBD interface, one state was defined to each which assigns the *Read/Write* privilege. For the CGW, four states were defined which correspond to the remaining four privileges. Security mechanisms are not considered here for reasons of simplicity. To create transitions, it was assumed that an attacker or tester has access to the OBD interface and wants to gain access to the internal vehicle network via the CGW. To model transitions between the states, we apply our privilege model as illustrated in Figure 2. This results in a transition from *State 1* to *State 2* and from *State 2* to *State 3 - State 6* respectively. It can be switched arbitrarily between the states of the CGW using a corresponding transition. The only exception here is *State 6*, since we assume that the *Full Control* privilege includes the other three privileges. Finally, a transition leads from *State 5* and *State 6* to *State 7* as explained in Figure 2. A formal description of the EFSM presented in Figure 3 is not further discussed here. Only the syntax and semantics of transitions is revisited in the next section to explain our concept for attack path generation based on attacker behavior and penetration tester experience.

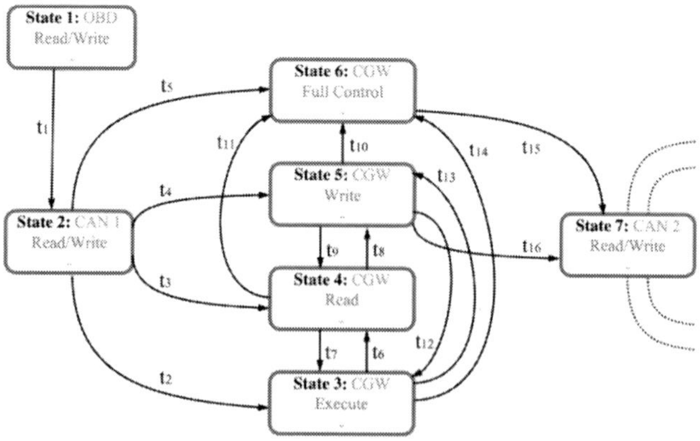

Figure 3. Security model based on an E/E architecture consisting of an OBD interface, a Central Gateway (CGW), and two CAN buses.

IV. Attack Path Generation using an Attack Database

In this section, we explain how attacker behavior based on our attack database [1] can be used to derive attack paths from the security model presented in Section III. First, we explain the transitions within our model. In general, transitions within an EFSM have the following structure:

$$Source \xrightarrow{Event\ [Guard]\ /\ Action} Target$$

A transition enables the change from a source state to a target state. The transition is triggered when an *Event* occurs (e.g., reception of a message or an input). In addition, a *Guard* condition must be met (e.g., message has a matching identifier) for a state change to occur. If an event occurs and the guard condition is met, the state will change and an output *Action* (e.g., sending an acknowledgement) will be triggered. We use these semantics to model an occurrence of attacks (exploitation of a vulnerability) in our security model. This results in the following structure as an example application to the transition t_2 from Figure 3:

$$State\ 2 \xrightarrow[\{Privilege,\ Violated\ Security\ Property\}]{Exploit\ [Vulnerability]\ /} State\ 3$$

To get from *State 2* (CAN 1 with *Read/Write* privilege) to *State 3* (CGW with *Execute* privilege), an attacker must employ an *Exploit* based on a *Vulnerability* leading to this state. The question now is, which exploits and which vulnerabilities can be used and how are they described. This is where our attack database [7] is applied, which currently (as of June 2022) contains 361 publicly known security attacks on vehicles. Overall, these attacks consist of 621 individual attack steps. To provide a uniform description of these attacks and steps, we published an attack taxonomy in [1] and classified our database accordingly. This taxonomy has different categories for describing an attack step, such as used tools, interfaces, brief description of the attack, requirements and restrictions, etc. For the transitions of the security model presented in this paper, the taxonomy categories shown in Figure 4 are particularly relevant. For each database attack step, there is a category *Component* and *Interface*, which specify affected components (e.g., ECU, Sensor, or Actuator) or interfaces (e.g., OBD or CAN interface). Furthermore, the *Violated Security Property* and the achieved *Attacker Privilege* are given for each step. To describe the *Vulnerability*, we use the Common Weakness Enumeration (CWE™) [26] provided by *The MITRE Corporation*. CWE is a systematic and hierarchically classified listing of software and hardware weaknesses, which are also used, for example, in the National Vulnerability Database (NVD) [27]. To describe exploits of a transition, we use the STRIDE classification [28]. STRIDE divides an attack into the categories *Spoofing, Tampering, Repudiation, Information Disclosure, Denial of Service, and Elevation of Privilege*.

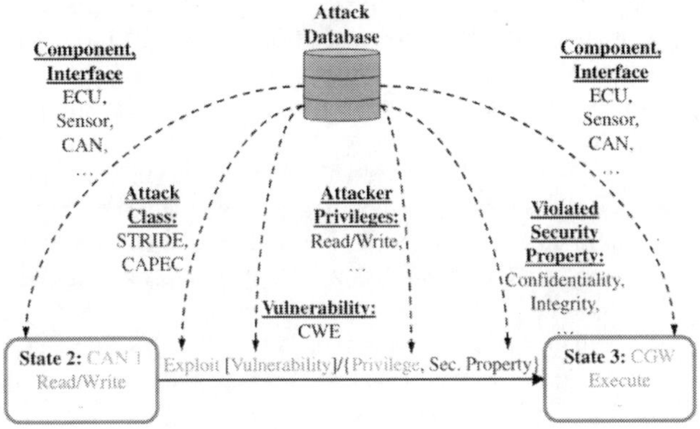

Figure 4. General application of the attack database to transitions of the security model.

In addition, we use the Common Attack Pattern Enumeration and Classification (CAPEC™) [29], which like the CWE is provided by MITRE. CAPEC provides a hierarchical description scheme for attack patterns (attack techniques/methods). These have a direct link to the CWE elements, which could be exploited by a respective attack pattern. The application of CAPEC is diverse. Currently, CAPEC suggests 26 different use cases. One of which is using attack patterns as a metric to comply with standards. Thus, CAPEC can be used to comply with automotive threats of the UN R155. All elements of a transition can be described by data of our attack database. This allows an application of all database attack steps to the security model. Thus, the model can be analyzed for the presence of real-world attack paths. In principle, this can be done in two ways. On the one hand, it can be checked whether an attack path is found exactly as described in the database. For example, if an attack consists of four attack steps, it can be analyzed whether these four explicit steps and their order can be mapped to the model. On the other hand, it is also possible to search for attack paths in the model which are composed of attack steps of several different attacks. This makes it possible to find new attack paths in our model based on the permutation of existing attack steps.

Since our security model is based on a formal EFSM, the entire process from model creation to analysis and generation of attack paths can be completely automated through a software tool. For this purpose, the E/E architecture of a vehicle, implemented security mechanisms, and the *Attacker Privileges* have to be provided. We plan on creating such a tool in future work. This would allow an attack or vulnerability analysis to take place at model level in an automated way (for example, by employing search algorithms). Furthermore, concrete attack paths to the vehicle under test can be derived, which can be used for security or penetration testing.

V. Attack Path Generation based on Penetration Tester Experience

In the previous section, we demonstrated how existing attacks from our attack database can be used to analyze a security model for existing attack paths. In this section, we present a proposal on how that process can be used to derive attack paths based on experience of penetration testers. Since penetration testing is experience-based and explorative, it is hard to be automated. The main problem is how to handle and capture the experience of a tester. A tester usually gains experience by performing several penetration tests on different systems. This builds up knowledge about which systems are more likely to have vulnerabilities, or which attack techniques are more likely to succeed. For example, the ECUs of a particular vendor might be more vulnerable against buffer overflow attacks. Thus, in this case the tester would first try to execute buffer overflow attacks to other ECUs of that vendor in further tests of other vehicles. This accumulated knowledge is used again in subsequent tests, i.e., a tester first tries to find known vulnerabilities in the system based on his experience. In order to capture that experience, the attack database from the previous section should first be examined again. This database is a collection of successful security attacks on vehicles. These were almost exclusively carried out from an attacker's perspective with little knowledge of the vehicle systems, even in cases where attacks were carried out by security researchers. The attack database can thus be seen as a collection of attacker experience, behavior, and knowledge. If there is a database containing successful penetration tests instead of or in addition to the attack database, the experience and knowledge of penetration testers can be captured in the same way. Such a database could be maintained by testers, for example, within a penetration testing vendor, in order to use it in the same way as the attack database (see Section IV). Creating that database can be done iteratively over several penetration tests. Our idea is inspired by the capture-replay principle from testing Graphical User Interface (GUI) applications as described by Liu et al. [30]. Here, inputs made manually by a user in a GUI application are logged and transferred to test scripts. These can then be reused for new and automated test executions. In Figure 5, this process is illustrated for our automotive use case. The security model (see Section IV) of the vehicle under test could be made available to penetration testers within a software tool. The tester uses his experience to exploratively find vulnerabilities in the SUT through appropriate testing, attacks, etc.

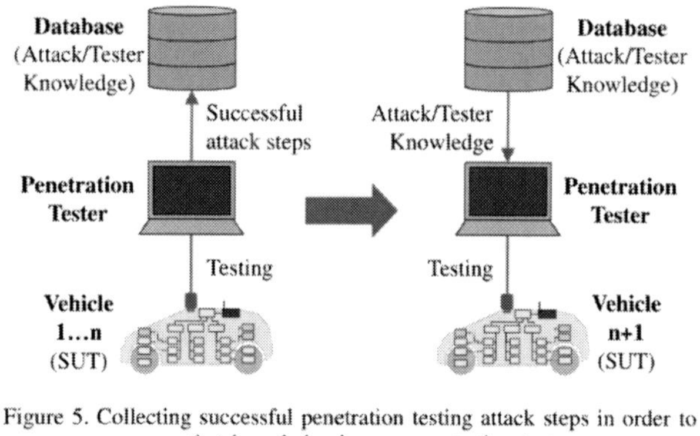

Figure 5. Collecting successful penetration testing attack steps in order to reuse that knowledge in new penetration tests.

Successful attack steps are then logged/recorded by the tester in the model, i.e., exploited paths are selected in the model and respective information (e.g., a specific attack technique used and vulnerability exploited) is specified for each attack step. Successful attack paths are then transferred to a database. If this process is carried out over several tests or different testers, an experience-based penetration testing knowledge database can be created. This can be used within model-based testing methodologies (as in the previous section) and associated tools, or within an expert system to support penetration testers in future testing. We also see a benefit of this approach for novices just entering the security testing domain, as they can benefit from an accumulated knowledge of experienced testers.

VI. Discussion

In this section, the presented approach is discussed to address use cases, current challenges, and limitations. In order to derive attack paths from a security model, only a vehicle's E/E architecture and an attack/tester database are required. For this reason, our method can be used at an early stage in the development process. This enables an application even previous to penetration testing, e.g., at the integration and system test stage. In this way, potential vulnerabilities can be found and eliminated at an early stage. It is also possible to link that process to TARA, which is carried out as part of vehicle development. In principle, there is a high degree of similarity between a TARA and the approach shown here, as both processes aim to identify threats/vulnerabilities and attack paths. An applicability of the *Attacker Privilege* model explained in Figure 2 in the context of TARA has already been shown in [5]. However, our model-based security testing approach targets the testing process. We consider aspects, such as security mechanisms, as well as concrete exploits for potential vulnerabilities and detailed technological characteristics of vehicle systems. At the time of performing a TARA, such details are usually not yet available. One challenge of our approach is the transferability of attacks stored in our database to new vehicle systems or network architectures. In particular, if the network of a vehicle under test differs significantly from the network of an already attacked vehicle, there can be a risk that an attack path is not transferable. This problem can be circumvented by combining/permutating attack steps from different database attacks. Whether resulting attack paths actually reveal vulnerabilities in a vehicle, however, can only be determined by the tester. Furthermore, we want to highlight that it would make sense to carry out further testing activities. In general, our approach can be seen as a black-box test method. Even if we have detailed information about elements of the vehicle E/E architecture, our security model does not cover all aspects, such as software code. In case an attack path generated from our model reveals a vulnerability, we only know that there is a vulnerability. This does not mean that the root cause of that vulnerability is also known. Thus, additional grey-box or white-box-based test methods should be applied in this case to find the root cause. As a final aspect, we discuss how our approach can be evaluated. In [5], we were already able to show that critical attack paths can be found by applying the *Attacker Privilege* model to vehicle architectures. In addition, we were able to determine in initial investigations that security models based on E/E architectures of attacked vehicles from our database (for example, from publications, such as Miller and Valasek [31]) contain new attack paths, which were also exploited in reality. These investigations should be extended to a detailed case study in future work.

VII. Conclusion

In this paper, an approach to enable automation of the security testing process was shown. In particular, we presented a formal security model, which can be analyzed for possible attack paths based on existing attacks from our attack database. We further demonstrated how paths for security testing can be derived. In addition, a proposal was presented on how knowledge and experience of penetration testers can be captured and reused to derive test paths. The approach is designed to deal with an increasing complexity of modern vehicles by automating sub-processes of the security testing process, in particular test planning and test case generation (attack paths). This enables early system analysis (e.g., as model-in-the-loop tests) and early testing. Further, estimations of security test effort can be made. For a practical implementation of the presented method, future work is to develop a software tool. This enables the creation of a security model, an analysis of that model, and the derivation of security testing paths. The tool can also be used to support penetration testers, as it provides knowledge about attacks or knowledge of testers in a comprehensive way. In addition, our approach should be evaluated in the context of a case study. Initial investigations have shown that existing attack paths from our database can also be found in other E/E architectures. A larger case study should therefore be carried out to examine this in detail.

Acknowledgment

This work was developed in the project SecForCARs-SAVE (reference number: 16KIS0796) which is funded by the German Ministry of Education and Research (BMBF).

References

[1] F. Sommer, J. Dürrwang, and R. Kriesten, "Survey and classification of automotive security attacks," *Information*, vol. 10, no. 4, p. 148, 2019.

[2] ISO/SAE 21434:2021, "Road vehicles — cybersecurity engineering," 2021.

[3] UNECE, "Un regulation no. 155 - uniform provisions concerning the approval of vehicles with regards to cyber security and cyber security management system: E/ece/trans/505/rev.3/add. 154," 03/2021. [Online]. Available: https://unece.org/sites/default/files/2021-03/R155e.pdf (Accessed 2022.07.12).

[4] S. Marksteiner and Z. Ma, "Approaching the automation of cyber security testing of connected vehicles," in *Proceedings of the Third Central European Cybersecurity Conference*, 2019, pp. 1–3.

[5] J. Dürrwang, F. Sommer, and R. Kriesten, "Automationin automotive security by using attacker privileges," in *Proceedings of the 19th escar Europe 2021*, pp. 137–152.

[6] F. Sommer, R. Kriesten, and F. Kargl, "Model-based security testing of vehicle networks," in *2021 International Conference on Computational Science and Computational Intelligence (CSCI)*, 2021, pp. 685–691.

[7] F. Sommer and J. Dürrwang, "Ieem-hska/aad: Automotive attack database (aad)," 2019. [Online]. Available: https://github.com/IEEM-HsKA/AAD (Accessed 2022.07.12).

[8] M. Felderer, P. Zech, R. Breu, M. Büchler, and A. Pretschner, "Model-based security testing: a taxonomy and systematic classification," *Software Testing, Verification and Reliability*, vol. 26, no. 2, pp. 119–148, 2016.

[9] L. Wang, E. Wong, and D. Xu, "A threat model driven approach for security testing," in *Proceedings of the Third International Workshop on Software Engineering for Secure Systems*, 2007, p. 10.

[10] C. Nickerson et al., "The penetration testing execution standard," 2014. [Online]. Available: http://www.pentest-standard.org/index.php/Main_Page (Accessed 2022.06.27).

[11] M. Meucci et al., "Owasp testing guide, v3," 2008. [Online]. Available: https://owasp.org/www-project-web-security-testing-guide/assets/archive/OWASP_Testing_Guide_v3.pdf (Accessed 24.08.2022).

[12] M. Ring, "Systematische security-tests von kraftfahrzeugen (systematic security tests of vehicles)," Dissertation, Universität Ulm, Ulm, 2019.

[13] S. Bayer, K. Hirata, and D. K. Oka, "Towards a systematic pentesting framework for in-vehicular can," *14th ESCAR Europe*, 2016.

[14] ISO 11898-1:2015, "Road vehicles – controller area network (can) – part 1: Data link layer and physical signalling," 1993.

[15] ISO 14229:2006, "Road vehicles — unified diagnostic services (uds) — specification and requirements," 2006.

[16] C. Smith, *The Car Hacker's Handbook: A Guide for the Penetration Tester*. San Francisco: No Starch Press, 2016.

[17] J. Dürrwang, J. Braun, M. Rumez, R. Kriesten, and A. Pretschner, "Enhancement of automotive penetration testing with threat analyses results," *SAE International Journal of Transportation Cybersecurity and Privacy*, vol. 1, no. 11-01-02-0005, pp. 91–112, 2018.

[18] M. Utting, A. Pretschner, and B. Legeard, "A taxonomy of model-based testing approaches," *Software Testing, Verification and Reliability*, vol. 22, no. 5, pp. 297–312, 2012.

[19] M. Cheah, S. A. Shaikh, O. Haas, and A. Ruddle, "Towards a systematic security evaluation of the automotive bluetooth interface," *Vehicular Communications*, vol. 9, pp. 8–18, 2017.

[20] C. A. R. Hoare, "Communicating sequential processes," *Communications of the ACM*, vol. 21, no. 8, pp. 666–677, 1978.

[21] Bluetooth Special Interest Group, "Bluetooth core specification v5.0," 2016. [Online]. Available: https://www.bluetooth.com/specifications/bluetooth-core-specification (Accessed 2022.07.12).

[22] P. S. Oruganti, M. Appel, and Q. Ahmed, "Hardware-in-loop based automotive embedded systems cybersecurity evaluation testbed," in *Proceedings of the ACM Workshop on Automotive Cybersecurity*, 2019, pp. 41–44.

[23] M. Appel, P. S. Oruganti, Q. Ahmed, J. Wilkerson, and R. Sekar, "A safety and security testbed for assured autonomy in vehicles," *SAE International*, p. 8, April 14, 2020.

[24] T. Volkersdorfer and H.-J. Hof, "A concept of an attack model for a model-based security testing framework: Introducing a holistic perspective of cyberattacks in software engineering," in *SECURWARE 2020 : The Fourteenth International Conference on Emerging Security Information, Systems and Technologies*, pp. 96–101.

[25] V. S. Alagar and K. Periyasamy, *Specification of software systems*, 2nd ed. Springer Science & Business Media, 2011.

[26] The MITRE Corporation, "Common weakness enumeration (cwe)," 2022. [Online]. Available: https://cwe.mitre.org/ (Accessed 2022.07.12).

[27] H. Booth, D. Rike, and G. Witte, "The national vulnerability database (nvd): Overview," Gaithersburg, 2013. [Online]. Available: https://www.nist.gov/publications/national-vulnerability-database-nvd-overview (Accessed 2022.07.12).

[28] L. Kohnfelder and P. Garg, "The stride threat model," 2009. [Online]. Available: https://docs.microsoft.com/en-us/previous-versions/commerce-server/ee823878(v=cs.20) (Accessed 2022.07.12).

[29] The MITRE Corporation, "Common attack pattern enumeration and classification (capec)," 2022. [Online]. Available: https://capec.mitre.org/index.html (Accessed 2022.07.12).

[30] C. H. Liu et al., "Capture-replay testing for android applications," in *2014 International Symposium on Computer, Consumer and Control*, 2014, pp. 1129–1132.

[31] C. Miller and C. Valasek, "Adventures in automotive networks and control units," *Def Con*, vol. 21, pp. 260–264, 2013.

Security Information Quality Provided by News Sites and Twitter

Ryu Saeki[1] and Kazumasa Oida[2]
Department of Computer Science and Engineering
Fukuoka Institute of Technology
Fukuoka, 811-0295 Japan
e-mails: [1]mfm22105@bene.fit.ac.jp, [2]oida@fit.ac.jp

Abstract—**Twitter is widely used as a tool for disseminating and collecting information related to security incidents. The quality of information provided by Twitter, however, has not been studied in detail so far, where quality in this paper refers to the detailedness, real-time performance, and reliability of the information. This paper evaluates the quality of Twitter information by comparing with that of information provided by a news site that publishes a large number of security-related articles as a baseline. Our analysis showed that Twitter was significantly better in terms of detailedness and real-time performance. On the other hand, a news site was slightly better in terms of reliability.**

Keywords-Emotet; real-time performance; security; Twitter; reliability.

I. INTRODUCTION

Social Networking Services (SNS) and cybersecurity-focused news sites are two media for investigating ongoing security attacks on the Internet. SNSs can provide a large amount of fresh security information because information is transmitted in real time from a variety of sources [1]. On the other hand, news sites publish daily articles on security incidents and new vulnerabilities, with coverage by trusted security experts. In order to clarify the differences in the quality of security information provided by these two media, this study collected data on Emotet attacks in Japan provided by Twitter and Security NEXT as a case study.

Emotet is a Trojan horse that spreads primarily through spam e-mails and is raging worldwide. The most common Emotet attack method is to infect computer systems with various types of malware using malicious files attached to spam e-mails. Japan has been a major target for Emotet since 2019 [2]. Twitter includes links to external sites in its tweets and disseminates Indicators of Compromise (IoCs) from a variety of sources, including malware sandboxes, security vendor blogs, etc. It has been reported that Twitter captures ongoing malware threats, such as Emotet variants and malware distribution sites, better than other public threat intelligence [1]. Security NEXT, on the other hand, is a news site specializing in information related to security incidents in Japan, with a large number of postings and free access to all articles.

This study compared the detailedness, real-time performance, and reliability of information provided by Twitter and Security NEXT. We found that Twitter excelled in terms of detailedness and real-time performance of information about Emotet. The rest of the paper is structured as follows. In Section II, we present the process of collecting and analyzing Emotet data. In Section III, we discuss the visualized results. Finally, we conclude the work in Section IV.

II. PROGRAM STRUCTURE

We created a program that visualizes information on Emotet provided by Twitter and Security NEXT in Japanese for the period from January 1, 2019 to August 31, 2020. The following describes the program execution sequence.

1. Collect URLs posted on Twitter and Security NEXT as follows. In the case of Twitter, collect all shortened URLs (http://t.co/) in every tweet containing the term "emotet", and then convert all the shortened URLs to the original URLs. Next, check all duplicate sites (the same URL, same title, or same text) to exclude them. In the case of Security NEXT, collect all URLs contained in all of the articles of the news site.
2. Collect text areas (the areas enclosed by tag <p>) of Japanese websites of the URLs obtained above if their titles include "emotet."
3. Extract words (nouns and compound nouns) from the texts collected above using a morphological analysis library janome [3].
4. Group all collected words into several categories because they contained a variety of words including synonyms.
5. Create a histogram representing the frequency of the classified categories.

III. CALCULATION RESULTS

Table I shows the number of web sites from which information was retrieved, the total number of words, and the program execution time. Much of the program execution time is spent on the program execution sequence 1-2 in Section II. Table I shows that Twitter has more than 20 times more words than Security NEXT and that the program execution time for Twitter is more than 10 times longer. In other words, while Twitter has more detailed information than Security NEXT, it takes longer to retrieve the information.

Emotet distributes malware through spam e-mails with malicious file attachments. Therefore, we visualize the previous and current trends in Emotet's attack strategy by focusing on malware types, extensions of attachments, and subject lines of spam e-mails. Figures 1 and 2 show yearly frequencies of malware distributed by Emotet [4]-[6]. These figures show that fewer types of malware appear in Security NEXT articles than in Twitter. Figures 3 and 4 show the yearly frequencies of malicious file extensions. These figures demonstrate similar result in that the ZIP format has the highest percentage in 2020, followed by the DOC format (including the DOCM format), and then the PDF format. However, in Figure 4, data for 2019 and 2021 are missing. Figures 5 and 6 show the yearly frequencies of spam e-mail subject lines. Figure 5 shows that five to six categories appear in every year, while Figure 6 shows six categories appearing only in 2020. Accordingly, Twitter tends to provide detail Emotet attack characteristics (malware, extension, subject) every year. On the contrary, Security NEXT may provide no information during the periods when Emotet attacks are less frequent.

Table II compared the dates when Twitter and Security NEXT reported the Emotet malware names for the first time. As shown in the table, Twitter reported at least 220 days earlier for all malware types. Although not mentioned in this paper, Twitter also provided quicker reports on malicious file extensions and spam e-mail subject lines.

Table III compares Twitter and Security NEXT on eight reliability measures of 20 randomly sampled websites. Here we measure the reliability of information on Twitter and Security NEXT based on website reliability. The table shows that Security NEXT is slightly better. Twitter is dependable in that it mostly has links to information sources, but the probability of link errors is not negligible. Twitter sometimes does not include writers' contact information and privacy policy statements.

TABLE I. DATA SET SIZES AND EXECUTION TIMES.

	Twitter	Security NEXT
Number of Websites	1,660	91
Number of different words	42,347	2,091
Execution time (h)	63	6

TABLE II. DATES MALWARE NAMES WERE FIRST REPORTED.

Malware name	Twitter	Security NEXT
TrickBot	Apr. 13, 2019	Nov. 28, 2019
QakBot	Apr. 13, 2019	Oct. 8, 2020
Ryuk	Apr. 22, 2019	Nov. 28, 2019
IcedID	Apr. 1, 2019	Nov. 10, 2020

TABLE III. COMPARISON FROM EIGHT RELIABILITY MEASURES.

	Reliability measure	Twitter	Security NEXT
1	Writer name	20/20	20/20
2	Writer' s contact info.	13/20	20/20
3	Published/updated date	20/20	20/20
4	SSL certificate	20/20	20/20
5	Information sources	14/20	1/20
6	No link errors	8/20	20/20
7	No misspellings	18/20	20/20
8	Privacy policy	13/20	20/20
	Total	113/160	141/160

IV. CONCLUSIONS AND FUTURE WORK

Today, security experts significantly depend on Twitter information. This paper quantitatively evaluated the quality of Twitter information in terms of detailedness, real-time performance, and reliability. Our results showed that the quality of Twitter information was excellent in terms of detailedness and real-time performance. On the other hand, a news site was slightly better when measured based on reliability. In the future, we will evaluate the reliability of Twitter information using other methods such as language-based and knowledge-based approaches.

REFERENCES

[1] H. Shin, W. Shim, S. Kim, S. Lee, Y. G. Kang, and Y. H. Hwang, "# twiti: Social listening for threat intelligence," in Proceedings of the Web Conference 2021, 2021, pp. 92-104.

[2] "The ever-changing malware "EMOTET" is causing more damage in Japan," 2019. [online]. Available from: https://blog.trendmicro.co.jp/archives/22959. [retrieved: August, 2022].

[3] Japanese morphological analysis engine written in pure python". [online]. Available from: https://github.com/mocobeta/janome/. [retrieved: August, 2022].

[4] "Three threats: TrickBot deployment by Emotet and data theft and Ryuk proliferation by TrickBot," 2019. [online]. Available from: https://www.cybereason.co.jp/blog/cyberattack/3613/. [retrieved: August, 2022].

[5] "Threat Actor Profile: TA542, From Banker to Malware Distribution Service," 2019. [online]. Available from: https://www.proofpoint.com/us/threat-insight/post/threat-actor-profile-ta542-banker-malware-distribution-service. [retrieved: August, 2022].

[6] "Threat Spotlight: Panda Banker Trojan Targets the US, Canada and Japan," 2018. [online]. Available from: https://blogs.blackberry.com/en/2018/10/threat-spotlight-panda-banker-trojan-targets-the-us-canada-and-japan. [retrieved: August, 2022]

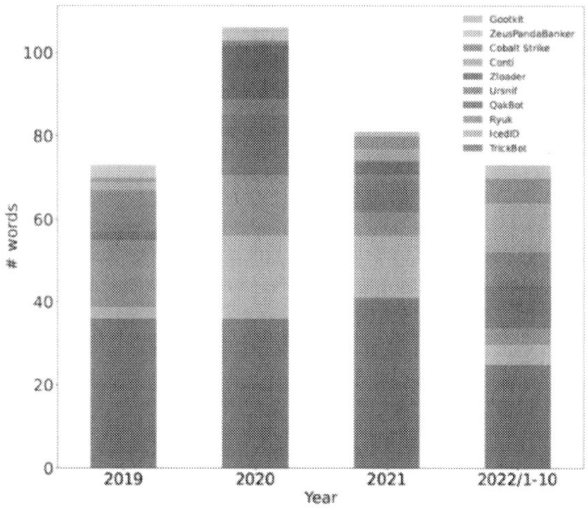

Figure 1. Malware distributed by Emotet (Twitter)

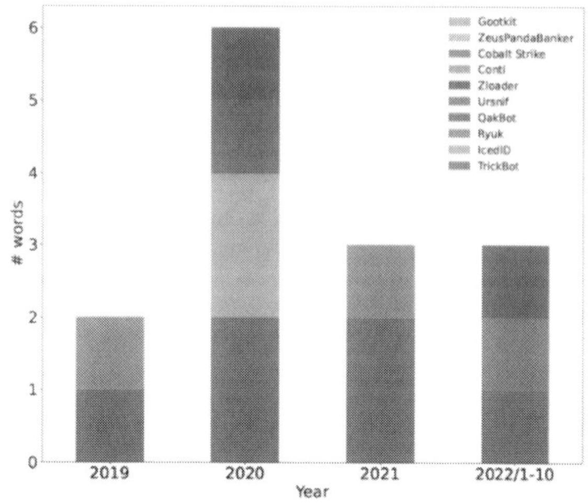

Figure 2. Malware distributed by Emotet (Security NEXT)

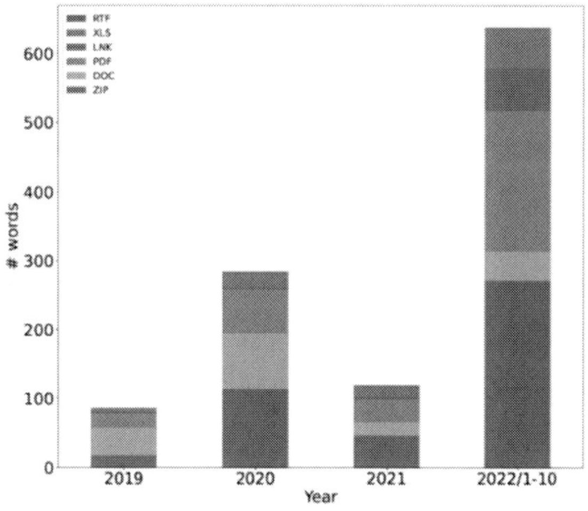

Figure 3. Malicious file extension (Twitter)

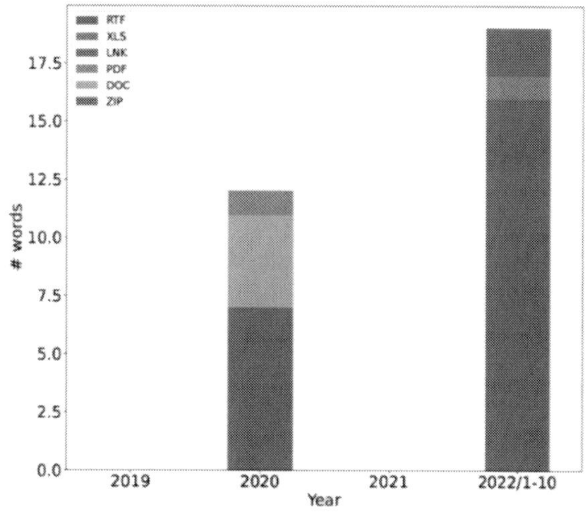

Figure 4. Malicious file extension (Security NEXT)

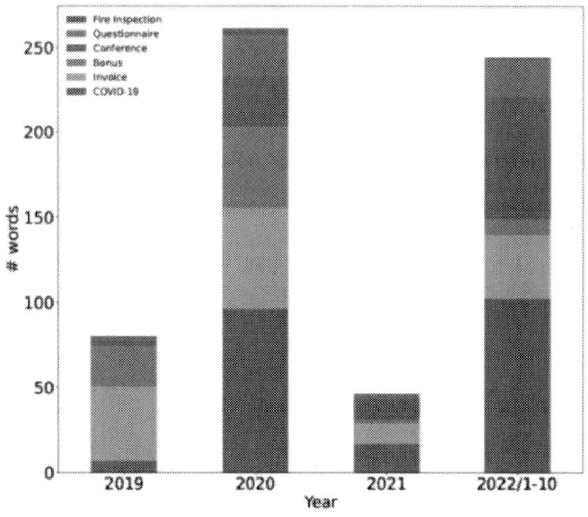

Figure 5. Spam e-mail subject line (Twitter)

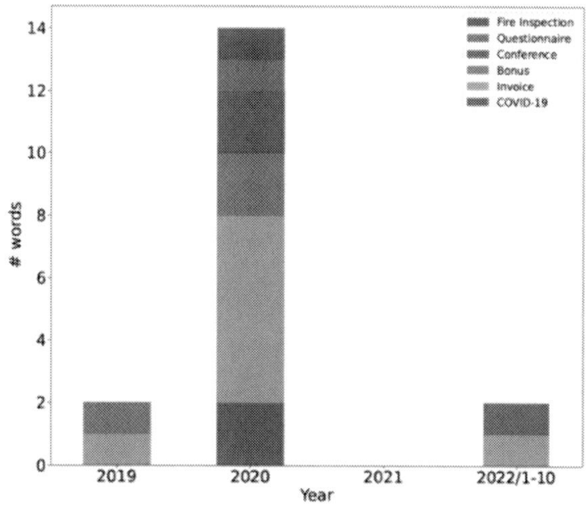

Figure 6. Spam e-mail subject line (Security NEXT)

A Survey on Artificial Intelligence Techniques in Cybersecurity Management

Mercy Ejura Dapel
Faculty of Arts, Science and Technology
University of Northampton
Northampton, United Kingdom
e-mail: mercy.dapel@northampton.ac.uk

Mary Asante
Faculty of Arts, Science and Technology
University of Warwick
Coventry, United Kingdom
e-mail: mary.asante@warwick.ac.uk

Chijioke Dike Uba
Faculty of Business and Law
University of Northampton
Northampton, United Kingdom
e-mail:Chijioke.Uba@northampton.ac.uk

Michael Opoku Agyeman
Faculty of Arts, Science and Technology
University of Northampton
Northampton, United Kingdom
e-mail:Michael.OpokuAgyeman@northampton.ac.uk

***Abstract*—The rapid development in Internet Services led to a significant increase in cyber-attacks. The need to secure systems and operations has become apparent as cybersecurity has become a global concern. Cybersecurity involves techniques that protect and control systems, networks, hardware, software, and electronic data from unauthorized access. Developing an effective and innovative defensive mechanism is an urgent requirement as conventional cybersecurity solutions are becoming inadequate in safeguarding information against cyber threats. There is a need for cybersecurity methods that are capable of making real-time decisions and respond to cyber-attacks. To support this, researchers are focusing on approaches like Artificial Intelligence (AI) to improve cyber defense. This study provides an overview of existing research on cybersecurity, using AI technologies. AI technologies made a remarkable contribution in combating cybercrimes with significant improvement in anomaly intrusion detection.**

Keywords-Artificial Intelligence; Cybercrime; Cyber-attacks; Cybersecurity; Security Threats.

I. INTRODUCTION

The rapid development in Information and Communication Technology (ICT) created positive implication to the global economy. The internet has improved the quality of life by providing a platform that facilitates knowledge sharing, communication and interaction, which is important for development and daily life [1]. In view of the benefits, the dark side abound. Cyber criminals exploit the vulnerability of individuals and organizations [2]. Providing security for systems have become difficult. Hackers are becoming smarter and more innovative in exploiting individuals and organizations. With cyber-attacks and data breaches coming to light daily, cyber-attacks have been ranked among the top 5 most likely sources of severe global risk [3]. Cyber fraud has become complex to track as cyber theft can originate from any part of the world. Organizations have become challenged with the complexity of cyber-attacks which calls for the adoption of intelligent methods like AI to mitigate them. AI is a thriving field that has been deployed in application areas such as manufacturing [4], healthcare [5], education [6], agriculture [7] and Cybersecurity. According to Abraham et al. [8], AI algorithms can predict previously seen and unseen attacks, it is effective in detecting cyber-attacks with low false alarm rate. Advancement in AI have produced technologies that can learn from past patterns to improve future experiences. Researchers and developed countries have adopted cybersecurity solutions like AI to improve cyber defense [9]. Some existing studies have discussed and summarized cybersecurity issues. To the best of my knowledge, none focused on AI in cybersecurity management systematically. Figure 1 summarized the key trends of events related to cybercrime over 2 decades as identified by Alqurashi [39]. Ransomware attacks have increased drastically over the last decade as illustrated. This article summarized progress in applying AI to tackle cybersecurity. The effectiveness of these solutions in detecting and preventing cyber-attacks is demonstrated. The remainder of this paper is structured as follows: Section II presents the background of study and related work. Section III presents the review methodology used to conduct the study. Section IV presents findings on AI in cybersecurity. Section V discusses future direction of AI in cybersecurity management. Section VI presents the research validation, limitation and concludes the paper.

II. BACKGROUND LITERATURE

A. Artificial Intelligence for Cybersecurity

With persistent cyber threats and advanced cyber-attacks emerging, cybersecurity researchers agree that information security is important. Consequently, a number of studies attempted addressing information security by adopting improved techniques such as anomaly intrusion detection and prevention systems, firewall setups and data encryption algorithms. Although some studies have argued that cybersecurity can be effectively tackled by focusing on human behavior. However, others argued that human behavior alone is insufficient.

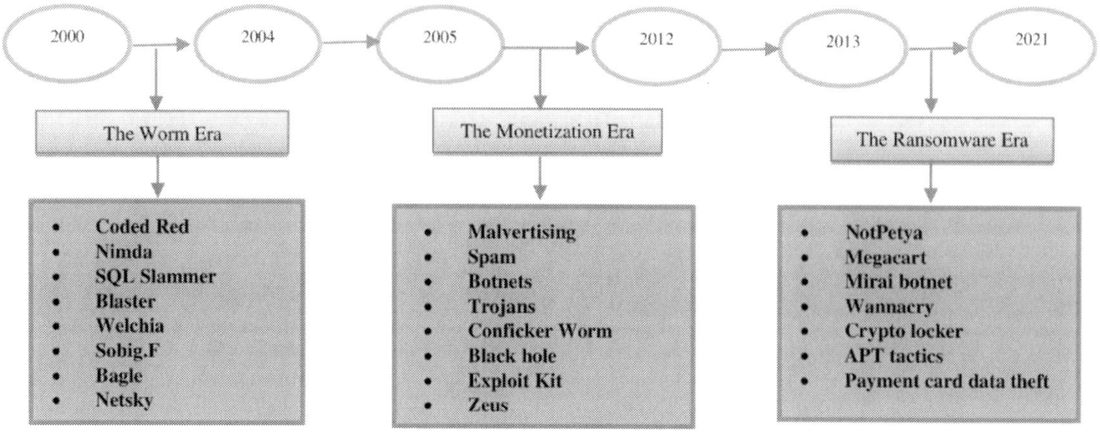

Fig. 1 20-year retrospective on cyber threats.

For instance, the volume of information handled by organizations calls for automation. Hence the need for balance between humans and technology in organizational security activities. Conventional cybersecurity approaches depend on tedious and manual processes, they rely on detect and respond measures that can't keep pace with the volume and velocity of current threats. Furthermore, the first generation of antivirus were designed to identify virus by scanning its bit signature, the assumption of this concept is that virus has the same structure and bit pattern in all instances. These signatures are fixed. Although the catalog of signatures are updated when devices are connected to internet network, the regular release of sophisticated malwares make this approach ineffective. The introduction of signature-less approaches that are capable of detecting and mitigating cyber-threats using newer methods such as AI and behavioral detections have been argued to be effective.

Advancements in AI applications made it possible to design an effective and efficient system that automatically detect and prevent malicious activities in cyberspace. These advancements have been adopted to support existing technologies as they provide mechanisms that better prevent and control cyber-attacks. In view of all the benefits AI provides, emerging cyber threats make it extremely difficult for researchers to identify the most efficient technique and its impact in cyberspace. The general perception among researchers suggest that AI has improved information security. To the best of our knowledge, these claims has not been substantiated. Existing studies have either demonstrated how their innovation outperformed a selection of existing methods or a sample of systems that compare algorithms to access their performance. Accordingly, a literature review is required to provide summary on issues, challenges and future research direction.

TABLE I
GOAL QUESTION METRIC

Purpose	The study analyzes
Issue	Publication trends, application domain, methods, impact, performance and future direction
Object	Existing articles on AI in cybersecurity
Viewpoint	Between 2018 to 2022

B. Related Work

Several existing studies have reviewed literatures on AI in cybersecurity management. For instance, Chan et al. [47] described the intrusion detection ability of AI while identifying false positives and using predictive analysis for storing data. Although their study provides meaningful insights to help people understand AI better, it is not systematic in presenting discussions. Li [48] summarized the intersection of AI and cybersecurity by reviewing the use of AI related algorithms. Their study classified AI applications and contributions as promising for integrated cybersecurity. However, the method used for the survey was not defined, it is open to bias, and therefore their survey cannot claim to be systematic when compared with guidelines proposed by Kitchenham et al. [50].

Waife et al. [51] conducted a systematic mapping review of AI for cybersecurity using quantitative and qualitative methods to analyze several articles. AI made a significant contribution in combating cybercrimes with improvement in false alarm rate for Intrusion Detection Systems (IDS). Al- though the study provides meaningful insights to researchers, the articles selection process was limited to the IEEE and ACM digital libraries. Therefore, their findings cannot be generalized. Sarker et al. [52] surveyed popular AI-driven cybersecurity concepts for protecting inter-connected systems from cyber-threat. The survey revealed that expert systems are used to tackle cybersecurity issues like unauthorized access intelligently, they explained the importance of intelligent cybersecurity management but failed to present an overview of trends in the domain, Johansson [49] explored a study on coordinated cyber-attacks towards power grid systems by utilizing IDS to provide internal network protection, he utilized qualitative approach and identified countermeasures suitable. However, the study did not follow Kitchenham et al. [50] guidelines, but it provides a foundation.

III. REVIEW METHODOLOGY

PRISMA, a Systematic Literature Review (SLR) protocol, is used in this paper to obtain insight on the application of AI in cybersecurity management as proposed by Kitchenham et al. [50]. PRISMA is a SLR that uses a well-defined methodology to identify, evaluate, and interprete relevant research by using unbiased, trustworthy, rigorous and repeatable methodology. By using PRISMA, the research method can be replicated. A set of keywords were used to identify studies related to AI in cybersecurity management through several database search engines. Keywords used in the search are Artificial Intelligence, Cybersecurity, cyber threats and Information Security. The words were combined to form a search phrase, they are Artificial Intelligence and/or cybersecurity, cyber threats and/or cybersecurity, cyber threats and/or Information security. The viewpoint for the search was limited to studies published from 2018 to 2022. This allowed for consideration of the most recent articles. IEEE xplore digital library, science direct, Google Scholar and other sources were used to select several literatures as mentioned by Kitchenham et al. [50] as they make up the majority of databases used for literature reviews. This was done to avoid bias and ensure that a wide database is covered in the selectionprocess.

250 articles were initially identified. All articles were sub- jected to inclusion and exclusion criteria to identify the state- of-the-art literature before analysis. Conference papers, jour- nals, and short papers etc. were all included. The wide search was to ensure that no relevant article was left out to avoid bias. Titles of articles that did not suggest the application of AI in cybersecurity management were excluded. Articles that are less than 4 pages and are written in languages other than English were also excluded. Abstracts that did not strongly discuss AI in cybersecurity were discarded to reduce bias in the selection process. In total, 67 articles were selected and included in the study.

The process employed is illustrated in Figure 2, it is a diagrammatic representation of the review process. In addition to the rationale of the study, research questions were identified. The search strategy and data extraction are based on inclusion and exclusion criteria. This is grouped into phases as suggested by Kitchenham et al. [50]. Review questions were formulated during the planning stage which forms the foundation for the study. The Goal Question Metric Approach (See Table 2) was adopted by Basili [35]. This approach has also been demonstrated by Yahya et al. [36] to be effective for eliciting the objectives of systematic reviews. This section gave a review of the methodology used to obtain insight into the application of AI in cybersecurity management.

TABLE II
RATIONALE AND REVIEW QUESTIONS

	Research Question	Motivation
RQ1	What publications featured AI in cybersecurity management?	To identify studies and countries where AI con- tributed to cybersecurity management with view- point from 2018 to 2022.
RQ2	What threats was AI ad- dressing in cybersecurity management?	To identify AI solutions applied in cybersecuritymanagement.
RQ3	What impact does AI have in cybersecurity manage- ment?	To classify and identify impact/performance of AI in cybersecurity manage ment.
RQ4	What is the future direc- tion for AI research?	To identify future direction of AI in cybersecurity management. This will provide direction for current and future researchers whose area of interest is cybersecurity management.

IV. REVIEW OF FINDINGS ON AI IN CYBERSECURITY

Information regarding the publication year, publication out lets with more than two articles on AI in cybersecurity and al- gorithms used was recorded. This study analyzed, summarized, and discussed the impact of existing methods. Below is the discussion of findings from the study.

A. Publication Trends on AI in Cybersecurity

The results in Figure 3 show that research publications on AI in cybersecurity have increased considerably. AI techniques started gaining rapid attention years before the viewpoint of this review (2018 to 2022), however from the year 2018, the margin of articles increased. The articles reviewed for the year 2018 accounted for 33% of the total selected articles for the primary study. The publications increased from 2019 to 2022. This indicates that studies on AI in cybersecurity management are increasing. The findings in Figure 4 indicate that publications are represented in different publishing outlets. Out of 67 articles on AI, 33 were published in IEEE Access journals and 9 were published at IEEE transactions on Informatics Forensics and Security Journal. These publication outlets listed above accounted for 40% out of the total number. See Figure 4 for the chart on publication distribution according to publication outlets.

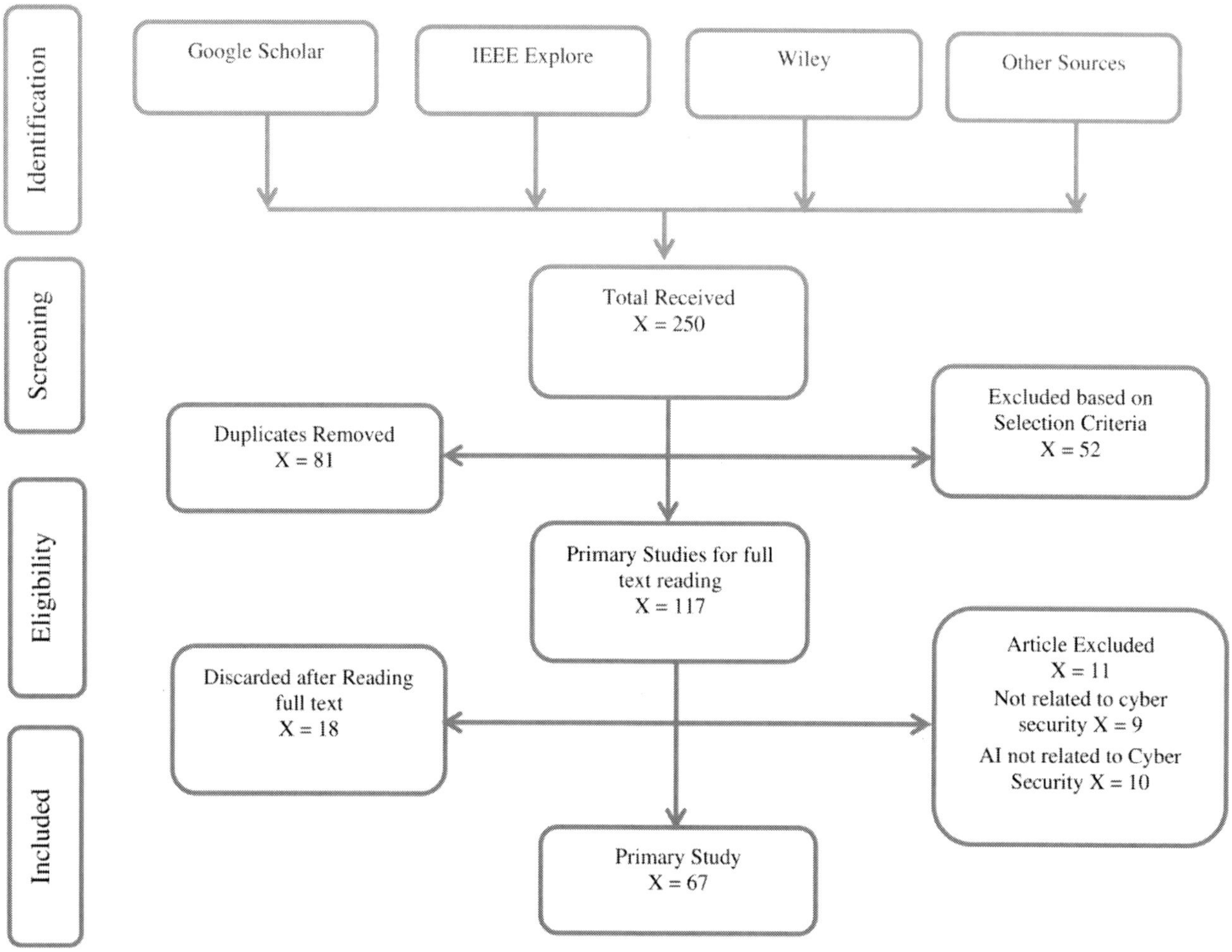

Fig. 2. Diagrammatic representation of PRISMA protocol.

The chart presents outlets with more than two publications. The next publication outlet that recorded most articles is Science Direct which recorded 4 papers, Wiley and IEEE transaction on neural network & learning recorded 3 articles each. The remaining publication outlets recorded two or less studies. Some were published in Transaction Signal Information Process over networks while other publications were recorded in books, conference papers and journals such as Engineering application for artificial Intelligence to mention a few. Similarly, it was observed that the research was skewed geographically. The address of the authors revealed that majority of the studies originated from countries in Asia. It can be deduced from Figure 5 that 58% of the articles originated from Asia. China recorded the highest number of publications, followed by India. Sudan and Norway recorded one publication each.

B. AI in Cybersecurity

AI was proposed in 1956 by John McCarthy as a science concerned with making computers behave intelligently like humans [8]. AI application has evolved significantly, it has a plethora of benefits in education, biometric systems, Internet of Things and cybersecurity among others. AI algorithms contribute to solving security issues. The cost and average time of detection and response to cyber threats is greatly reduced with the intervention of AI [34]. Neural networks have been used to detect classifying data as normal and abnormal [30]. Swarm intelligence methods handles feature selection to identify new intrusions.

Technologies like expert systems and intelligent agents have been used to secure internet networks and improve intrusion detection performance [31].

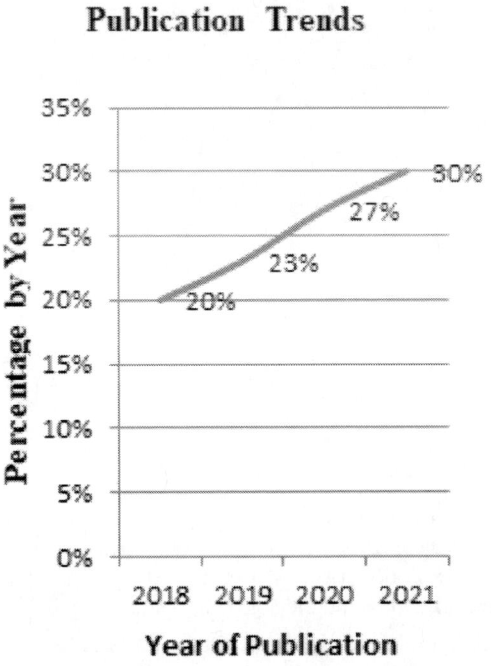

Fig. 3. Trends in primary studies from 2018 to 2021.

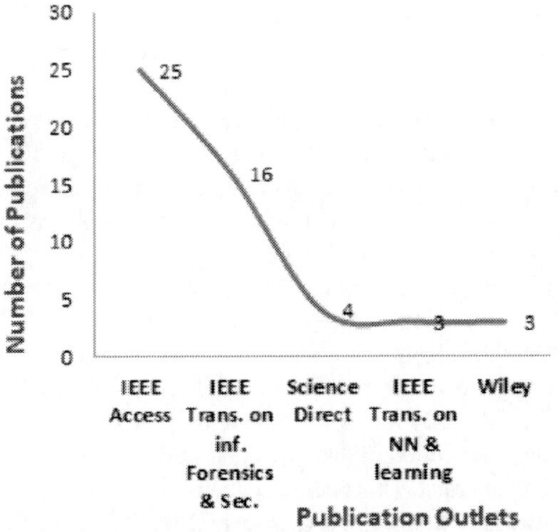

Fig. 4. Publication outlets with more than 2 articles on AI in Cybersecurity

With AI, complexity and model training time is reduced [32]. AI is quickly becoming a tool for automating threat detection and responding effectively than conventional human driven methods which are unable to keep up with volumes of viruses generated daily [30]. AI is relevant in threat detection, intrusion detection, fraud detection and cybersecurity, it has increased the accuracy and speed of cyber response. The major disciplines in AI are fuzzy logic, natural language processing, deep learning, machine learning, computer vision and robotics.

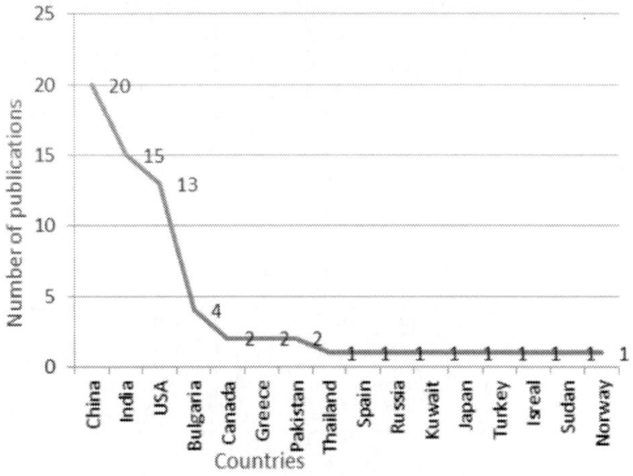

Fig. 5. Distribution of publication by country of origin of the corresponding author

This role of AI in cybersecurity have been displayed in applications that prevent and detect different types of attacks. Several studies that provide knowledge gaps and opportunities in the domain for current and future researchers were identified. The taxonomy informed the clustering in Table III.

C. AI as a Tool in Combating Cyber-attacks

With the pace and increase in cyber-attacks, human intervention alone is insufficient for timely and appropriate response. AI technology is becoming very essential to information security. It is capable of analyzing millions of data to detect and prevent cyber threats. It can deduce patterns and identify abnormalities in a computer network expeditiously. AI technologies use behavioral analysis to identify and detect anomalies that are indicative of an attack [32]. This technology gathers large amount of data to identify suspicious behavior that might lead to cyber threat. Processing and analyzing massive amount of data in seconds, using AI algorithms makes prediction of cyber threats possible before they occur, it also predicts future data breaches. With AI breaches can be responded to immediately an attack is detected by responding anonymously without human intervention and also by sending alerts and creating defensive patches [33]. According to a report by Capgemini, the effort and cost of detecting and responding to cyber threats is lowered by 15% in some organizations with AI, as more data is analyzed. This technology learns from

TABLE III
TAXONOMY: AI TECHNIQUES USED IN CYBERSECURITY

Techniques used	Purpose	References
DNN (RNN, ANN, CNN)	Anomaly intrusion detection, Data security, traffic identification-tion, classification and comparison	[50],[44],[10],[40]
DNN	Cyberattack detection, cybersecurity, intrusion detection, Comparison	[54]-[55]
DNN (RNN, CNN)	Spam detection	[56]
DNN (RNN, CNN)	Ransomware/malware detection	[57],[58],[59]-[60]
DNN (RNN, CNN)	Situational Awareness	[61]
CNN	Image detection, intrusion detection, threat detection, Pattern recognition, web security	[62], [63]-[64]
Deep Learning, LSTM	Fraud detection, cybersecurity, intrusion detection, pattern Detection	[9], [65]
ANN, swarm optimization (SO)	Intrusion Detection	[66],[67]
KNN, K prototype cluster-Ing	Anomaly detection, cybersecurity	[38],[42]
Regression Model	Awareness	[45]
Random Forest	Comparison, Anomaly detection, traffic detection, malware Detection	[8], [46]
SVM	Spam detection, anomaly intrusion detection, malware detec-tion, cybersecurity	[47],[56]

past patterns to become proficient in identifying suspicious activities thereby protecting information [34]. AI capabilities and adaptive behavior can overcome the deficiencies of conventional cybersecurity tools

D. AI Algorithms in Cybersecurity

Several algorithms were identified from the primary studies. The dominant algorithms are Random forest (RF), Long Short-Term Memory (LSTM), Decision Tree (DT), Naive Bayesian algorithm, Adaptive Boost (AdaBoost), J48, Support Vector Machines (SVM), K-Nearest Neighborhood (KNN), Convolutional Neural Network (CNN), Artificial Neural Network (ANN), Fuzzy logic, Particle swarm optimization (PSO), Logistic Regression and Recursive Neural Network (RNN).

E. Impact of AI in Cybersecurity Management

AI presents advantages in several areas, cybersecurity being one of them. AI is considered as one of the promising technologies for tackling cyber threats. It is capable of analyzing millions of datasets to identify and prevent cyber-attacks. The most significant contribution of AI is anomaly intrusion detection. To overcome cybersecurity issues, Vinayakumar et al. [10] proposed a highly scalable and hybrid deep neural network, to monitor network traffic and host level events that raise alert for unforeseen

They employed distributed and parallel machine learning algorithms with optimization techniques, making them capable of handling volumes of network and computing resources. Their framework stood out due to scalability and real-time detection of malicious activities from early warning signals. To increase training speed and avert over fitting, batch normalization and dropout approach was used. Deep neural network performed well by detecting and classifying unforeseen and unpredictable cyber- attacks in real-time.

Sokolov et al. [11] analyzed cybersecurity threats in cloud applications using deep learning techniques to monitor data. Suricata engine and module based on Google tensor flow framework was used. They proposed a system that used neural classifiers for network traffic, spam comments, spam email and images. The suricata engine monitored network security and prevented intrusion in real-time.

Fernandez et al. [12] explored a self-adaptive system for anomaly detection that identified cyber-threats in 5G mobile networks. Deep learning techniques was used to analyze network traffic by extracting features from network flows. The authors proposed a high-level cyber defense architecture consisting of virtualized infrastructure (VI), virtualized network function (VNF), management and orchestration (MANO), operations and business support systems. Anomaly symptom detection (ASD) and network anomaly detection (NAD) were proposed to achieve effective network anomaly detection. Once an anomaly is produced from traffic generated, it is communicated to the monitoring and diagnosis module. The experimental result showed that the architecture can self-adapt to anomaly detection based on the volume of network flow gathered from users in real-time.

A botnet is one of the significant threats infecting devices today. Abraham et al. [8] compared the performance of five (5) Machine learning approaches and identified useful features to classify malicious traffic.

Random forest proved to be more robust, it could generalize unseen bots' types.

Intrusion detection technology is a mechanism that monitors and prevents system intrusion. Zhang et al. [13] introduced a multiple-layer representation learning model for accurate detection of network-based attack and proposed a new data encoding scheme based on P-Zigzag to encode network traffic into two-dimensional gray-scale images for representation. Comparing the combination of gcForest and CNN allowed detection of imbalanced data with fewer hyper parameters, which increased computational efficiency. The experimental results showed that the combined algorithms outperformed single deep learning methods in terms of accurate detection and false alarm rate, thereby demonstrating its effectiveness in attack detection. The authors proposed a new intrusion detection method by combining random forest and LSTM to address the above challenges.

In view of the vast amount of data generated daily, and the increased interconnection of the internet infrastructure, Zhong et al. [14] proposed big data based on a hierarchical deep learning system that utilizes behavioral features. Companies can adapt it as a solution for the detection of intrusive attacks. The authors defined the hierarchical structure in five (5) phases. In the first phase, behavioral and content features are extracted using big data techniques. In the second phase, the dataset is separated into clusters, in the third phase, the root clusters of each sub tree is combined until the quality of the merged clusters dropped below the given threshold. In the fourth phase the deep learning model for each cluster was trained, while in the fifth phase, deep learning model was merged to select the most confident model. They concluded that it increased the detection rate of intrusive attacks when compared to a single model learning approach. Their strategy is effective in capturing data patterns for intrusive attacks.

A. Dey [15] utilized a 2018 dataset and proposed the effectiveness of attention mechanism for intrusion detection based on Convolutional Neural Network (CNN) and LSTM model. The authors observed increased performance based on LSTM.

Dawoud et al.'s [16] concept is based on unsupervised deep learning for revealing network threats and detecting anomalies by evaluating the use of restricted Boltzmann machines. This intrusion detection system is used to expose network threat and protect network assets. Their simulation study showed 99% detection accuracy with significant improvement.

Ishaque et al. [17] explored deep learning research by manipulating large amount of data using the functionality of computational intelligence. An important feature which the authors applied for dimensionality and attribute reduction is feature extraction. They concluded that the proposed system can detect attacks that are not hybridized.

Distributed denial of service (DDOS) attack has been a real threat to cyber infrastructure that can bring down ICT infrastructure. Isa et al. [18] adopted deep learning to analyze traffic, focusing on mitigating cyber-attacks with machine learning. Assembly module for statistics collection and adaptive machine learning module for analyzing traffic and enforcing policies are the two main functionalities that was proposed. Auto encoder and random forest algorithm possessed an accuracy of 98.4% with a decreased amount of training and execution time. The result proved that the model is optimally efficient for real-time intrusion detection.

Detecting cyber-attacks requires analyzing cyber-threats to match potential attack profiles. Malicious connections were filtered to improve the accuracy of threat detection and reduce false-positive rates. Lin et al. [19] focused their study on network intrusion detection, using enhanced CNN based on Lenets 5 to classify network threats. The authors developed an improved behavior-based model for anomaly detection by training a CNN to extract enhanced behavior features and identify threats. Their experiment showed overall prediction accuracy with 97.53% intrusion detection rate. The proposed model improves the accuracy of intrusion detection for threat classification.

Zeng et al. [20] proposed a Deep Full Range (DFR) framework comprising a network of encrypted traffic classification and intrusion detection. Three deep learning algorithms (CNN, LSTM and stack auto encoder SAE) were employed for traffic classification and intrusion detection. CNN was used to learn features of the raw traffic; LSTM was used to learn features from time-related aspects and SAE was used to extract features from coding characteristics. The full range consists of three algorithms capable of classifying encrypted and malware traffic within one framework without human intervention. The authors proved that the DFR could attain a robust and accurate performance on both encrypted traffic classification and intrusion detection.

Dey et al. [21] proposed Gated Recurrent Unit (GRU) - LSTM using Google's tensor flow that provided options to visualize network design. Their analysis showed that GRU - LSTM provided high accuracy with low false alarm rate. When compared, GRU-LSTM showed a strong potential in terms of accuracy for anomaly detection.

Hsu et al. [22] proposed a Deep Reinforcement Learning- based (DRL) for anomaly network intrusion detection. Their design revealed incoming network traffic by data sniffing and a pre-processing data module that checks the quality of data before it is fed for intrusion detection. This method can be adopted for self-updating and detecting abnormal incoming network traffic on real-time basis in company websites. SVM and Random Forest algorithms was utilized. They showed high anomaly detection accuracy and improved processing speed.

Privacy protection and national security in the cyber world depends on safe cyberspace. Network intrusion is one of the sophisticated actors stemming from cyber-threats. Sezari et al. [23] applied a deep feed forward network by modifying the parameters of the anomaly-based network. Their result demonstrated better performance with less complexity and a low false alarm rate. Therefore, their model is trustworthy and can be used to prevent intruders. It can detect unknown attacks based on its network features.

Naseer et al. [24] investigated the suitability of deep learning approaches for anomaly-based intrusion detection. They developed a model based on ANN, Auto encoder and RNN. The models were trained on NSL KDD training dataset and evaluated on the test dataset provided by NSL KDD. A Graphic Processing Unit (GPU) powered test bed using keras with theano backend was employed. A comparison between Deep Neural Network (DNN) and conventional machine learning models was carried out where both Deep Conventional Neural Network (DCNN) and LSTM models showed exceptional accuracy on the test dataset, this demonstrates the fact that Deep learning is a promising technology for intrusion detection.

Anomaly detection has received considerable attention in cybersecurity. The clandestine nature of cyber-attacks increased considerably where malware is installed through a supply chain. Malware eavesdrops and disrupts information exchange.

Huma et al. [27] proposed a detection approach deployed to secure incoming and outgoing traffic, they utilized the application of deep random neural network with multilayer perceptron and evaluated the scheme using two datasets DS205 and UNSW-NB15. They proposed a deep learning based cyber-attack detection system that detects cyber-attack 25 minutes after the attack was initiated to improve cybersecurity at its embryonic stage. It provided performance metrics like accuracy, precision, recall and F1 score which can be compared with several state-of-the-art attack detection algorithms. Classification of 16 different attacks was proposed, and accuracy of 98% and 99% was achieved.

Several industries have adopted the Industrial Internet of Things (IIoT) in smart homes, smart cities, connected cars and supply chain management which introduced new trends in business development. However, these edge devices have become exploitation points for intruders, it raised security and privacy challenge to the trustworthiness of edge devices by compromised devices that transmit false information to cloud servers. An IDS is widely accepted as a technique to monitor malicious activities [26].

The growth of modern cyber infrastructure made cybersecurity more important. It is estimated that a trillion devices will be connected to the Internet by 2022 [28]. IDS is an essential tool with objective to detect unauthorized use and abuse in the host network [29]. Sezari et al. [23] demonstrated the performance of a system while comparing the false alarm rate of models on KDD 1999 Cup dataset, they applied a highly optimized deep feedforward network by the modification of the model parameters. Their model achieved a highly accurate low false alarm and detection rate which can be used to detect and prevent intruders. Utilizing deep learning provided a system behavior model that selects abnormal behavior and is reliable with less complexity.

Khaw et al. [25] monitored network traffic to detect abnormal activities and ensured security of communication and information, using network intrusion simulation datasets (NSL-KDD and UNSW- NB15) on a real campus network. They proposed a Deep Reinforcement Learning-based (DRL) system with self-updating ability to detect abnormal incoming traffic. Dawoud et al. [16] explored the applicability of deep learning to detect anomaly in Internet of Things (IoT) architecture. They proposed an anomaly detection framework by evaluating the use of Restricted Boltzmann machines as generative energy-based model against auto encoders. The study showed approximately 99% detection accuracy. Deep learning algorithms showed positive results and achieved highest detection accuracy with high-performance speed that is effective in detecting false alarm rate (FAR), they can detect previously seen and un- seen threats, however deep neural network could perform better when given more data. Securing a large network in real-time is a challenge that was identified. Several studies focused on intrusion detection to analyze network traffic by extracting features from network flows and traffic fluctuation.

Deep learning algorithm can self-adapt to anomaly intrusion detection and predict network attacks, this was demonstrated in a study conducted by Fernandez et al. [12]. Abraham et al. [8] compared several machine learning algorithms, Random Forest had a superior model, it performed optimally for anomaly detection using cross-validation, and their overall result revealed that previously seen and unseen anomaly-based intrusion can be detected. An improvement in the reduction of false-positive alerts that enabled rapid response to cyber-threat was observed while using ANN [40]. CNN can detect anomalies in industrial control systems by detecting majority of attacks with low false positive rate [41]. A study conducted by Hashim et al. [42] showed that LSTM has high detection accuracy in securing websites from external breaches. Vinayakumar et al. [10] analyzed ransomware attacks and focused on Twitter as a case study, they concluded that deep learning can be used to monitor online posts and provide early warning about ransomware spread.

TABLE IV. PUBLICATION YEAR AND AI SOLUTIONS (2018 TO 2022)

	Intrusion Detection	Spam detection	Malware detection	Image recognition	Traffic classification	Pattern recognition	Other	Total
2018	5	1	2	2	1		1	12
2019	3	1	4				5	13
2020	7	1	5	1	1		1	16
2021	9	2	11			1	3	26
Total	24	5	22	3	2	1	10	67

V. FUTURE DIRECTION OF AI METHODS IN CYBERSECURTY MANAGEMENT

Research directions in AI applications for cybersecurity records broad areas of application. Challenges in cybersecurity continue to emerge which makes it difficult for further research to focus on a specific area. Studies within similar areas are experimenting with different AI algorithms. From table IV, algorithms classified as other were identified to have been used in less than two applications. Researchers are adopting newer techniques. In particular, anomaly intrusion detection needs improvement by reducing model training time in complex systems. Accordingly, future studies may opt for novel techniques. There is a need for applications to be efficient and have performance that reduce computational complexity. However, it was emphasized that for neural networks to present best accuracy with low error, it must be given large dataset. Researchers should advocate a scalable framework that can learn from traffic without manual intervention and can be used in real time to raise alert of possible cyber-attacks.

Future studies may opt for LSTM that have shown improved performance with high accuracy and low computation time.

In recent years, AI applications for cybersecurity have gained interest from researchers. Remarkable contributions have been made in combating cybercrime linking to issues like anomaly intrusion detection and malware detection. Several applications demonstrated improvement with impact in various areas. These areas include prediction of network attacks, presenting best accuracy with the lowest error rate, detecting previously seen and unseen threats and monitoring online post to provide early warning about cyber-threats. The nature of recent research suggests promising result. However, there are some challenges. A significant number of studies did not state the algorithm used or the domain applied. Also, the variety of algorithms identified suggests that researchers are not accepting newer methods, but they are comparing the available algorithms to determine which algorithm is best for an identified situation. Therefore, it is necessary for researchers to investigate further as the latest trends are tending towards IoT. Gradually new modern world activities have moved to the cloud. It is now possible for systems to be connected to the internet and controlled from anywhere in the world. Internet of Things connects these devices to the internet. If companies and organizations can secure their devices with intelligent solutions, consumer confidence will increase.

VI. RESEARCH VALIDATION, LIMITATION AND CONCLUSION

This paper presented a survey of existing research on the application of AI in cybersecurity management. We reviewed the use of AI technologies (Algorithms) in detecting and preventing attacks in cyberspace. The importance and impact of AI in cybersecurity management was discussed. This study covered research centered on viewpoint from 2018 to 2022. Several scholarly databases with related studies were considered. The use of journals, conference papers short papers and more were used to avoid bias in the selection process.

This study confirms that deep learning is not only viable for intrusion detection but is also a promising technology for detecting known and unknown threats. The complexity of cyber-attacks requires techniques that are effective. AI has proven to be effective while maintaining low computation time with a focus on LSTM that have shown low training and computation time.

Over the years, information and communication technology has advanced and cyber-attack surface continued to grow rapidly. Increased frequency of cyber-attacks has reinforced the need for cybersecurity initiatives. Conventional techniques have become inadequate in mitigating complex cyber-attacks, therefore solutions that are capable of tackling cyber threats in real-time is required. AI has shown effectiveness in terms of computational complexity while maintaining low training time

AI is a technology with a range of computational models and algorithms. It deals with the design of intelligent systems that mimic human intelligence. Although AI can be used to fight cybercrime, it could also be exploited hackers. These intelligent security solutions can be considered and integrated into a comprehensive system in countries with low record of publications. AI can be considered as a holistic approach. The advantage of utilizing the above intelligent security solutions is greatly publicized, the integration remains open for further investigations.

REFERENCES

[1] S. Xu, "Cybersecurity Dynamics: A Foundation for the Science of Cybersecurity," Adv. Inf. Secur., vol. 74, pp. 1-31, 2019, doi: 10.1007/978-3-030-10597-6_1.

[2] K. F. Steinmetz and M. Yar, "Cybercrime and society,"_Cybercrime and Society, pp. 1–368, 2019.

[3] P. Ping, W. Qin, Y. Xu, C. Miyajima, and K. Takeda, "Impact of driver behavior on fuel consumption: Classification, evaluation and prediction using machine learning," IEEE Access, vol. 7, pp. 78 515–78 532, 2019.

[4] M. Ghahramani, Y. Qiao, M. Zhou, A. O. Hagan, and J. Sweeney, "AI based modeling and data-driven evaluation for smart manufacturing processes," IEEE/CAA Journal of Automatica Sinica, vol. 7, no. 4, pp. 1026–1037, 2020.

[5] K.-H. Yu, A. L. Beam, and I. S. Kohane, "Artificial in- telligence in healthcare," Nature biomedical engineering, vol. 2, no. 10, pp. 719–731, 2018.

[6] M. Chassignol, A. Khoroshavin, A. Klimova, and A. Bilyatdinova, "Artificial intelligence trends in education: a narrative overview," Procedia Computer Science, vol. 136, pp. 16–24, 2018.

[7] M. J. Smith, "Getting value from artificial intelligence in agriculture," Animal Production Science, vol. 60, no. 1, pp. 46–54, 2018.

[8] B. Abraham et al., "A Comparison of Machine Learning Approaches to Detect Botnet Traffic," Proc. Int. Jt. Conf. Neural N. Intell. Yr Retrosp. Two/New/A Hardware-Trojan Classif. Method Util. Bound. net Struct, vol.-July, doi: 10.1109/IJCNN.2018.8489096.

[9] R. Abdulhammed, M. Faezipour, A. Abuzneid, and A. Abumallouh, "Deep and Machine Learning Approaches for Anomaly-Based Intrusion Detection of Imbalanced Network Traffic," IEEE Sensors Lett., vol. 3, no. 1, pp. 2019–2022, doi: 10.1109/LSENS.2018.2879990.

[10] R. Vinayakumar et al., "Deep Learning Approach for Intelligent Intrusion Detection System," IEEE Access, vol. 7, pp. 41525–41550, doi: 10.1109/ACCESS.2019.2895334.

[11] S. A. Sokolov, T. B. Iliev, and I. S. Stoyanov, "Analysis of cybersecurity threats in cloud applications using deep learning techniques," 42nd Int. Conv. Inf. Commun. Technol. Electron. Microelectron. MIPRO - Proc., pp. 441–446, doi: 10.23919/MIPRO.2019.8756755.

[12] L. Fernandez et al., "A Self-Adaptive Deep Learning-Based System for Anomaly Detection in 5G Networks," IEEE Access, vol. 6, pp. 7700–7712, doi: 10.1109.2018.2803446.

[13] X Zhang, J Chen, Y. Zhou, L. Han and J. Lin, A multiple-layer representation learning model for network- based attack detection. IEEE Access, 7, pp.91992-92008. 2019.

[14] W. Zhong, N. Yu, and C. Ai, "Applying big data based deep learning system to intrusion detection," Big Data Min. Anal., vol. 3, no. 3, pp. 181–195, 2020, doi: 10.26599/BDMA.2020.9020003.

[15] A. Dey, Deep IDS. A deep learning approach for Intrusion detection based on IDS, 2nd Int. Conference Sustain. Technology Ind. 4.0, vol. 0, pp. 19–20, doi 10.1109/STI 50764.2020.9350411.

[16] A. Dawoud, O. A. Sianaki, S. Shahristani, and C. Raun, "Internet of Things Intrusion Detection: A Deep Learning Approach," IEEE Symp. Ser. Comput. Intell. SSCI, pp. 1516–1522, doi: 10.1109/SSCI47803.2020.9308293.

[17] M. Ishaque and L. Hudec, "Feature extraction using Deep Learning for Intrusion Detection System," 2nd Int. Conf. Comput. Appl. Inf. Secur. ICCAIS doi: 10.1109/CAIS.2019.8769473.

[18] M.M. Isa and L. Mhamdi, Native SDN intrusion detection using machine learning. In 2020 IEEE Eighth International Conference on Communications andNetworking (ComNet), pp. 1-7, IEEE. 2020.

[19] W. H. Lin, H. C. Lin, P. Wang, B. H. Wu, and J. Y. Tsai, "Using convolutional neural networks to network intrusion detection for cyber-threats," Proc. 4th IEEE Int. Conf. Appl. Syst. Innov. ICASI, pp. 1107–1110, doi:10.1109/ICASI.2018.8394474.

[20] Y. Zeng, H. Gu, W. Wei, and Y. Guo, "Deep-Full- Range: A Deep Learning Based Network Encrypted Traf fic Classification and Intrusion Detection Framework," IEEE Access, vol. 7, pp. 45182–45190, doi: 10.1109/AC-CESS.2019.2908225.

[21] S. K. Dey and M. M. Rahman, "Flow based anomaly detection in software defined networking: A deep learning approach with feature selection method," 4th Int. Conf. Electr. Eng. Inf. Commun. Technol. iCEEiCT, pp. 630–635, doi: 10.1109/CEEICT.2018.8628069.

[22] Y. -F. Hsu and M. Matsuoka,.A Deep Reinforcement Learning Approach for Anomaly Network Intrusion Detection System," 2020 IEEE 9th International Conference on Cloud Networking (CloudNet), 2020, pp. 1-6, doi: 10.1109/CloudNet51028.2020.9335796.

[23] B. Sezari, D. P. F. Moller, and A. Deutschmann, "Anomaly-Based Network Intrusion Detection Model Using Deep Learning in Airports," Proc. - 17th IEEE Int. Conf. Trust. Secur. Priv. Comput. Commun. 12th IEEE Int. Conf. Big Data Sci. Eng. Trust pp. 1725–1729, doi: 10.1109/TrustCom/BigDataSE.2018.00261.

[24] S. Naseer et al., "Enhanced network anomaly detection based on deep neural networks," IEEE Access, vol. 6, pp. 48231–48246, doi: 10.1109/ACCESS.2018.2863036.

[25] Y. M. Khaw et al. "A Deep Learning- Based Cyberattack Detection System for Transmission Protective Relays," IEEE Trans. Smart Grid, vol. 12, no. 3, pp. 2554–2565, doi: 10.1109/TSG.2020.3040361.

[26] S. Qureshi et al. "A Hybrid DL-Based Detection Mechanism for Cyber-threats in Secure Networks," IEEE Access, vol. 9, pp. 1–1, doi: 10.1109/access.2021.3081069.

[27] Z. E. Huma et al., "A Hybrid Deep Random Neural Network for Cyberattack Detection in the Industrial Internet of Things," IEEE Access, vol. 9, pp. 55595–55605, doi: 10.1109/ACCESS.2021.3071766.

[28] L. Santos, C. Rabadao, and R. Gonçalves, "Intrusion detection systems in internet of things: A literature review," in 2018 13th Iberian Conference on Information Systems and Technologies (CISTI). IEEE, 2018, pp. 1–7.

[29] M. Wang, K. Zheng, Y. Yang, and X. Wang, "An Explain- able Machine Learning Framework for Intrusion Detection Systems," IEEE Access, vol. 8, pp. 73127–73141, doi: 10.1109.2020.2988359

[30] S. Zeadally, E. Adi, Z. Baig, and I. A. Khan, "Harnessing artificial intelligence capabilities to improve cybersecurity," IEEE Access, vol. 8, pp. 23 817–23 837, 2020.

[31] S. Aljawarneh, M. Aldwairi, and M.B. Yassein, Anomaly-based intrusion detection system through feature selection analysis and building hybrid efficient model. Journal of Computational Science, 25, pp.152- 160, 2018

[32] P. Mishra, V. Varadharajan, U. Tupakula, and E.S. Pilli, A detailed investigation and analysis of using machine learning techniques for intrusion detection. IEEE Communications Surveys & Tutorials, 21(1), pp. 686-728, 2018.

[33] P. Parrend, J. Navarro, F. Guigou, A. Deruyver, and P. Collet, Foundations and applications of artificial Intelligence for zero-day and multi-step attack detection. EURASIP Journal on Information Security, 2018(1), pp.1-21. 2018

[34] B. Naik, A. Mehta, H. Yagnik, and M. Shah, "The impacts of artificial intelligence techniques in augmentation of cybersecurity: a comprehensive review," Complex & Intelligent Systems, pp. 1-18, 2021.

[35] V. R. Basili, "Goal question metric paradigm," Encyclopedia of software engineering, pp. 528–532, 1994.

[36] F. Yahya, R. J. Walters, and G. B. Wills, "Using goal- question-metric (gqm) approach to assess security in cloud storage," in International Workshop on Enterprise Security. Springer, 2015, pp. 223–240.

[37] Z. Liu, T. Qin, X. Guan, H. Jiang, and C. Wang, "An integrated method for anomaly detection from massive system logs," IEEE Access, vol. 6, pp. 30 602–30 611, 2018.

[38] R. K. Alqurashi, M. A. AlZain, B. Soh, M. Masud, and J. Al-Amri, "Cyber-attacks and impacts: A case study in Saudi Arabia," International Journal, vol. 9, no. 1, 2020.

[39] I. Siniosoglou et al., "A unified deep learning anomaly detection and classification approach for smart grid environments," IEEE Transactions on Network and Service Management, 2021.

[40] J. Lee, J. Kim, I. Kim, and K. Han, Cyber threat detection based on artificial neural networks using event profiles. IEEE Access, 7, pp.165607-165626, 2019.

[41] M. Kravchik, and A. Shabtai, Detecting cyberattacks in industrial control systems using convolutional neural networks. In Proceedings of the 2018 Workshop on Cyber-Physical Systems Security 2018, pp. 72-83.

[42] A. Hashim, R. Medani, and T.A. Attia, Defences against web application attacks and detecting phishing links using machine learning. In 2020 International Con ference on Computer, Control, Electrical, and Electronics Engineering (ICCCEEE), pp. 1-6, IEEE. , 2021.

[43] A. Iliev, N. Kyurkchiev, A. Rahnev, and T. Terzieva, Some models in the theory of computer viruses propagation. LAP LAMBERT Academic Publishing, 2019.

[44] W.H. Lin, H.C. Lin, P. Wang, B. H. Wu, and J.Y. Tsai, Using convolutional neural networks to network intrusion detection for cyber threats. In 2018 IEEE International Conference on Applied System Invention (ICASI) , pp. 1107-1110, IEEE , 2018.

[45] Z. Ma, H. Yuanyuan, and J. Lu, "Trojan traffic detection based on machine learning," in 2020 17th International Computer Conference on Wavelet Active Media Technology and Information Processing (IC- CWAMTIP). IEEE, 2020, pp. 157-160.

[46] A. Alzahrani and D. B. Rawat, "Comparative study of machine learning algorithms for sms spam detection," in 2019 Southeast Con. IEEE, 2019, pp. 1-6.

[47] L. Chan et al., "Survey of AI in cybersecurity for information technology management," in 2019 IEEE technology & engineering management conference(TEMSCON). IEEE, 2019, pp. 1–8.

[48] J.-h. Li, "Cyber security meets artificial intelligence: A survey," Frontiers of Information Technology & Electronic Engineering, vol. 19, no. 12, pp. 1462–1474, 2018.

[49] J. Johansson, "Countermeasures against coordinated cyber-attacks towards power grid systems: A systematicliterature study," 2019.

[50] B. Kitchenham et al., "Systematic literature reviews in software engineering-a systematic literature review," Information and software technology, vol. 51, no. 1, pp. 7–15, 2009.

[51] I. Wiafe et al., "Artificial intelligence for cybersecurity: a systematic mapping of literature," IEEE Access, vol. 8, pp. 146 598–146 612, 2020.

[52] I. H. Sarker, M. H. Furhad, and R. Nowrozy, "AI-driven cybersecurity: an overview, security intelligence modeling and research directions," SN Computer Science, vol. 2, no. 3, pp. 1–18, 2021.

[53] Q. Chang, X. Ma, M. Chen, X. Gao, and M. Dehghani, "A deep learning based secured energy management framework within a smart island," Sustainable Cities andSociety, vol. 70, p. 102938, 2021.

[54] L. Malhotra, B. Bhushan, and R. V. Singh, "Artificial intelligence and deep learning-based solutions to enhance cyber security," Available at SSRN 3833311, 2021.

[55] S. Wang et al., "Detecting android malware leveraging text semantics of network flows," IEEE Transactions on In- formation Forensics and Security, vol. 13, no. 5, pp.1096–1109, 2017.

[56] Z. Zhang and Q. Yu, "Modeling hardware trojans in 3d ics," in 2019 IEEE Computer Society Annual Symposium on VLSI (ISVLSI). IEEE, 2019, pp. 483–488.

[57] Z. Fang et al., "Statistical modeling of computer malware propagation dynamics in cyberspace," Journal of Applied Statistics, pp. 1–26, 2020.

[58] S. Y. Yerima and S. Sezer, "Droidfusion: A novel multilevel classifier fusion approach for android malware detection," IEEE transactions on cybernetics, vol. 49, no.2, pp. 453–466, 2018.

[59] G. Iadarola, F. Martinelli, F. Mercaldo, and A. San- tone, "Towards an interpretable deep learning model for mobile malware detection and family identification," Computers & Security, vol. 105, p. 102198, 2021.

[60] P. Feng, J. Ma, C. Sun, X. Xu, and Y. Ma, "A novel dynamic android malware detection system with ensemble learning," IEEE Access, vol. 6, pp. 30 996–31 011, 2018.

[61] S. Srinivasan et al., "Deep convolutional neural network based image spam classification," in 2020 6th Conference on data science and machine learning applications (CDMA). IEEE, 2020, pp. 112–117.

[62] B. Bayar and M. C. Stamm, "Constrained convolutional neural networks: A new approach towards general purpose image manipulation detection," IEEE Transactions on Information Forensics and Security, vol. 13, no. 11, pp. 2691–2706, 2018.

[63] A. Lakshmanarao, P. S. P. Rao, and M. B. Krishna, "Phishing website detection using novel machine learning fusion approach," in 2021 International Conference on Artificial Intelligence and Smart Systems (ICAIS). IEEE, 2021, pp. 1164–1169.

[64] A. Dal Pozzolo et al. "Credit card fraud detection: a realistic modeling and a novel learning strategy," IEEE transactions on neural networks and learning systems, vol. 29, no. 8, pp. 3784–3797, 2017.

[65] J. Lee, J. Kim, I. Kim, and K. Han, "Cyber threat detection based on artificial neural networks using event profiles," IEEE Access, vol. 7, pp. 165 607–165 626, 2019

[66] A. S. Sadiq et al., "An efficient ids using hybrid magnetic swarm optimization in wanets," IEEE Access, vol. 6, pp. 29 041–29 053, 2018.

[67] G. Kabanda, "Performance of machine learning and other artificial intelligence paradigms in cybersecurity" Oriental journal of computer science and technology 13.1, 2020, pp. 1-21.

Sterilized Persistence Vectors (SPVs): Defense Through Deception on Windows Systems

Nicholas Phillips
Department of Computer and Information Sciences
Towson University, Towson, MD, USA
nphill5@students.towson.edu

Aisha Ali-Gombe
Division of Computer Science and Engineering
Louisiana State University, Baton Rouge, AK, USA
aaligombe@lsu.edu

Abstract—**The vicious cycle of malware attacks on infrastructures and systems has continued to escalate despite organizations' tremendous efforts and resources in preventing and detecting known threats. One reason is that standard reactionary practices such as defense-in-depth are not as adaptive as malware development. By utilizing zero-day system vulnerabilities, malware can successfully subvert preventive measures, infect its targets, establish a persistence strategy, and continue to propagate, thus rendering defensive mechanisms ineffective. In this paper, we propose sterilized persistence vectors (SPVs) - a proactive *Defense by Deception* strategy for mitigating malware infections that leverages a benign rootkit to detect changes in persistence areas. Our approach generates SPVs from infection-stripped malware code and utilizes them as persistent channel blockers for new malware infections. We performed an in-depth evaluation of our approach on Windows systems versions 7 and 10 by infecting them with 1000 different malware samples after training the system with 1000 additional samples to fine-tune the learning algorithms. Our results, based on a memory analysis of pre-and post-SPV infections, indicate that the proposed approach can successfully defend systems against new infections by rendering the malicious code ineffective and inactive without persistence.**

***Keywords—* Malware, Computer Security, Reverse Engineering, Persistence, Rootkit.**

I. Introduction

Malware is a continued threat against cyber systems. Characterized by stealthiness, persistence, and mutation, new-generation malware often utilizes various system vulnerabilities for infection and then leverages standard system functionality to maintain persistence. With a suitable persistence strategy, malware can remain active and prolong its existence on a host system. One of the strengths of modern malware development is its adaptability: methodologies mutate rapidly, targeting areas where security measures are weaker or nonexistent. In both related literature and practice, many malware defensive techniques have been proposed - (1) anti-virus and host-based intrusion detection [29], (2) integrity checking [27], [38], detection [7], [24], [36], [37] and (3) after-effect or post-mortem analysis [2], [9], [30], [40], [41] of modern malware. However, as evidenced by the continued rise in stealthier attack scenarios, new samples, and variant development [15], these existing defensive approaches fall short in addressing a growing threat. The common theme of these techniques is identifying the problem either before infection through signature or anomaly detection or after infection through system scans. Neither provides a general means to stop malware due to its adaptability. These ideas of a responsive or reactionary approach to detecting and preventing malware infections, in many respects, play to malware's strengths. Because of the limitations mentioned above, we propose SPVs - a Defense by Deception approach. The goal of our methodology is to drastically reduce malware infections by reducing the available areas of persistence for a malicious actor's exploits, including zero-day attacks. Our approach employs the use of malware code segments to defend a target system against future infection, thus serving as a defensive mechanism. This novel technique is a drastic shift from the conventional utilization of malware code for signature detection and fingerprinting. In our proposed approach, we place blockers called SPVs in critical areas of persistence on target systems. These SPVs are persistence and deployment elements stripped from the various malware samples analyzed. Essentially, SPVs prevent a new malware infection by either blocking it from writing its own vector or overwriting the persistence vector associated with already established malware. With this approach, malware loses its ability to persist and is prevented from executing its payloads, and consequently propagating further. We implemented the prototype of our SPV by manually building a library of 75 payload-stripped SPVs into the Defense by Deception code base, which is then compiled into a target system and deployed at system startup. The Defense by Deception code called the *SPVExec* is then administered as a malware defensive apparatus on a need basis automatically at system runtime without user intervention. The empirical results of the evaluation on Windows 7 and 10 for pre- and post SPV deployment infected of 1000 malware samples showed that the use of SPVs is a very effective strategy for malware defense. For 99% of the samples in the data set, the SPV Defense by Deception process rendered them inert - the malware sets were not able to execute their payloads, persist, or propagate.

Contributions - Our proposed novel SPV strategy provides the following salient features:

- **Defense Against Malware**: The development of a practical approach to preventing new malware infections by simulating and inventing the perception that the system is already infected.
- **Fully Automated Deployment Process**: The deployment and rendering of the SPVs at runtime is done without human intervention.
- **Efficiency**: The SPV code incurs very minimal overhead on run-time system resources.
- **Usability**: The generated SPVs are reliable and seldom flagged as malware by system defense and antiviral tools. Furthermore, the proposed system allows for legitimate programs to be installed without hindrance based upon internal whitelisting.

The rest of the paper is organized as follows: Section 2 presents the problem statement and an overview of rootkit infection; Section 3 provides a detailed description of the SPV process; Sections 4 and 5 present the implementation and evaluation of our research, respectively; Section 6 reviews the related literature; and Section 7 concludes the paper.

II. Related Work

Means of malware detection have grown more stagnant in the last ten years. As shown in Tahir, Alsmadi, and El Merabet [42], [43], [44], most of the improvements have been focused on implementing machine learning. This implementation is worked by classifying individual features within malware samples and rejecting non-specific elements found within a large number of malware samples. While this is an improvement upon the standard malware detection means, there is the limitation that they are process intensive, both in the means of teaching algorithms for detection also in the scanning of the multitude of files that are presented to the system. The remainder of the detection methodologies can be broken down into Host-based detection, Hypervisor-based detection and Post-mortem analysis.

A. Host-based Detection

The more traditional technique for rootkit detection is a host-based intrusion detection system that checks for anomalies or footprints of known malware. For example, the System Virginity Verifier verifies the validity of in-memory code for critical system DLLs and kernel modules; [35] checks the legitimacy of every kernel driver before it is loaded into the operating system; Panorama [36] is designed to perform behavioral runtime tracking; and SBCFI [22] detects threats by examining the control flow integrity of the kernel code. A smaller subset of methods, such as Autovac, utilizes forensics snapshot comparison engines to detect the execution of malware on the system to prevent it [34]. Other host-based rootkit detection systems include HookFinder [36] and HookMap [32]. These techniques use systematic approaches to detect and remove malware hooks in target operating systems. One major drawback of traditional host-based detection methodologies is the ability of the malicious entity to evade detection, since it is running with the same level of privilege as the detection systems. Since most of these tools are designed to probe for the rootkit signature and/or behavior, malware can easily subvert this effort by hiding its footprint. Malicious actors can employ obfuscation techniques, such as altering the checksums, implementing collection encryption, and setting file wiping [7] to thwart analysis. The SPV code does not scan for malware footprint or traits; instead, it takes the more aggressive approach of hijacking the persistence area of a potential rootkit, leaving the malware with no place to hide. Furthermore, the SPV code is built so that the malware cannot eject or terminate its process.

B. Hypervisor-based Detection

Integrity checking is a technique that requires continuous monitoring of the kernel code for changes to signatures, control flow, and kernel data structures. For kernel-level rootkits, the most practical approach for maintaining kernel integrity is hypervisor-based systems that leverage virtual machine introspection (VMI) [1], [13], [14], [24], [26], [27], [38], [39]. VMI systems and tools are built to introspect the virtual environment through the hypervisor. Since the hypervisor runs at a much lower level than the virtual OS, these mechanisms are often seen as an effective means of detecting rootkits and monitoring their behavior. However, their major limitation is the fact that they target only virtualized environments and cloud infrastructures and cannot be applied to introspect real hardware-based systems. Moreover, most kernel integrity-check-based systems are susceptible to return-oriented rootkit attacks [13]. Methods used to detect the integrity of a system have been proven to be limited based upon the existence of UEFI bootkits. These malicious code elements work by making the operating system accept that malicious code pieces are a legitimate portion of the system's code [8], [12], [23], [33]. With our proposed SPV Defense by Deception process, the system is designed to execute on both hardware and virtual systems, thus circumventing this limitation.

C. Post-mortem Analysis

The last category of rootkit detection methods is postmortem analysis systems, designed to analyze the after-effects of rootkit execution. These forms of analysis are often passive and involve examining kernel memory snapshots looking for evidence of rootkit infection, persistence, and stealth. Disk forensics tools, such as [2], [9], [30], [40] are used for general system incident response. These tools can examine a target system for file modifications, running processes, network activities, and more. In much the same way as integrity checkers, disk forensics tools are limited by their coverage. If malicious code hides its elements in specific system files or structures, these will generally be missed by the aftereffect analysis [6]. With memory forensics, aftereffect analysis is carried out on a snapshot of volatile memory. The most widely used memory analysis framework is the volatility framework [41]. This methodology is restricted to current events and processes. Terminated malware behaviors cannot be retrieved. Furthermore, modern rootkits can evade detection from memory forensics tools by performing direct kernel object manipulations that hide their presence from registering in major kernel structures or by altering the memory collection or imaging process as a whole [17]. In comparison to a more passive malware detection approach, our SPV process is an offensive approach that prevents malware infections in real time. The SPVs are designed to block malware from executing, thus forcing the malware to terminate its process.

D. Problem Statement

Malware has always had the strength of its adaptability, which enables it to use multiple mechanisms to infect and evade detection or bypass many of the elements of system defense [11]. Either through using out-of-date signatures, exploiting unknown vulnerabilities, or targeting the weakest link - the human - malware will cause the defense to fail, even if only one of these falls short. Current detection and prevention tools are at a significant disadvantage in that malware is evolving at a much faster rate than defense tools. Stealthy zero-day attacks are becoming increasingly common, and it takes only a single unknown offense or human error to bring down the whole gauntlet of defenses [16].

Thus, we present the SPV Defense by Deception process - a novel technique that attempts to hijack the areas in which malware in general and rootkits in particular can land their persistence vectors. Rootkit persistence vectors are specifically selected in this research because they are the most common persistence mechanism used by malware of all families [11].

The motivation to use persistence vectors stems from the fact that, in practice, infection vectors are unpredictable, meaning that exploits, especially zero-day exploits used to launch malware attacks, evolve with newly found vulnerabilities. However, the persistence vectors with which the malware maintains a presence on a victim's machine are often deterministic. As such, the most effective way to curtail rootkit infections and ultimately render them ineffective is to place blockers in the potentially persistent channels in the system. Long-term malware campaigns, specifically those utilized by Advanced Persistent Threats (APTs), do not wish to bring a targeted system down immediately. Instead, they wish to complete target profiling against the network, exfiltrate sensitive data, and work further into the system. It can sometimes be months before the threat actors launch their final attack target. For this, they require a means to remain in the system. They require persistence. One of the longest of these types of campaigns was the Harkonnen Operation. Malicious actors could utilize their malware persistence and operate on a network for twelve years before they were finally detected. During this time, the malware implanted could assist with further target development, stealing essential data, such as corporate financial documentation, and pilfering money for the attackers [19]. Our approach injects the SPV code into the system startup process and can be rendered on both bare hardware and virtualized environments. The SPV process blocks all malware by first detecting in real-time when the malware deploys its persistence vector. It then hijacks the malware area of persistence by automatically selecting and overwriting the malware code with certain SPVs. This process consistently blocks target malware from maintaining a presence on a defended system. Although our approach is currently limited to the categories of malware containing persistence vectors, "fileless" malware has only existed substantially since 2002. It is still not utilized as substantially as persistent malware [20], thus making this limitation minimal.

III. The SPV - Defense by Deception Process

The SPV process is a code implementation of "sterilized" malware, or malware that has had its malicious content removed, injected via a common infection mechanism. It is a technique designed to prevent malware persistence on a system. SPV process involves injecting a malware persistence vector into a clean system to block potential malware from maintaining access. This process requires combining standing entries consisting of stripped malware persistence vectors and infection code fragments with filler code. With SPVs, the malicious payload code fragments are entirely stripped off while retaining the core elements of malware, such as API hooking, process manipulation, and service control in the SPV. The workflow for our proposed approach is made up of the SPV development phase and SPVExec code deployment and integration.

A. Development Phase

This phase begins with the identification and extraction of malware persistence vectors, followed by the reprogramming of the extracted persistence code fragments into one executable module.

1) Persistence Extraction: The mechanism in this stage requires manual extraction through detailed reverse engineering. We completed our reverse engineering via both static and dynamic malware analysis techniques. Malicious samples were collected from virus repositories: VirusShare [1] and Malshare [21]. One thousand samples were run through the two phases of reverse engineering. This was completed in a series of virtualized environments of the Windows operating system: Windows 7 and 10, with two copies of each, one for dynamic analysis and one for static analysis. Each machine had two 2.4 GHz cores and 4 GB RAM. For each target malware, we ran the sample against an unpacker to remove any possible common packers and cryptors, leaving behind the bare-bones malware code that would be evaluated by the analysis tools. In this initial phase, the stripped malware code was executed in a custom-built dynamic analysis sandbox running ProcMon, CaptureBat, CFF Explorer, API Monitor, and RegShot.

This static analysis identifies specific part of the executable targeted during the dynamic analysis phase. Such code construct include specific API invocation, non-normal network traffic, registry modification, and file creation. We executed the samples through a debugger and disassembler for the dynamic analysis, specifically IDAPro and OllyDbg, targeting the identified elements in static analysis. Then through the utilization of the HexRay program within IDAPro, the code section was removed and converted to a C program snippet.

2) SPV Generation: With the elements of persistence and infection identified and removed from the base malware code, we developed the SPVs. Since the identified persistence code was disassembled, we began this stage by converting the assembly code into C programming language.

PVs upon extraction reflect specifically that individual sample of the malware, but additionally can be utilized against the majority of the samples of that specific malware family of that generation. For example, an extracted persistence vector from Zeus Botnet would identify not only that specific file but also the different samples in that same generation of Zeus. Specific PVs could also be utilized against other families, dependent upon source code sampling utilized by the author upon its creation. Prior or future versions would require additional PV extractions depending on the evolution of the malware sample.

Figure 1 shows the PV extracted from Necurs Rootkit. The Necurs sample persists using multiple techniques but notably the implementation of boot and registry modification. These specific PVs were identified through our two-phased reverse engineering and exported for inclusion in the SPV library.

These 800 individual SPV extracted from the 1000 malware samples are loaded into the SPV Defense, including the deployment

```
        // Installing the boot loader
        Status = BkSetupWithPayload(BootLoader, BootSize, Payload, PayloadSize);
        vFree(BootLoader);

        if (Status != NO_ERROR)
        {
            DbgPrint("BKSETUP: Installation failed because of unknown reason.\n");
            break;
        }

        // Creating program key to mark that we were installed
        if (RegCreateKey(HKEY_LOCAL_MACHINE, KeyName, &hKey) == NO_ERROR)
            RegCloseKey(hKey);

        Status = NO_ERROR;
        DbgPrint("BKSETUP: Successfully installed.\n");
    } while(FALSE);

    if (hMutex)
        CloseHandle(hMutex);

    if (Payload)
        vFree(Payload);

    if (KeyName)
        vFree(KeyName);

    if (MutexName)
        vFree(MutexName);

    if (IsExe)
        DoSelfDelete();
```

Fig. 1. Extracted PV

code elements. These were selected as they covered the range of persistence vectors and allowed for broad defense of the SPVs when deployed on the system.

To build a stronger SPV defensive process, we developed an SPV library consisting of a combination of multiple SPVs.

B. SPVExec Deployment and Integration

The proposed SPV mechanism uses these extracted PVs to form a benign rootkit of the SPV and implements persistence elements in the areas extracted in the SPV code called the SPVExec. Additional persistence scanning mechanisms, like the Wingbird scanning ability for its infections, were added to the code to overwrite non-whitelisted persistence modifications. Additionally, previously removed malware functionality deployed a FAT32 file system within the bootstrap code section was added to the system. This area was used for SPV library, whitelisting, and the SPV Defense base code. The data remained encrypted, utilizing a 256-bit key to protect against registering on scans. The SPVExec was implemented as a single Windows executable program loaded alongside the essential boot files at system startup. The prototype is approximately 1800 lines of code in the C programming language. The code is a collection of SPVs, filler code consisting of protective measures extracted from malware, dynamic white- and blacklisting, the learning algorithm, and the SPV launcher.

1) Infection Code Scanning and Rewriting: After successful loading of the SPVExec, the persistence vectors employ two scanning techniques to validate and ensure that an intruder has not altered the injected SPVs at runtime. The first check utilizes time-based scans, similar to those employed by current protective tools. In the current implementation, this check runs a scan every second. Our secondary scanning technique leverages API hooking to check for malware intrusion. The SPV instances are injected into kernel-level processes. Any attempts to access the protected area of persistence are redirected to one of the SPV Defended DLLs. Both scanning techniques utilize hash lookups. During SPV code deployment, a hashmap of the injected SPVs and the region of persistence are stored. The rewriters dynamically replace code elements within the SPVExec codebase and are designed to look up any changes to the injected SPVs. The dynamically computed hashes of the injected vectors are then compared against the hashes of the SPVs that are expected to be at those regions. If any of the values return no match, then the code rewrites those SPVs as expected.

IV. Evaluation of the SPV Defense by Deception Process

We evaluate the effectiveness of our proposed SPV defense mechanism by performing four major experiments that answered the following questions:

- **Persistence of the SPV Defense process** - Can the SPV Defense survive and persist through system restarts and power removal?
- **Defense against malware** - Can the SPVs be used as an effective strategy to block potential malware from writing to protected areas of persistence?
- **Defense Through Deception** - Does the SPV Defense identify as malware to other malware and legitimate to legitimate programs?
- **System Performance** - Can the SPV Defense process be used as an efficient apparatus for system defense without depleting system resources?
- **White Listing Capability** - Does the SPV Defense allow legitimate programs to install without being replaced with SPV code?

A. Test Environment

To test SPVs across operating systems, we generated Testbed-3 and Testbed-4, utilized Windows testbeds using the same baseline operating systems as in the persistence extraction phase, i.e., Windows 7 and Windows 10. They both contain sets of virtual machines and bare metal with two 2.4 GHz cores and 4 GB RAM. Testbed-1 remained at the same level of security as that of the persistence extraction environment; this removes the chance of malware failing to infect because of patching or security tools. Unlike in persistence extraction, however, this testbed has most of its nonsecurity functionality restored. This allows the system to act similarly to a standard user system that would be part of a normal network. Testbed-2, Testbed-3 and Testbed-4 are equipped with system security monitoring tools, such as operating system inbuilt defense, i.e., Windows Defender, Host-based Security System, and other commercial off-the-shelf antivirus products. For all the testbeds, user programs were installed to simulate a working system that would be on a network and typical applications that are often targeted for compromise. To provide better containment during our analysis and testing, we implemented FakeDNS to resolve any network traffic.

B. Post-Mortem Analysis Environment

We leverage an in-depth analysis of the extracted memory snapshots of the target systems to evaluate the accuracy, resilience, and performance of the overall SPV Defense process. To perform forensic examinations of the memory dumps, we created a separate system equipped with FTK and Volatility. Additionally, to protect the data from being compromised on the system after malware infection, the collection tools were loaded on a USB. This allowed the acquisition to have a limited impact on the system while also keeping the tools from being impacted by any potential built-in anti-analysis approach.

C. Experiments

1) Experiment I: Persistence: Vital to the functionality of the SPVExec benign rootkit is its ability to maintain persistence. To test this functionality, we took the Testbed-2 system post SPV deployment and saved it as "X-Security-TestingPost." We then performed a power cycle. An start up alert was entered into the code to present a popup if the SPV remained in tact. This alert displays the first SPV value and

Windows 7	True Positive	True Negative	False Positive	False Negative	Overall Accuracy
Symantec	999	0	0	1	99.9%
McAfee	981	0	0	11	98.1%
Kaspersky	987	0	1	12	98.7%
SPV	999	0	1	0	99.9%
Windows 10	**True Positive**	**True Negative**	**False Positive**	**False Negative**	**Overall Accuracy**
Symantec	999	0	0	1	99.9%
McAfee	981	0	0	11	98.1%
Kaspersky	987	0	1	12	98.7%
SPV	999	0	1	0	99.9%

Fig. 2. SPV Evaluation: Regular Testing

a "Hello World" message. Upon powering the system on, a memory collection was completed utilizing FTK Imager. The memory image was processed by Volatility Memory Framework with the following plugins: psxview, malfind, ldrmodules, apihooks, dlldump, procdump, and threads. Processes and Dynamic Link Libraries (DLLs) of the SPVExec were found that proved that it could maintain its persistence, and a popup was displayed.

2) Experiment II-A: Defense Against Malware: The primary functionality of the SPVExec is its ability to stop malware attacks against the system. To provide a sufficient test of the defensive capabilities of our approach, we conducted this experiment with 1000 malware samples with diverse infection and persistence vectors and varying degrees of stealthiness. We utilized Testbed-2, Testbed-3, and Testbed-4 and executed the SPVExec; the image was saved as "X-Post-SPV," with X representing the OS. Each malware sample was then executed, and a snapshot and memory collection were taken. The system was then reset with the "Post-SPV" images and infected with the next malware sample. As each memory dump was analyzed with Volatility with the above mentioned plugins, the persistence elements of the SPV were found without the markers of the malware surviving. This proves that the SPV Defense was able to prevent the malware from taking effect and rendered it inert, on the same level as other security tools. Comparisons of our process to standard antivirus software indicated that our proposed approach achieves the same level of accuracy as other COTs anti-viruses as shown in Figure 2.

D. Experiment II-B: Reversion Testing

For this experiment, an additional image was generated of Testbed-2, Testbed-3, and Testbed-4, titled "X-SecurityReversion-TestingPost." The commercial antivirus software had the signature libraries reverted back three iterations, allowing for newer malware to be tested as though it were a zero-day exploit. The sample repository listed above was run on both virtual machines. Compared to standard antivirus detection rates, SPV Defense was able to maintain consistent rates. However, during the zero-day detection experiment, it was able to double the detection rates of standard antivirus software, as shown

Windows 7	True Positive	True Negative	False Positive	False Negative	Overall Accuracy
Symantec	525	0	100	375	52.5%
McAfee	495	0	105	400	49.5%
Kaspersky	500	0	25	475	50.0%
SPV	999	0	1	0	99.9%
Windows 10	**True Positive**	**True Negative**	**False Positive**	**False Negative**	**Overall Accuracy**
Symantec	525	0	100	375	52.5%
McAfee	495	0	105	400	49.5%
Kaspersky	500	0	25	475	50.0%
SPV	999	0	1	0	99.9%

Fig. 3. SPV Evaluation: Regression Testing

in Figure 3. This proves that SPV Defense is capable of performing far better than commercial malware detection tools against unknown threats due to its targeting only the persistence vectors.

1) Experiment III: Deceptive Capability: For this experiment, the SPVExec was run against two unique phases. One phase determined if malware identified SPVs as similar malware, avoiding infections. The second is if legitimate programs, such as Antivirus, saw the SPVs as a benign code structure. For defense through deception testing, the system was reverted to a save of the SPV defended state presented in Testbed-1. The Necurs malware sample was run against the system. This particular sample was chosen because it has a built-in function searching for already modified keys signaling an infected system. A total of ten instances of the malware were executed in attempts to infect the system; each time, memory collections were completed. Upon analysis of the memory samples via the Volatility analysis, no signs of the Necurs malware were present. Benign testing was conducted against a pool of fifteen antiviruses that ran against the SPV code base. All tests returned negative, indicating that none of the antiviruses flagged the SPVs as malicious.

2) Experiment IV: System Performance: In this experiment, we evaluate the effectiveness of our approach on system resources, particularly the impact of the SPV Defense process on memory and CPU utilization.

(i) CPU Utilization: Utilization was recorded in two separate instances to obtain a baseline for the pre- and postdeployment system. Baseline scores for each of these system performances were recorded. Next, multiple applications were opened to simulate a typical user's desktop, including two Microsoft Word documents, a single instance of Google Chrome, and one instance of the Windows file structure. The system was then left under these conditions for a period of 10 minutes. In the same way as most effective rootkits perform malicious activities without overloading the system, SPVs run in the background without exhausting CPU resources. The CPU usage overhead is on par with that of average antivirus software or an IDS/IPS, which is approximately 2 percent on average [29].

(ii) Memory Utilization The amount of memory utilized by the SPVs, specifically as they spawn processes, is also crucial. Too much memory utilization can cause an internal denial of service, making the method unusable. Utilizing the same parameters as in the CPU overhead test, the system was run with the same software instances for the 10-minute implementation. The baselines were again compared. This result also showed minimal impact on the system resources.

3) Experiment V: White Listing Capability: All the experiments conducted above were able to prove the ability of the proposed method to block future malware infections. However, this would be moot if normal programs were unable to make low-level system modifications and maintain their persistence. For this experiment, we attempted to install 10 "legitimate" programs on an SPV Defended system and determined that all were still installed after system restart. These programs were PyCharm, Visual Studio, BitRise, Atom, BlueFish, CodePen, Crimson Editor, Eclipse, Komodo Edit, and NetBeans. Each of these software programs was examined by the same methodology as malware to determine the major system changes made to ensure their own persistence. Individual snapshots from the "X-Post-SPV" series had one of the above ten programs installed. Memory collection was completed, and a snapshot was taken, titled "XPost-SPVTool", with X being the software installed. Upon powering on, a second memory collection was completed. Finally, the application was tested for functionality by launching the program. In all instances, both the SPV Defense and the program were operational and maintained persistence.

V. Conclusion and Future Works

In this paper, we present a new SPV Defense by Deception strategy that leverages sterilized persistence vectors extracted from a real malware corpus to block potential malware infections. Our system utilizes code from malware samples, not as signatures but as defensive strategies that stop new infections from attempting to write into persistence regions. Compared to existing COTs and techniques described in the literature for malware detection and prevention, our approach is designed to be more robust and versatile, with the ability to block malware both on bare hardware and in virtualized environments. Additionally, our methodology does not require a signature or agnostic of the target malware behavior. Through an in-depth evaluation of 1000 malware samples with pre- and post SPV infection, we demonstrate that our proposed SPV Defense by Deception mechanism can be used to effectively defend systems against malware infections with 1-3 percent CPU and memory overhead while not limiting the ability to install legitimate programs properly.

While this is a strong defense against malware implementation, it is currently limited to Windows OS. Additional work can be conducted into the persistence vectors that are different and unique to other OSes, which could prove beneficial, especially in the Unix-based system, as this portion of the computing world is expanding greatly due to the Internet of things, which bulk have some flavor of Unix driving them.

References

[1] I. Ahmed, A. Zoranic, S. Javaid, and G.G. Richard III. "Modchecker: Kernel module integrity checking in the cloud environment". In2012 41st International Conference on Parallel Processing Workshops 2012 Sep 10 pp. 306-313. IEEE.

[2] D. Byers and N. Shahmehri. "A systematic evaluation of disk imaging in EnCase® 6.8 and LinEn 6.1". Digital Investigation. 2009 Sep 1;6(1-2):61-70.

[3] Z. Gittins and M. Soltys. "Malware persistence mechanisms". Procedia Computer Science. 2020 Jan 1;Vol.176. pp. 88-97.

[4] M.U. Rana, M.A. Shaha, and O. Ellahi. "Malware Persistence and Obfuscation: An Analysis on Concealed Strategies". In2021 26th International Conference on Automation and Computing (ICAC) 2021 Sep 2 pp. 1-6. IEEE.

[5] B.V. Prasanthi. "Cyber forensic tools: a review". International Journal of Engineering Trends and Technology (IJETT). 2016;Vol.41(5). pp.266-271.

[6] M. Carbone, W. Cui, L. Lu, W. Lee, M. Peinado, and X. Jiang. "Mapping kernel objects to enable systematic integrity checking". InProceedings of the 16th ACM conference on Computer and communications security 2009 Nov 9 pp. 555-565.

[7] E. Chan, S. Venkataraman, F. David, A Chaugule, and R. Campbell. "Forenscope: A framework for live forensics". InProceedings of the 26th Annual Computer Security Applications Conference 2010 Dec 6 pp. 307-316.

[8] B.N. Flatley. "Rootkit Detection Using a Cross-View Clean Boot Method". AIR FORCE INST OF TECH WRIGHT-PATTERSON AFB OH GRADUATE SCHOOL OF ENGINEERING AND MANAGEMENT; 2013 Mar 1.

[9] S.L. Garfinkel. "Automating disk forensic processing with SleuthKit, XML and Python". In2009 Fourth International IEEE Workshop on Systematic Approaches to Digital Forensic Engineering 2009 May 21 pp. 73-84. IEEE.

[10] Z. Gu, B. Saltaformaggio, X. Zhang, and D. Xu. "Face-change: Application-driven dynamic kernel view switching in a virtual machine". In2014 44th Annual IEEE/IFIP International Conference on Dependable Systems and Networks 2014 Jun 23 pp. 491-502. IEEE.

[11] I.U. Haq, S. Chica, J. Caballero, and S. Jha. "Malware lineage in the wild". Computers Security. 2018 Sep 1; Vol.78. pp.347-63.

[12] O.S. Hofmann, A.M. Dunn, S. Kim, I. Roy, and E. Witchel. "Ensuring operating system kernel integrity with OSck". ACM SIGARCH Computer Architecture News. 2011 Mar 5; Vol.39(1). pp. 279-290.

[13] R. Hund, T. Holz, and F.C. Freiling. "Return-oriented rootkits: Bypassing kernel code integrity protection mechanisms". InUSENIX security symposium 2009 Aug 10 pp. 383-398.

[14] X. Jiang, X. Wang, and D. Xu. "Stealthy malware detection through VMM-based 'out-of-the-box'semantic view". In14th ACM Conference on Computer and Communications Security (CCS), Alexandria, VA (November 2007) (Vol. 10, No. 1315245.1315262).

[15] A. Kapoor and R. Mathur. "Predicting the future of stealth attacks". InVirus Bulletin Conference 2011 Oct pp. 1-9.

[16] J.D. Kornblum and ManTech CF. "Exploiting the rootkit paradox with windows memory analysis". International Journal of Digital Evidence. 2006;Vol. 5(1). pp. 1-5.

[17] T.K. Lengyel, S. Maresca, B.D. Payne, G.D. Webster, S. Vogl, and A. Kiayias. "Scalability, fidelity and stealth in the DRAKVUF dynamic malware analysis system". InProceedings of the 30th annual computer security applications conference 2014 Dec 8 pp. 386-395.

[18] L. Litty, H.A. Lagar-Cavilla, and D. Lie. "Hypervisor Support for Identifying Covertly Executing Binaries". InUSENIX Security Symposium 2008 Jul 28. Vol. 22, p. 70.

[19] R. Luh, S. Schrittwieser, and S. Marschalek. "TAON: An ontology-based approach to mitigating targeted attacks". InProceedings of the 18th International Conference on Information Integration and Web-based Applications and Services 2016 Nov 28 pp. 303-312.

[20] D. Patten. The evolution to fileless malware. Retrieved from. 2017.

[21] Malshare. www.malshare.com. (2019, October).

[22] N.L. Petroni Jr and M. Hicks. "Automated detection of persistent kernel control-flow attacks". InProceedings of the 14th ACM conference on Computer and communications security 2007 Oct 28 pp. 103-115.

[23] F. Raynal, Y. Berthier, P. Biondi, and D. Kaminsky. "Honeypot forensics". InProceedings from the Fifth Annual IEEE SMC Information Assurance Workshop, 2004. 2004 Jun 10 pp. 22-29. IEEE.

[24] R. Riley, X. Jiang, and D. Xu. "Guest-transparent prevention of kernel rootkits with vmm-based memory shadowing". InInternational Workshop on Recent Advances in Intrusion Detection 2008 Sep 15 pp. 1-20. Springer, Berlin, Heidelberg.

[25] J. Rutkowska. "System virginity verifier: Defining the roadmap for malware detection on windows systems". InHack in the box security conference 2005 Sep 28.

[26] M. Schmidt, L. Baumgartner, P. Graubner, D. Bock, and B. Freisleben. "Malware detection and kernel rootkit prevention in cloud computing environments". In2011 19th International Euromicro Conference on Parallel, Distributed and Network-Based Processing 2011 Feb 9 pp. 603-610. IEEE.

[27] A. Seshadri, M. Luk, N. Qu, and A. Perrig. "SecVisor: A tiny hypervisor to provide lifetime kernel code integrity for commodity OSes". InProceedings of twenty-first ACM SIGOPS symposium on Operating systems principles 2007 Oct 14 pp. 335-350.

[28] M.I. Sharif, W. Lee, W. Cui, and A. Lanzi. "Secure in-vm monitoring using hardware virtualization". InProceedings of the 16th ACM conference on Computer and communications security 2009 Nov 9 pp. 477-487.

[29] O. Sukwong, H. Kim, and J. Hoe. "Commercial antivirus software effectiveness: an empirical study". Computer. 2011 Mar 1; Vol. 44(03). pp. 63-70.

[30] S. Vömel and H. Lenz. "Visualizing indicators of Rootkit infections in memory forensics". In2013 Seventh International Conference on IT Security Incident Management and IT Forensics 2013 Mar 12 pp. 122-139. IEEE.

[31] J. Wang, A. Stavrou, and A. Ghosh. "Hypercheck: A hardware-assisted integrity monitor". InInternational Workshop on Recent Advances in Intrusion Detection 2010 Sep 15 pp. 158-177. Springer, Berlin, Heidelberg.

[32] Z. Wang, X. Jiang, W Cui, and X. Wang. "Countering persistent kernel rootkits through systematic hook discovery". InInternational Workshop on Recent Advances in Intrusion Detection 2008 Sep 15 pp. 21-38. Springer, Berlin, Heidelberg.

[33] M. Xu, X. Jiang, R. Sandhu, and X. Zhang. "Towards a VMM-based usage control framework for OS kernel integrity protection". InProceedings of the 12th ACM symposium on Access control models and technologies 2007 Jun 20 pp. 71-80.

[34] Z. Xu, J. Zhang, G. Gu, and Z. Lin. Autovac: Automatically extracting system resource constraints and generating vaccines for malware immunization. In2013 IEEE 33rd International Conference on Distributed Computing Systems 2013 Jul 8 pp. 112-123. IEEE.

[35] J. Rutkowska. "System virginity verifier: Defining the roadmap for malware detection on windows systems". InHack in the box security conference 2005 Sep 28.

[36] H. Yin, Z. Liang, and D. Song. "HookFinder: Identifying and understanding malware hooking behaviors".

[37] H. Yin, D. Song, M. Egele, C. Kruegel, and E. Kirda. "Panorama: capturing system-wide information flow for malware detection and analysis". InProceedings of the 14th ACM conference on Computer and communications security 2007 Oct 28 pp. 116-127.

[38] H.A. Lagar-Cavilla and L. Litty. "Patagonix: Dynamically Neutralizing Malware with a Hypervisor".

[39] Y. Oyama, T.T. Giang, Y. Chubachi, T. Shinagawa, and K. Kato. "Detecting malware signatures in a thin hypervisor". InProceedings of the 27th Annual ACM Symposium on Applied Computing 2012 Mar 26 pp. 1807-1814.

[40] O. Vermaas, J. Simons, and R. Meijer. "Open computer forensic architecture a way to process terabytes of forensic disk images". InOpen Source Software for Digital Forensics 2010 pp. 45-67. Springer, Boston, MA.

[41] A. Mohanta and A. Saldanha. "Memory Forensics with Volatility". InMalware Analysis and Detection Engineering 2020 pp. 433-476. Apress, Berkeley, CA.

[42] R. Tahir. "A study on malware and malware detection techniques". International Journal of Education and Management Engineering. 2018 Mar 1; Vol. 8(2). pp. 20.

[43] N. Idika and A.P. Mathur. "A survey of malware detection techniques". Purdue University. 2007 Feb 2;Vol. 48(2). pp. 32-46.

[44] H. El Merabet and A. Hajraoui. "A survey of malware detection techniques based on machine learning". International Journal of Advanced Computer Science and Applications. 2019; Vol. 10(1).

Efficiency of an Artificial Intelligence-based Chatbot Support for an IT-Awareness and Cybersecurity Learning Platform

Dominik Fanta, Farhan Sajid, Michael Masssoth and Lennart Kruck
Department of Computer Science
Hochschule Darmstadt (h_da) - University of Applied Sciences Darmstadt,
Darmstadt, Germany
e-mail: {dominik.fanta, farhan.sajid}@stud.h-da.de , {michael.massoth, lennart.kruck}@h-da.de

Abstract-**The IT awareness learning platform with Artificial Intelligence (AI) learning chatbot imparts target group-specific expert knowledge on the topics of IT awareness and cybersecurity. The user interactively controls the AI chatbot by making selections and asking questions. There is also the option that the AI chatbot questions the user and the user has to answer the questions. The AI chatbot is an expert in 23 IT security topics, including malware, but also in the areas of sexting or catfishing. The goal is to provide a fully comprehensive IT awareness and cybersecurity learning platform. In order to best adapt the AI chatbot to the needs of the users, it was important to conduct surveys with the target group in order to best recognize the respective spelling of the users so that there are no problems with the recognition of the input at the beginning. IT awareness knowledge is imparted by means of the AI chatbot through efficient dialog-based learning in a low-threshold, mobile way, "in small bites", and "for in between".**

Keywords— Artificial Intelligence; chatbot; it-awareness; learning platform; chat flow; ecosystem security.

I. INTRODUCTION

Due to the SARS-CoV2-pandemic, the threat situation in the digital space is intensifying. Employees are operating in their home offices, in some cases outside the company's own protected IT infrastructures.

IT infrastructures, and mobile devices are increasingly being used. Criminals are exploiting the global pandemic situation technically and, above all, as a thematic starting point for social engineering and other attacks.

The Proofpoint Human Factor Report 2019 proves, "more than 99 percent of cyberattacks rely on a human interaction in the process, making the individual user the last line of defense." The report shows that more than 99 percent of observed threats required a human interaction, whether it was activating a macro, opening a file, clicking a link or opening a document. To significantly reduce risk, organizations need a holistic approach to cybersecurity that focuses on the individual employee. Essential to this is the sensitization of all people in the company as well as effective security awareness training.

Through AI-based IT awareness training and education, companies and government agencies are strengthening the digital defenses of the entire workforce. AI chatbots enable efficient conversational learning. Learning with AI chatbots is thus comparable to learning through discussion rounds. As a rule, people remember content more easily when it is conveyed during a dialogue, rather than through a frontal presentation. AI chatbots make it possible to convey IT awareness knowledge in a short, mobile and interactive way.

This project aims to improve the aforementioned efficiency of AI-based learning chatbots in the context of IT knowledge training.

This paper is organized as follows:

Section II reviews the relevant terminology and advantages of AI chatbots. Section III describes the current state of the art considering related works. Section IV describes the IT awareness chatbot approach. In Section V, the implementation and structure of an AI learning chatbot. In Section VI, initial test results of a user testing are disclosed. Section VII deals with the efficiency of learning chatbots and the learning gains that can be achieved with them.

II. BACKGROUND

IT and cybersecurity awareness [Definition]: IT and cybersecurity awareness mean problem awareness and secure behavior. In everyday dealings with IT systems, awareness is an elementary security measure. First, this means creating an awareness of the problem of cyber security attacks and threats. Building on this, it is possible to achieve a change in behavior toward secure digital use. Security awareness measures are successful if they empower the target groups and motivate individuals to improve their cyber security. It is important to develop awareness at eye level and in a practical manner [1].

AI learning chatbot [Definition]: An AI learning chatbot is a computer program that uses Artificial Intelligence (AI) and Natural Language Processing (NLP) to understand learners' questions and automate responses to them, simulating human conversation. Users can ask questions to which the system responds in natural language [2].

Advantages of an AI chatbot: AI chatbots in use for IT awareness can help:

• Reduce costs. AI chatbots can support processes through automation and thus reduce process costs. Here specifically the costs for necessary awareness measures and presence training.

• Relieve employees. AI chatbots are able to take on uncomplicated cases in the call center or self-services. This can significantly reduce the workload of employees; and they are given the opportunity to focus fully on the critical IT security cases where they are really needed.

• Improve the user experience through efficient dialog-based learning.

All advantages of AI chatbots at a glance:

• Chatbots are available 24/7
• Chatbots never drop out due to illness or vacation
• Chatbots learn constantly and get better the longer they are deployed
• Chatbots eliminate waiting time for learners and users
• Chatbots are fast and effective
• Chatbots are scalable

Benefits for around 150,000 employees in the state of Hesse:

In Hesse alone, there are around 150,000 employees (full-time equivalents) at the state level who can be users of IT awareness training with AI chatbots.

III. Related Work and Research Question

State of research and technology:

If we take a closer look at the topic of chatbots, we can see that it has become increasingly important in recent years. It has therefore also been shown in several studies that it is possible to learn with a chatbot. The authors in [8] have shown in their study that it is possible to learn with a chatbot. For this purpose, they took 2 study courses with once 167 and once 124 students. Of the 167 and 124 students, 121 and 87 passed respectively. At the end of the semester, the students who had passed were able to fill out a questionnaire in which 187 had responded. The analysis of the questionnaires showed that 133 times (71.13%) the chatbot provided correct suggestions. In 30(16.04%) cases, the chatbot has the correct suggestion but not suitable for the students' needs. Only in 24 (12.83%) cases, the chatbot provided wrong suggestion.

In order to make learning with a chatbot more interesting, the authors in [7] showed that it is necessary to come up with a suitable gamification strategy to make users learn longer with it. Badges, different levels, quests, countdown, rule and reward or leaderboards are mentioned here as possible approaches, all of which should be considered when designing a AI learning chatbot.

However, good chances of success or a good gamification concept are only secondary for chatbots; it is much more important that the users can interact with the chatbot. Yin-Chun Fung and Lap-Kei Lee [6] conducted a survey with 20 participants to test an AI chatbot for cybersecurity awareness in their survey, it was found that 75% of the respondents know how to use an AI chatbot. It was also found that using a cybersecurity awareness chatbot can increase cybersecurity awareness, so 75% of the respondents agreed and the remaining 25% were neutral.

An extensive literature search has not yet been able to find any studies or research results on the use and effectiveness of AI chatbots in IT awareness training. IBM Germany also informed the project manager that Darmstadt University of Applied Sciences is conducting the first project in the area of AI learning chatbots for IT awareness in Germany [as of 01/2022]. The objective of the project goes beyond the current state of research and does real pioneering work.

Research questions and objectives: It is investigated how the existing knowledge about IT awareness and cybersecurity can be increased in a target group-specific way by using an AI chatbot. Target groups are especially users without detailed knowledge about information security, as well as executives and IT administrators. The goal of the research project is to determine the effectiveness and efficiency of an AI chatbot for raising awareness among employees of the Hessian state administration and government in a target group-specific manner. The AI-based learning chatbot will be tested and optimized on selected target groups.

IV. Idea and Approach

An IT awareness learning platform with AI chatbot:

An AI-based learning chatbot is an intelligent, voice-respectively text-based dialog system that allows chatting with an Artificial Intelligence. Such an AI-based learning chatbot is to be used and tested for the first time as part of an IT awareness training for basic sensitization of employees. The AI chatbot conveys the most relevant learning content on the topic of IT awareness to the learner in a simple, and in some cases even playful, dialog. In the process, AI chatbots divide the knowledge into small "morsels" and send them to the user one by one.

Solution: The IT awareness learning platform with AI chatbots imparts expert knowledge about IT awareness and cyber security to specific target groups: Low-threshold, "in small bites", "for in between".

The user controls the AI learning chatbot through his questions/choices/selections.

The following **specialist topics** are already included in the current IT awareness learning platform with AI chatbots and optimized for **detection rates of over 75%.**

TABLE I. SUBJECT MATERIALS

Malware	Phishing	Secure handling on the web	Good and secure passwords
Social engineering	Data protection on the web	Blackmail Trojan	Computer viruses
Spying on data	Botnets and DDoS attacks	Cyber and computer crime	Voice assistants
Hacking - my online bank data on the web	Industrial and commercial espionage	Cyberbullying and cyberstalking	Fake stores, fraud, subscription traps
Skimming	ICT criminal law	Sexting on the web	Catfishing

The **AI-based IT awareness training** starts with a **self-assessment** of the user and a **placement test** and is then based on the knowledge level of the individual participants. In this way, the strengths and weaknesses, as well as the individual learning type of the employee are taken into account and a training adapted to the respective person is guaranteed.

V. Structure of the AI Chatbot

Learning scenario 1:
Answering questions from learners

The AI-based learning chatbot shall be able to answer frequently asked questions, a precise analysis of the most frequently asked questions per subject had to be carried out first. Based on this analysis, a knowledge base was then developed for the AI chatbot answers. If the AI chatbot detects a similarity between a new question and a question in the knowledge database, it outputs the corresponding answer.

Important success factor:
Helping users to ask questions

With an A/B/C-usability test it was conducted in which the participants were to test the learning platform by asking the chatbot questions. Group A was given no additional tools on the learning webpage, group B was given a mind map diagram as an additional tool to ask questions, and group C was given an additional info-video (but no mind map). As result of the A/B/C-usability test, it turned out, that group B achieved the greatest success, in which they were able to achieve the greatest learning gain and asked the most amount of questions to the chatbot [3]. The example mind map diagram in Figure 1 is intended to give users who are not familiar with the topic some clues and ideas as to what they can ask the chatbot.

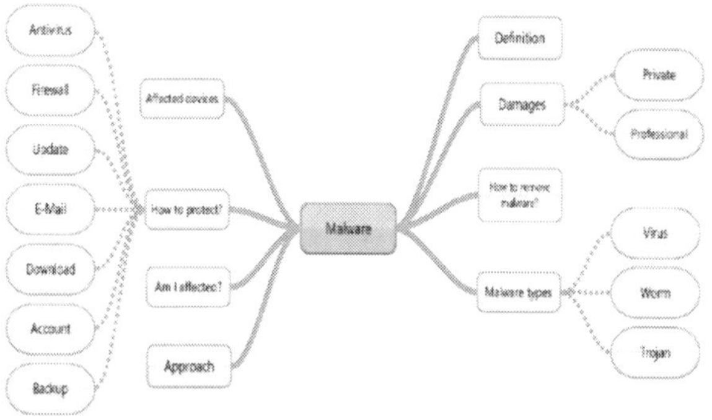

Figure 1. Example of a mind map diagram

Learning scenario 2:
Inquire about and deepen (prior) knowledge

The AI chatbot is used to determine the (prior) knowledge of a learner. To do this, the AI chatbot asks a series of predefined questions (**chat flow**) and evaluates the answers. Unlike multiple-choice tests, there are no predetermined answers. The AI chatbot can provide solution hints and feedback immediately after the answer. The prerequisite for such a dialog is that the test questions have been defined beforehand and the AI chatbot knows the correct answers. Using intent matching, the AI chatbot can estimate whether a correct or incorrect answer was given.

Test scenario:
Knowledge check to certify a training measure

The guided chat flow (from learning scenario 2) is used to test the knowledge of a learner. Here there are 3 different levels of difficulty (easy, medium, hard). The learner can collect 15 points per training unit. Once a certain number of points has been reached, a successful IT awareness training session can be certified.

A. *Structure of the questioning chatbot*

The chatbot is set up in such a way that the learner can prove his knowledge with the help of a quiz in the chatbot, where the chatbot asks the learner questions. By entering a keyword or trigger, such as "Malware Quiz", the chat flow in the chatbot is addressed and the quiz is started. The learner collects points by correctly answering the questions posed by the chatbot. The chatbot asks the learner five questions per difficulty level and topic. Depending on whether the learner answered the question correctly or incorrectly, he or she receives points and a short explanation of the correct answer.

1) Game method

There are 2 methods of play to successfully complete the quiz. The first method is based on the fact that the learner has already unlocked all difficulty levels at the beginning, whereas in the second method, the learner can only select the difficulty level at the beginning and unlock the other levels first. difficulty level at the beginning and has to unlock the other levels first. must first unlock the other levels.

a) Method 1: Difficulty level selectable

In the first method, the learner can choose any difficulty level, but the learner must play through all three difficulty levels for the chosen subject to be considered successful. For each question answered correctly, the learner receives one point. This means that the learner must achieve 15 points to successfully complete the quiz for the selected subject.

In the example, the chatbot was addressed with the trigger "test quiz" and the chatbot gives the learner the opportunity to select the difficulty level.

b) Method 2: Unlock difficulty level

In the second method of play, the learner must first successfully complete the easy difficulty to unlock the intermediate level, and then the learner must successfully complete this to unlock the hard difficulty.

This method gives the learner the feeling that he is in a game and must make progress to unlock the so-called "end level", the level difficult. In this method of playing, the learner does not have a free choice to select the difficulty level, but the learner can start the quiz or also read through the rules of the game.

2) Chat flows

To conduct the quizzes, so-called chat flows are used. Here there are connections that can be used to insert many branches into the chat flows. The learner can use these to navigate to a specific point. For example, in the quiz there are paths, depending on whether the learner's answer is correct or incorrect, the learner is forwarded to the particular branch. As a result of how many questions the learner answers correctly, he gets his points by advancing in the particular path. In this quiz, each correct answer directs the user down one level in the tree diagram and in the left direction; if an answer is incorrect, the branch at the bottom right is taken. On the whole, the chat flow is similar in structure to the normal Chat bot, in which the learner asks the chatbot questions, also a so-called Question and Answers. The special feature here, however, is that you can create a direct connection from one conversation to the next. In order not to put the performance of the chatbot under high load, a chat flow and a difficulty level has only five questions. By answering all the questions correctly, the node redirects the user to a new chat flow at the end, where he can continue with the quiz. This allows the learner to be guided through a multi-level dialogue, for example, to request several pieces of information or to define a problem in more detail. This function is also used, for example, to create a ticket for support. In Figure 2, you can see what the tree structure looks like with the various branches and how complex it can become, depending on the number of questions.

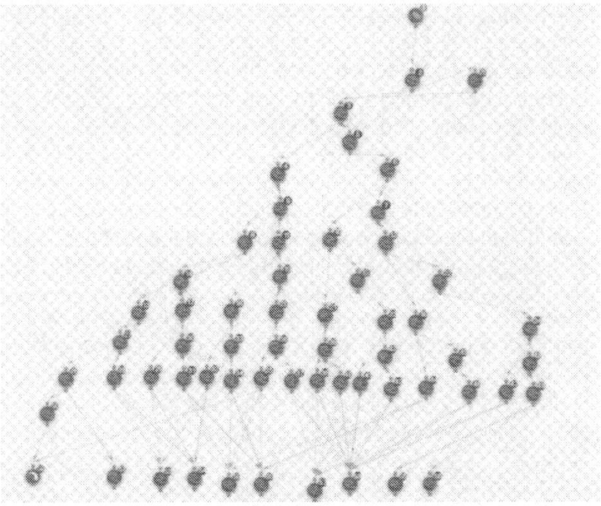

Figure 2. Chatflow of a Multiple-Choice Quiz

3) Future outlook

To bring out the full potential of the AI-based learning chatbot, and for learners to achieve even better success, it is necessary to conduct surveys to find out the learning behavior of users. Therefore, some surveys about the learning behavior will take place in the coming weeks. On the one hand it will be tested if the learners prefer to learn via multiple choice or if they prefer a variant where they have to enter the complete answer manually. It will also be tested which of the above-mentioned game modes lead to a better game experience or to an increased learning gain. In addition, it is still checked which requirements are optimal for the awarding of a certificate so that it has a relevant value. After completion of the surveys, the results will be evaluated and based on these, the chatbot will be further improved. In addition, a final test with subsequent certification will be implemented. In order for the certification to have a value that is recognized in society, an attempt will be made to accredit the complete IT awareness chatbot.

VI. User Experience Testing

A User Experience Questionnaire (UEQ) consists of 6 predefined UX factors: Attractiveness, Efficiency, Perspicuity, Dependability, Stimulation and Novelty. For many other products or applications, however, the above-mentioned UX factors are not really relevant. The extension of the User Experience Questionnaire (UEQ+) therefore does not consist of 6 predefined UX factors, but of a question catalogue consisting of 20 UX factors, which can be adapted to the needs of your product. Since each UX factor consists of 4 pairs of opposing characteristics and the importance of the UX factor is also asked, it is advisable not to use more than 5 or 6 of the 20 UX factors so that the length of the UEQ+ questionnaire is within a reasonable range. A user experience questionnaire is now conducted with a representative number of test persons in order to obtain values that are as accurate as possible. During the test, the test persons have to rate the pairs of opposites on the basis of a predefined question. As can be seen in Figure 3, the evaluation is done on a scale of 1 to 7, with the more negative characteristics on the left and the positive characteristics on the right [4].

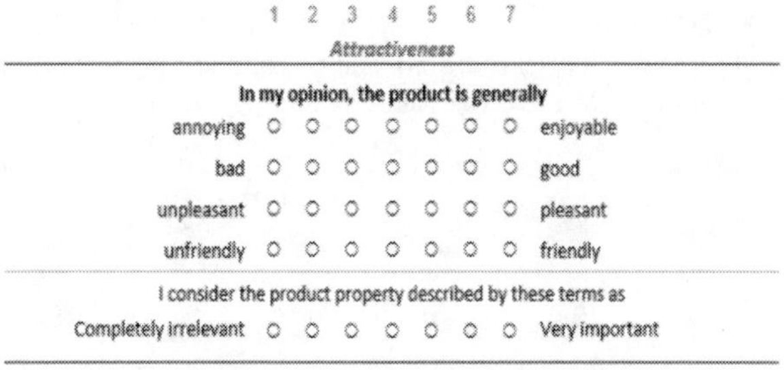

Figure 3. Example of a UEQ+ UX factor

After conducting the User Experience Questionnaire with a representative number of test persons, it can be analysed with an Excel table provided by UEQ+ and the mean value, standard deviation and confidence range for each individual UX factor are obtained. The confidence interval indicates the range that includes the mean value of a distribution with a certain probability. For this purpose, the upper and lower limits of the confidence interval are additionally determined and presented in the evaluation. These are represented by black lines within the associated mean values of the respective UX factors.

There is also the option of displaying the importance of the individual UX factors, the evaluation is carried out as explained above. The aim is to get an overview of how well the respective UX factors are implemented and which factors need to be addressed.

A. *User Experience Questionnaire+ for AI learning chatbots*

Testing the user experience of an AI learning chatbot requires a good testing method. The UEQ+ is the best testing method for AI learning chatbots because it allows UX factors to be specifically tailored to the chatbot under test. However, since there are no studies yet on which UX factors are particularly well suited for an AI learning chatbot, a small study was conducted with 30 computer science students from the Darmstadt University of Applied Sciences as part of this project. The goal of the study was to find out which UX factors are particularly suitable for AI learning chatbots and to obtain initial user feedback on the existing AI learning chatbot. For the study, the 30 subjects filled out a user experience questionnaire with 18 of the 20 UX factors. The UX factors haptics and acoustics were deliberately neglected, as our AI learning chatbot does not generally communicate acoustically and cannot be touched. Then, the mean values of each UX factor were measured and the best 6 factors were selected based on the result. Figure 4 shows that it is especially important for a learning AI chatbot to be a reputable source that is good to learn with. After the best 6 UX factors were collected, they were then evaluated. Figure 5 shows that the learning AI chatbot already performs very well in many of the 6 relevant UX factors.

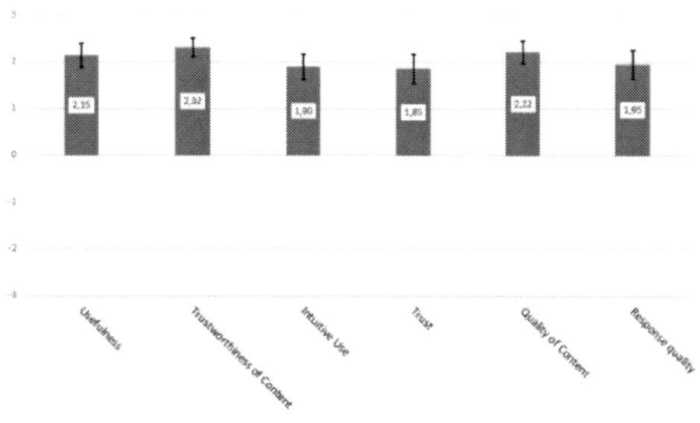

Figure 4. Importance Rating of an AI learning Chatbot

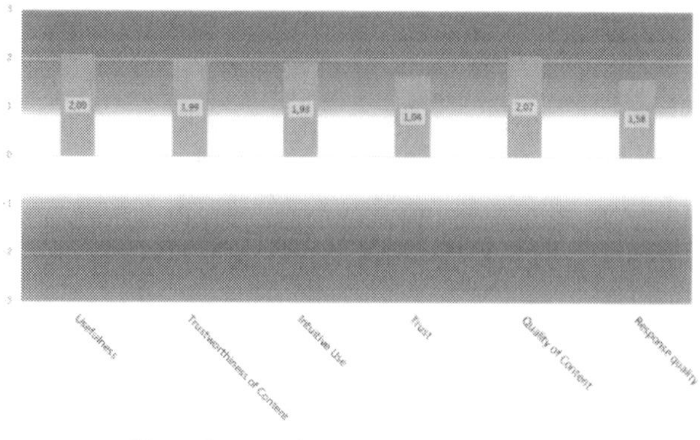

Figure 5. General evaluation of the AI chatbot

VII. Results

Initial user experience tests on the AI chatbot yielded the following results:

- The AI chatbot was very well received by test persons
- Subjects found it very enjoyable to use
- Easy use of the chatbot
- High recommendation rate

In order to measure the efficiency of an AI learning chatbot, learning growth was measured in addition to the UEQ+ mentioned above. For this purpose, a study was conducted with 30 computer science students from Darmstadt University of Applied Sciences, in which they were able to interact and learn with the AI learning chatbot. The study was structured in such a way that the subjects first had to complete the entrance test on a specialized topic (Table 1) and then ask questions to the chatbot in the learning area based on a mind map (Figure 1). In the next step, the subjects had to be questioned by the chatbot to verify the previously learned knowledge. Finally, the subjects had to complete the final test, which contained the same questions as the initial test. At the end, the points achieved in the initial test were subtracted from the points in the final test to measure the learning progress. The subjects had to complete this run for all subject topics. As can be seen in Figure 6, a learning gain of 15.73 % was achieved, even though the test subjects were computer science students who are at least in their 4th semester and who already have prior knowledge in the area of cybersecurity due to their studies.

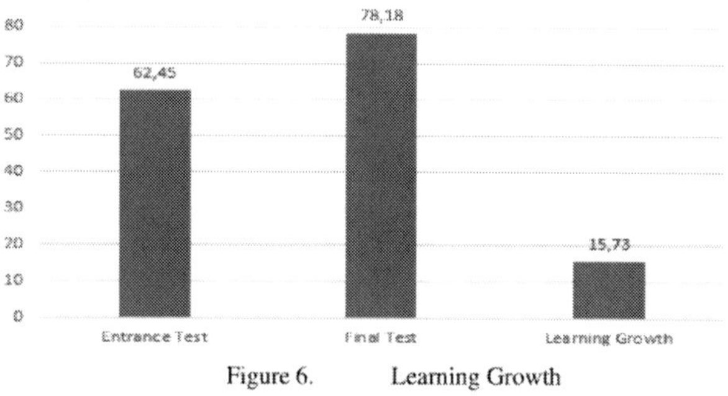

Figure 6. Learning Growth

Percentile:

Of all the valid tests for the individual subjects, the scores achieved on the entrance tests were used to calculate percentiles. In total, the results of 266 entrance tests were considered. Depending on the prior knowledge of the test subjects, between 0 and 100 points could be achieved on the entrance test. Table 2 shows that half of the test subjects (median) already scored 70 points or more on the entrance test. The best 10% of the test persons even achieved 90 points or more in the entrance test. The results in Table 2 clearly show that our test group had sound prior knowledge of all the specialist topics of IT awareness and IT security and cannot be regarded as beginners or laypersons.

TABLE II. PERCENTILES OF 266 ENTRANCE TEST

Percentile	Value (points) [Up to max. 100]	Meaning and discussion
5 percent percentiles	20	95% of the testers scored at least 20 points or more on the entrance test
10 percent percentiles	20	See line above (5 percent percentiles).
50 percent percentiles	70	50% of the testers scored at least 70 points or more on the entrance test
90 percent percentiles	90	The best 10% of the testers already achieve entrance test score 90 points or more
95 percent percentiles	100	The top 5% of testers already achieved the maximum possible entrance test the maximum possible 100 points

ACKNOWLEDGMENT

This work was supported by the Hessian Ministry of the Interior and Sports HMdIS, Government of the Federal State of Hessen; Research funding program: Cybersecurity. R&D project: "Awareness Training with AI chatbots"

REFERENCES

[1] Federal Office for Information Security (BSI), Germany; https://www.bsi.bund.de/EN/Home/home_node.html; last accessed on 2022-06-12

[2] IBM Chatbots: https://www.ibm.com/cloud/learn/chatbots-explained; last accessed on 2022-06-12

[3] A. D. S. Fernandes, " Implementation, evaluation and optimization of the user experience and IT security of an IT awareness learning platform with AI chatbots. ", Bachelor thesis 2021 at Darmstadt University of Applied Sciences at the Department of Computer Science

[4] UEQ+_Handbook_V2: ueq-research.org

[5] D. Bahcecioglu, "Development and optimization of an IT awareness learning platform with AI chatbots with regard to quality assurance through UX testing.", Bachelor thesis 2022 at Darmstadt University of Applied Sciences at the Department of Computer Science

[6] Y. C. Fung and L. K. Lee, "A Chatbot for Promoting Cybersecurity Awareness", Cyber Security, Privacy and Networking, 2022 - Springer

[7] I. Hidayatulloh, S. Pambudi, H. D. Surjono and T. Sukardiyono, "Gamification on Chatbot-Based Learning Media: a Review and Challenges", ELINVO (Electronics, Informatics, and Vocational Education), Mei 2021; vol 6 (1):71-80, ISSN 2580-6424 (printed), ISSN 2477-2399 (online,) DOI: 10.21831/ elinvo.v6i1.4370

[8] F. Colace, M. D. Santo, M. Lombardi, F. Pascale and A. Pietrosanto, "Chatbot for E-Learning: A Case of Study", International Journal of Mechanical Engineering and Robotics Research Vol. 7, No. 5, September 2018.

Black Swan or Just an Ugly Duckling?

Can potentially crippling cyber situations be foreseen and mitigated?

Anne Coull
Objective Insight
Sydney, Australia
Email: anne.objectiveinsight@gmail.com

Abstract— Black Swan situations and their consequences are considered extremely unlikely before they happen and make perfect sense afterwards. Two malicious exploits that triggered Black Swan situations, Emotet and WannaCry, are assessed, along with their attack sequences comprising of multiple attack vectors operating in sequence and targeted at known vulnerabilities. The early warning signs and the practical actions to prevent these types of Cyber Black Swan situations are outlined. Prevention is based on practical defence in depth controls, along with effective ongoing maintenance, with situational awareness guiding the cyber teams as to where to focus their response efforts.

Keywords- Black Swan; Emotet; WannaCry; Early Warning Indicator; Critical Vulnerability; Situational Awareness; Response.

I. INTRODUCTION

As an Australian, the notion of a Black Swan as an unexpected event is counter intuitive. While the swans in Europe may be white, in Australia the native swans are black. In a country of jumping kangaroos and duck-billed platypus, the unexpected is modus operandi. In his book: "Antifragility, things that gain from disorder," Nassim Taleb [41] uses the term *Black Swan* to describe unexpected situations with 3 attributes: Before the situation occurs, it is considered extremely unlikely, if not impossible; When it occurs its consequences are significant, either in changing belief, or in consequence; After it has occurred, it makes perfect sense as something that could happen [14][41].

With Australian insight it becomes clear that unusual creatures and events do not just suddenly appear, they evolve over time. Similarly, Black Swan situations develop over time and show early warning indicators. Noticing these early signs, and acting upon them, will make the difference between a dramatic event, a well-managed situation, or just another day doing business. The proposed mitigation on these Black Swans is based on situational awareness, basic, practical, and well-maintained cyber controls, and response to emergency situations.

Two black swan cyber situations, the Emotet Trojan, and the WannaCry Worm, are reviewed along with their attack vectors and the vulnerabilities they target. These two cyber attacks that triggered Black Swan situations were selected due to their scale and impact, which in turn can be attributed primarily to the preparation and response of the target organisations. These attacks differed in their initial access approach, their style of attack, and the combinations of attack vectors they utilised [4][36]. For each of these black swan cyber situations, the potential for predictability and reduced impact through stringent maintenance and monitoring, situational awareness, and response to early warning indicators is assessed.

Section 2 outlines the Emotet and WannaCry exploits and their respective impacts. Section 3 analyses their attack sequences for access, escalation, persistence, scanning, spread, exfiltration, and assault [43]. Section 4 looks at how these events could have been foreseen by reading the early warning indicators. Section 5 outlines how these attacks and others like them can be mitigated using practical cyber defence in depth with effective ongoing maintenance, situational awareness, and timely response.

II. EMOTET AND WANNACRY EXPLOITS AND THEIR IMPACTS

Over the last decade two of the most successful cyber attacks, in terms of scale and impact, have been Emotet and WannaCry. Both utilised a combination of exploits to target Microsoft vulnerabilities and gain access to organisations, establish persistence, escalate privileges, and exfiltrate data whilst concurrently spreading, infecting, and implementing assault strategies across the network [4][5][16][20][27][33][34][37]-[40].

Emotet started as a banking Trojan and has continued to evolve since it was first identified in 2014. In 2019, Emotet was responsible for approximately 60% of malware email spam [36]. By 2020 it had morphed into Botnet as a Service with global distribution. Infected devices themselves become C2 bots. In May 2019, 310 unique infected IP addresses were identified, of which two thirds (208) were confirmed bots, and 8% (17) of these were also infected with Trickbot [36] (see Figure 1).

In January 2021, the German Bundeskriminalamt (BKA) federal police agency coordinated a combined effort of law enforcement agencies to shut down the global botnet of hundreds of Emotet servers [34]. The Trojan malware, or a copycat, returned in November 2021 and infected an estimated 1.2 million systems in 2022 [34].

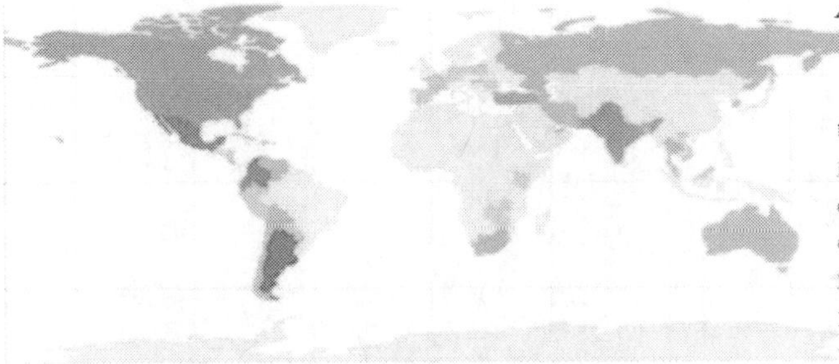

Figure 1. Geographic distribution of Emotet Botnet IP addresses, June 2019 [36].

In May 2017, after infecting more than 300,000 computers and crippling 150+ organisations worldwide. WannaCry was dubbed "the largest ransomware event in history." The WannaCry ransomware attack was stopped by a MalwareTech cyber researcher [19] who identified a key design flaw and purchased the URL WannaCry referenced in its attack sequence (see Figure 2).

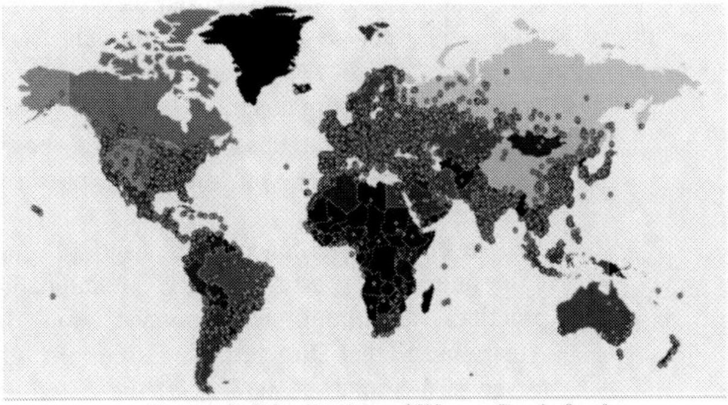

Figure 2. Distribution of WannaCry infections 14 May 2017, after 24 hours [5][19].

The situations triggered by WannaCry and Emotet could both be regarded as Black Swans. Each was considered extremely unlikely before they were experienced and identified. Each gained the attention of Europol and Eurojust due to their scale and the significant and costly consequences for those affected [34]. WannaCry brought the British NHS to a standstill [12], including the closure of public hospitals. Emotet was estimated as costing in excess of $1 million for every organisation it infected [4][34].

III. ATTACK SEQUENCE ANALYSIS

While there are some commonalities in the zero-day exploits targeting Microsoft SMB remote control vulnerabilities, Emotet and WannaCry utilise different attack vectors in the infection process.

A. *Emotet access, escalation, persistence, scanning, spread, exfiltration, and assault*

Emotet utilises social engineering phishing campaigns to entice recipients to click on a link that downloads a macro-infected Microsoft office file. These emails appear to come from a friend or colleague, or from a known organisation and include PayPal receipts, shipping notifications, or "past-due" invoices [4] (see Figure 3). The macro executes the payload malware for the next stage where it establishes persistence using auto-start registry keys and services to embed a scheduled task at startup [4][33][34].

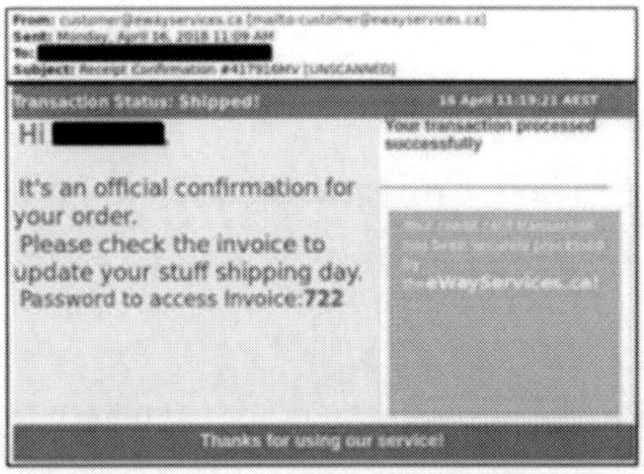

Figure 3. Emotet malicious email Emotet [4].

Emotet spreads by extracting contact lists from infected users' email accounts and using these to send phishing emails, so they will appear to come from a friend or colleague. Concurrently, Emotet spreads to systems across the network by enlisting a credential enumerator with service and bypass components. It utilises publicly available tools to recover passwords stored on: (i) the user's system and external drives; (ii) web-browsers such as Google Chrome, Internet Explorer, Mozilla etc.; and (iii) email providers such as Gmail, Outlook, Hotmail etc.

It concurrently utilises a malicious-actor-developed spreader module that applies brute force with enriched password lists to move through the Windows Admin Shares. It uses these credentials to access accounts and copy itself to the ADMIN$ of other network hosts, before using Server Message Block (SMB) to schedule execution on these hosts. It locates writable share drives and infects the entire disk by writing the Emotet service component onto the network [4][33][34] (see Figure 4).

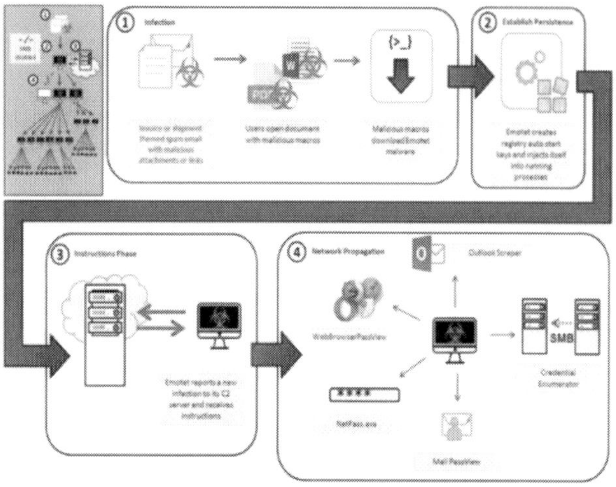

Figure 4. Emotet infection process [4].

From 2016 Emotet incorporated a Trickbot banking trojan which evolved to exploit the Microsoft Windows SMBv1 and NBT Remote Code Execution Vulnerabilities (CVE-2017-0144, CVE-2017-0147), and the Windows SMB Remote Code Execution Vulnerabilities (CVE-2019-0630, CVE-2019- 0633) [4][33]. The Trickbot is used to launch the malware payload, bypass Microsoft security measures, communicate with the command-and-control infrastructure, upload data and download DLL updates [33].

B. *WannaCry access, escalation, persistence, scanning, spread, exfiltration, and assault*

WannaCry identified its targets using EternalBlue to scan externally facing hosts across the internet where TCP ports 139 and 445 were open [42]. These ports are used to communicate using the SMB network protocol that enables remote code execution in MS Windows & sharing across networks [5][16][40].

When it identified the Microsoft SMB Windows Server Remote Code Execution Vulnerability (CVE-2017-0144) and the Microsoft SMB Windows Server Remote Code Execution Vulnerability (CVE-2017-0145) [39] which enabled remote code execution over SMB v1, EternalBlue then accessed the vulnerable target systems and installed the DoublePulsar exploit for persistence [5][20][27]. It continued to scan, access and replicate while it encrypted files and destroyed backups on every computer it infected: disrupting businesses by denying users access to their critical data [13][37]-[39]. It then displayed a ransomware image to the users of infected devices (see Figure 5).

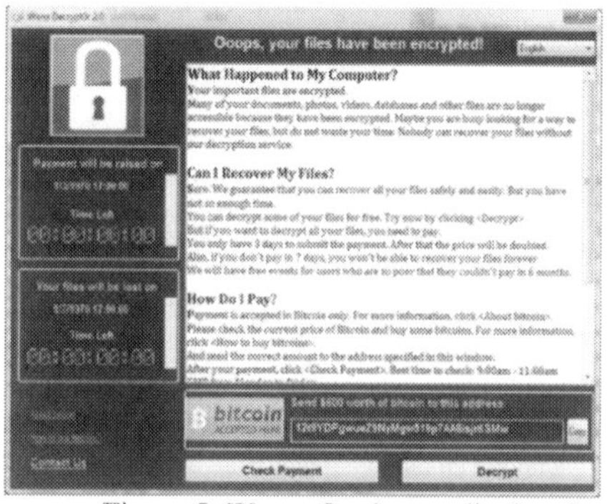

Figure 5. WannaCry image displayed on infected user's desktop [5][18].

IV. Proactively Looking for the Early Warning Indicators

Situational awareness is key to preventing malicious exploits developing into Black Swan situations. It enables organisations to notice the early warning signs and prepare for and respond to emerging situations. The early warning signs are there for Emotet and WannaCry, but they will only be noticed by those who actively seek them out. The early warning signs include:

1. The current state of the organisation:
   a. The cyber-risk awareness of personnel, based on their click-rate on targeted phishing campaigns.
   b. The level of compliance with standards and guidelines for basic defence maintenance practices, including compliance to the Australian Signal Directorate's Essential Eight cyber mitigations, in particular: the extent of unpatched Microsoft windows systems; privileged access management; ability to download macro-enabled email attachments; and availability of separately stored backup data [6].
2. Critical vulnerability reports:
   a. Microsoft CVE-2017-0144, CVE-2017-0145, & CVE-2017-0147 vulnerability reports published in the Microsoft Vulnerability Update Guide on 14 March 2017 [22]-[24] and corresponding CVE reports [7]-[9] and NIST reports published on 16 March 2017 [28]-[30].
   b. Microsoft CVE-2019-0630 & CVE-2019-0633 vulnerability reports published in the Microsoft Vulnerability Update Guide on 12 February 2019 [25][26] and corresponding CVE reports [10][11] and NIST reports published on 3 May 2019 [31][32].

3. Threat alerts and reports:
   a. Threat alerts and reports are readily available through research centres such as MalwareTech [19], Metasploit [15], and Talos [17].
   b. Cyber teams in peer organisations sharing information. Organisations, such as the Australian Banks, openly share information in a joint effort to fight cyber crime.

V. Preventing these Black Swan Situations

Emotet, WannaCry and similar trojan and worm-based malware exploits can be prevented, and/or their effects limited by applying basic cyber defence maintenance practices.

1. Address the weakest link. Educate all people in the organisation on the risks and indicators of cyber exploits, such as emails with links and attachments. Educate people to *not* click on links and to run their mouse over to see where it links to, even if the email comes from a trusted colleague or friend. Educate them to *not* click on online advertisements, and to never share unencrypted sensitive information through external email or on the phone [4][6].

2. Incorporate desired cyber practices into policies. For example, implement a policy requiring users to forward suspicious emails to the security team [4].

3. Control who accesses to what, when. Implement Privileged Access Management based on the principle of least privilege [6].

4. Maintain a technology defence barrier. Keep all operating system and application patching up-to-date, by applying tested patches and updates as a priority. In particular, apply critical patches within 48 hours. Five weeks prior to the main WannaCry attack, Microsoft had released updated CVE reports and emergency patches to the Windows SMB vulnerabilities that enabled WannaCry's EternalBlue and DoublePulsar exploits [6].

5. Set a Firewall rule to restrict inbound SMB communication between client systems, using Windows Group Policy Object, or if using a non-windows host-based intrusion prevention system [HIPS], implement custom modifications for the control of client-to-client SMB communication [4].

6. Using antivirus programs on clients and servers, with automatic updates of signatures and software will mitigate against many other malware exploits that are signature based [4][6].

7. Whitelist IP addresses and block suspicious and known malicious IP addresses at the firewall. Filter out emails with known malspam indicators, such as known malicious subject lines, by implementing filters at the email gateway [4][6].

8. Block or scan file attachments commonly associated with malware, such as .dll and .exe and those that include macros, as well as attachments that cannot be scanned by antivirus software, such as .zip files [4][6].

9. Disable macros and PowerShell to prevent macro driven PowerShell commands, such as those utilised by Emotet [4][6].

10. Implement Domain-Based Message Authentication, Reporting & Conformance (DMARC), a validation system that minimises spam emails by detecting email spoofing using Domain Name System (DNS) records and digital signatures [4].

11. Be prepared for the worst. Take daily backups for timely recovery and restoration of service to the business and its customers. Ensure these are stored on a separate network and restoration is tested regularly to prevent failure when restoration is really needed [1][2][4][6].

12. Maintain current situational awareness. Stay abreast of alerts and threat reports.

13. Limit exposure of critical systems to zero-day exploits.Take vulnerable, critical systems off-line and/or restrict their external accessibility when a zero-day exploit is underway.

14. Apply emergency zero-day patches immediately. During the WannaCry event, Microsoft released emergency patches for out-of-support versions of MS Windows.

VI. Conclusion

The Black Swan situations generated by the Emotet and WannaCry malicious exploits demonstrate the potential for preventing these situations from developing.

Situational awareness enables organisations to notice the early warning signs, prepare for and respond to emerging vulnerabilities and threats. Preparation involves addressing the weakest link, privileged access management, maintaining a technical defence barrier and keeping reliable backups. Current situational awareness ensures the organisation can respond to zero-day exploits by limiting exposure of critical systems and immediately applying emergency patches to vulnerable systems.

The threat landscape is constantly changing and evolving, with new malicious actors entering the scene and malicious exploits being released into the wild that can easily be combined for increased effect. But the impact of these exploits is ultimately driven by the preparedness, situational awareness, and response of the target organisations.

REFERENCES

[1] ACSC, "Strategies to mitigate cyber security incidents, "Australian Government, Australian Signals Directorate, 2017, Available from: https://www.cyber.gov.au/acsc/view-all-content/publications/strategies-mitigate-cyber-security-incidents, accessed October 2022.

[2] ACSC, "Essential eight explained, Australian Government," Australian Signals Directorate, 2019, Available from: https://www.cyber.gov.au/sites/default/files/2020-01/PROTECT%20-%20Essential%20Eight%20Explained%20%28April%202019%29.pdf, accessed October 2020.

[3] Any run, "Emotet", 2021, Available from: https://any.run/malware-trends/emotet, accessed October 2022.

[4] CISA 2018-2020, "Alert [TA18-201A] Emotet Malware," Available from: https://www.cisa.gov/uscert/ncas/alerts/TA18-201A, accessed October 2022.

[5] A. Coull, "WannaCry Malware Case Study," Cyber Security Operations 2017, UNSW.

[6] A. Coull, "How much cyber security is enough," The Fourth International Conference on Cyber-Technologies and Cyber-Systems, CYBER 2019, September 22, 2019 to September 25, 2019 – Porto, Portugal, Available from: https://www.iaria.org/conferences2019/CYBER19.html/CYBER19.html, accessed October 2022.

[7] CVE, "CVE-2017-0144 - CVE.report," Available from: https://cve.report/CVE-2017-144, accessed October 2022.

[8] CVE, "CVE-2017-0145 - CVE.report," Available from: https://cve.report/CVE-2017-145, accessed October 2022.

[9] CVE, "CVE-2017-0147 - CVE.report," Available from: https://cve.report/CVE-2017-147, accessed October 2022.

[10] CVE, "CVE-2019-0630 - CVE.report," Available from: https://cve.report/CVE-2019-630, accessed October 2022.

[11] CVE, "CVE-2019-0633 - CVE.report," Available from: https://cve.report/CVE-2019-0633, accessed October 2022.

[12] J. Graham, "How to Rapidly Identify Assets at Risk to WannaCry Ransomware and ETERNALBLUE Exploit," Available from: https://blog.qualys.com/vulnerabilities-threat-research/2017/05/12/how-to-rapidly-identify-assets-at-risk-to-wannacry-ransomware-and-eternalblue-exploit, accessed October 2022.

[13] A. Hern and S. Gibbs, "What is 'WanaCrypt0r 2.0' ransomware and why is it attacking the NHS?," the guardian, Saturday 13 May 2017, Available from: https://www.theguardian.com/technology/2017/may/12/nhs-ransomware-cyber-attack-what-is-wanacrypt0r-20, accessed October 2022.

[14] H. Jankensgard, "The Black Swan problem: Risk management strategies for a world of wild uncertainty," 2022, John Wiley & Sons Ltd. The Atrium, Southern Gate, Chichester, West Sussex, P019 8sQ, United Kingdom.

[15] D. Kennedy, J. O'Gorman, D. Kearns, & M. Aharoni, "Metasploit: the penetration tester's guide," 2011, No starch press, 245 8th Street, San Francisco, CA 94103.

[16] L. Kessem, "How did the wannacry ransomware begin?" IBM Security, 26 May 2017, Available from: https://www.quora.com/How-did-the-Wannacry-ransomware-begin, accessed October 2022.

[17] P. Rascagneres and C. Williams, "Player 3 Has Entered the Game: Say Hello to 'WannaCry'," Talos Intelligence, 12 May 2017, Available from: http://blog.talosintelligence.com/2017/05/wannacry.html, accessed October 2022.

[18] LogRhythm, "A technical analysis of wannacry ransomware, LogRhythm Labs, " 16 May 2017, Available from: https://logrhythm.com/blog/a-technical-analysis-of-wannacry-ransomware/, accessed October 2022.

[19] MalwareTech, "Botnet tracker," MalwareTech, 2017, Available from: https://intel.j.com/botnet/wcrypt/?t=1h&bid=all, accessed October 2022.

[20] A. McNeil, "How did the WannaCry ransomworm spread?" Malwarebytes, 19 May 207, Available from: https://blog.malwarebytes.com/cybercrime/2017/05/how-did-wannacry-ransomworm-spread/, accessed October 2022.

[21] Metasploit, "Metasploit | Penetration Testing Software, Pen Testing Security," Available from: https://www.metasploit.com/, accessed October 2022.

[22] Microsoft, "Windows SMB Remote Code Execution Vulnerability CVE-2017-0144," 2017, Available from: https://msrc.microsoft.com/update-guide/vulnerability/CVE-2017-0144, accessed October 2022.

[23] Microsoft, "Windows SMB Remote Code Execution Vulnerability CVE-2017-0145," Available from: https://msrc.microsoft.com/update-guide/vulnerability/CVE-2017-0145, accessed October 2022.

[24] Microsoft, "Windows SMB Information Disclosure Vulnerability CVE-2017-0147," Available from: https://msrc.microsoft.com/update-guide/vulnerability/CVE-2017-0147, accessed October 2022.

[25] Microsoft, "Windows SMB Remote Code Execution Vulnerability CVE-2019-0630," Available from: https://msrc.microsoft.com/update-guide/en-US/vulnerability/CVE-2019-0630, accessed October 2022.

[26] Microsoft, "Windows SMB Remote Code Execution Vulnerability CVE-2019-0633," Available from: https://msrc.microsoft.com/update-guide/en-US/vulnerability/CVE-2019-0633, accessed October 2022.

[27] P. Muncaster, "Wannacry didn't start with phishing attacks," says Malwarebytes, Infosecurity, 22 May 2017, Available from: https://www.infosecurity-magazine.com/news/wannacry-didnt-start-with-phishing, accessed October 2022.

[28] NIST, "CVE-2017-0144 Detail," Available from: https://nvd.nist.gov/vuln/detail/CVE-2017-0144, accessed October 2022.

[29] NIST, "CVE-2017-0145 Detail," Available from: https://nvd.nist.gov/vuln/detail/CVE-2017-0145, accessed October 2022.

[30] NIST, "CVE-2017-0147 Detail," Available from: https://nvd.nist.gov/vuln/detail/CVE-2017-0147, accessed October 2022.

[31] NIST, "CVE-2019-0630 Detail," Available from: https://nvd.nist.gov/vuln/detail/CVE-2019-0630, accessed October 2022.

[32] NIST, "CVE-2019-0633 Detail," Available from: https://nvd.nist.gov/vuln/detail/CVE-2019-0633, accessed October 2022.
[33] A. Perin, "Emotet Re-emerges with Help from TrickBot," Available from: https://blog.qualys.com/vulnerabilities-threat-research/2022/01/06/emotet-re-emerges-with-help-from-trickbot, accessed October 2022.
[34] A. Petcu, "Emotet Malware Over the Years: The History of an Infamous Cyber-Threat," Available from: https://heimdalsecurity.com/blog/emotet-malware-history/, accessed October 2022.
[35] Qualys, "IT Security and Compliance Platform, " Available from: https://www.qualys.com/, accessed October 2020.
[36] Proofpoint, "Q4 2020 Threat Report," Available from: https://www.proofpoint.com/us/blog/threat-insight/q4-2020-threat-report-quarterly-analysis-cybersecurity-trends-tactics-and-themes, accessed November 2022.
[37] A. Rousseau, "WCry/WanaCry ransomware technical analysis," End Game, 14 May 2017, Available from: https://www.endgame.com/blog/ technical-blog/wcrywanacry-ransomware-technical-analysis accessed September 2022.
[38] Symantec, "WannaCry: Ransomware attacks show strong links to Lazarus Group," Symantec Security Response, 22 May 2017, Available from: https://www.symantec.com/connect/blogs/ wannacry-ransomware-attacks-show-strong-links-lazarus-group, accessed October 2022.
[39] Symantec, "Ransom.Wannacry", Symantec, 24 May 2017, Available from: https://www.symantec.com/ security_response/writeup.jsp?docid=2017-051310-3522-99, accessed September 2017.
[40] Symantec, "WannaCry variant protection details and information", Symantec Support, 26 May 2017, Available from: https://support.symantec.com/en_US/ article.INFO4361.html, accessed October 2022.
[41] N.N. Taleb, "Antifragile, things that gain from disorder", Random House, Penguin Random House LLC, New York, 2021.
[42] I. Thomson, "Wannacry: everything you still need to know because there were so many unanswered Qs", The Register, 20 May 2017, Available from: https://www.theregister.co.uk/2017/ 05/20/wannacry_windows_xp/ accessed October 2022.
[43] S. Winterfeld & J. Andress, "The basics of cyber warfare: understanding the fundamentals of cyber warfare in theory and practice", 2013, Elsevier, Inc, United States of America.

Investigating the Security and Accessibility of Voyage Data Recorder Data using a USB attack

Avanthika Vineetha Harish Kimberly Tam Kevin Jones
Faculty of Science and Engineering
University of Plymouth, Plymouth, United Kingdom
e-mail: {avanthika.vineethaharish, kimberly.tam, kevin.jones}@plymouth.ac.uk

***Abstract*— Voyage Data Recorders (VDR) or 'black boxes' for ships hold critical navigational and sensor data that can be used as evidence in an investigation. These systems have proven extremely useful in determining the cause of several previous shipping accidents. Considering the importance of the VDR and the increasing number of cyber-attacks in the maritime sector, the likelihood of it being attacked is high. This paper examines the security and accessibility of VDR data through a malicious USB device. A USB device is used after a series of tests, detailed in this paper, found it to be a viable way to compromise a VDR system. Intensive penetration testing was performed on a VDR, and this paper presents the four key highlights from the authors' tests. The results show that real-world VDR data might not be secure from an insider threat with little to no cyber knowledge, and future VDRs may open that up to more outsider attackers. For a device like VDR, where confidentiality, integrity and availability of data are critical, a cyber-attack could therefore lead to serious repercussions.**

Keywords- Maritime; Ransomware; USB Rubber Ducky; Voyage Data Recorder.

I. INTRODUCTION

With the maritime industry increasingly dependent on technology, cyber incidents have also been on the rise. The emergence of new technologies has led to the creation of new attack vectors, such as Wi-Fi access, poor network configuration, and unsecure third-party devices, which can cause critical damage to the industry. Maritime industries are targeted in a wide variety of ways, from phishing attacks on shipping company offices to attacks on communications and navigation systems on board ships. In the event of a major incident in the industry, a forensic investigation will be conducted to determine the cause for legal and reporting purposes, which will also help in correcting past mistakes. The study [1] observes that forensic readiness in the maritime sector, though it is not yet developed, can help in assessing cyber risks and mitigating attacks in the future.

A Voyage Data Recorder (VDR), often referred to as 'the black boxes for ships', plays a critical role in forensic investigations on ships. They store sensor data that can be retrieved following an incident, to construct the navigational plan and other factors that lead to the incident. Due to its importance, it is essential that the data stored is secure and tamper-proof, and the International Maritime Organization (IMO) clearly stipulates that VDRs should maintain a store with secure and retrievable information regarding the position, the physical status, and the command and control of the vessel over the period of the accident [2]. Interestingly, in some cases, the forensic investigators were not able to access the VDR or the data recorded. A few incidents have occurred when the VDR data disappeared mysteriously or the VDR status failed to record data at all [3]. There has been some previous research hacking a VDR (documented on a blog [3]) that exclusively used static analysis and Quick Emulator (QEMU) emulation on VDR software. In comparison, this paper builds on this previous understanding. As this study had full access to a VDR, experiments were done on the actual hardware and software of the system, and analyses were primarily dynamic for triggering real digital and physical effects. Our VDR was also connected to other real-world bridge systems, which it collected data from, adding a layer of realism beyond previous studies.

The disappearance of data can either be accidental human error, system malfunction or deliberate tampering. This paper aims to determine how plausible tampering is. With the increase in cyber-attacks in the maritime industry, the possibility of tampering with the VDR data to cover an incident or attacking the VDR itself cannot be eliminated. In addition, we examine if tampering could be simplified, so that even an unskilled insider, could be a significant threat. This is unlike previous work, as it demonstrates how attackers, but also system pen-testers, can more easily penetrate a system using modern-day pen-testing tools (i.e., pre-programmed USB, pre-installed Kali Linux tools, publicly available malware simulators). Moreover, while previous studies [3] examined only Furuno VDR software, which required specific knowledge, the proposed pen-testing USB stick in the paper could be used on any make or model, given there is a USB port.

As a critical part of incident investigations, the disappearance of VDR data can lead to investigation dead ends. As outlined in [30], which looked at incidents from 01/11/2020 to 31/10/2021, there were 275 incidents related to data breach by privilege misuse, and all these incidents were caused by insiders. It was reported that 78% of the incidents were motivated by financial gain, 9% by grudge, 8% by espionage, and 6% by convenience [30]. A device like VDR, which stores its data for months on board a ship, leaves the possibility of insiders tampering with the evidence [1].

Based on the assumption that the threat actor is an insider, this paper examines the security and accessibility of VDR data with a malicious USB device. [5] shows that USBs are one of the top cyber security threat vectors, with USB threats targeted specifically at industries including shipping growing from 37% in 2021 to 52% in 2022, while the number of threats targeted at Industrial Control Systems (ICS) increased from 30% to 32% over the same period. Most VDRs typically have USB ports for updating the system, and older VDRs can only be updated this way, so leaving them open and accessible to anyone is a risk. Therefore, using the attack path of USB access seemed reasonable when the threat is an insider.

The paper will provide an overview of VDR systems and their importance in Section 2 and then moves on to describe the tools used for testing the VDR in Section 3. In Section 4, the paper will discuss the key results and highlights of the testing, followed by a conclusion with discussions and future work.

II. Background

According to [6], the main purpose of a VDR is to collect and provide navigational data to aid in maritime accident investigations and to monitor system performance. A typical VDR system would consist of an electronics unit that gathers data from the sensors and saves it to a storage drive, with interfaces for communication and monitoring like USB, and Ethernet [4]. In addition, it will have an uninterruptible power supply, a hardened capsule, or a floating capsule for storing data and a monitor or console for performing tests [6]. The data collected include but are not limited to GPS data, heading and speed information, Electronic Chart and Display Information System (ECDIS), Automatic Identification System (AIS), data from Radar, voice feeds from bridge and rudder responses [7]. It is important to notice that VDRs currently do not have a mechanism for verifying the integrity of data to confirm if it has been tampered with. As a result, even if any of the data is manipulated, investigators might not be able to detect it.

The IMO requires all passenger ships and other ships except those passenger ships exceeding 3000 gross tonnages that are constructed on or after 1 July 2002, to be equipped with VDRs to comply with the regulations under Safety of Navigation of the International Convention for the Safety of Life at Sea (SOLAS) [2]. The Maritime Safety Committee of the IMO amended SOLAS chapter V regulation 20 in its 79th session to include requirements for VDR on cargo ships [2]. It states that cargo ships engaged in international voyages are required to have a VDR, which can be a simplified version of VDR (S-VDR) [2]. As per MSC Resolution 333.90, all VDRs installed after July 2014 must record continuously and retain data for a period of at least 30 days on the long-term storage medium and at least 48 hours on fixed or floating storage medium [8]. VDRs installed before July 2014 must retain data for a minimum of 12 hours and data will be overwritten at the end of the period. This implies that different ships will have different rules depending on the type of vessel and the date of device installation. Given the long-life span of ships before they are scrapped, there is a possibility that many ships out at sea may still be equipped with outdated VDRs that are prone to cyber-attacks and can compromise forensic investigations.

Investigating authorities like Marine Accident Investigation Board (MAIB) and US National Transportation Safety Board (NTSB) have extensively used and interrogated VDRs as evidence. An iconic investigation was the sinking of El Faro following hurricane Joaquin when NTSB and a few other organizations spent 11 months on 3 expeditions to retrieve the VDR [9]. From 26 hours of audio recordings on the vessel's bridge, a transcript of over 500 pages was produced and it significantly contributed to the discovery of the accident's cause [10]. Another incident was the grounding of Costa Concordia in the Tyrrhenian Sea off the coast of Italy. Italian authorities recovered the hard disk from the concentrator and converted the data to usable formats, generating radar screenshots, National Marine Electronics Association (NMEA) strings, and other data logs [4]. The investigators analyzed all this information together to understand key details, such as whether the vessel was being driven by a manual or automatic pilot, rudder instructions given and followed, and the status of watertight doors that controlled the flooding of compartments [4].

III. Tools Used

This paper examines whether the VDR data could be accessed or compromised and whether it could lead to unreliable data. Intensive penetration testing was performed to look for vulnerabilities and concerns that could lead to VDR data breaches and manipulation. Penetration testing or Pen-test is the method of attacking the system by authorised personnel, to identify and detect flaws in the system that could be exploited by attackers. Testing is carried out with several dedicated tools and custom scripts and this section will detail each of the tools and devices used to test an off-the-shelf VDR.

A. *System Under Test*

The System under Test (SuT) is an off-the-shelf VDR manufactured by a global shipping equipment manufacturer that is used by ships around the world. The specific make and model of the SuT are omitted for security purposes. The PC associated with the VDR runs Windows Embedded Standard 7 Operating System (OS). To monitor the system and test for vulnerabilities, an external attack machine that is running on Kali Linux OS is used. Kali Linux is a special OS distribution with pre-configured tools designed for penetration testing purposes. This 64-bit Kali Linux machine with 2048MB base memory is installed on a virtual box to isolate the attacks running from the host machine.

B. *USB Rubber Ducky*

A $59.99 (around £52.6) malicious device that resembles a USB stick, called USB Rubber ducky was used to execute the attacks [11]. USB Rubber Ducky was created by an information security company, Hak5, and the tool gained popularity in the security community due to its properties, like ease of use and powerful payloads [11]. When physically plugged in, the Rubber Ducky injects keystrokes into the computer it is connected to. Users can specify the keystroke combinations they want using a scripting language called Ducky Script. The script is written in a text file and then transferred to a File Allocation Table (FAT) formatted Secure Digital (SD) card. The SD card used for performing tests, in this case, is of size 128MB. For using this device, users need not have prior complex cyber security knowledge as it automates the keystrokes for the commands and if set up correctly, this could lead to heavily damaging the system. There are Rubber Ducky payloads and resources available as Github repositories, making them publicly accessible [12]. This tool is useful for automating tests, as explained in the following sections.

C. *Metasploit Framework*

The Metasploit framework is a powerful penetration testing tool with many features [13]. It contains several modules, which are exploits that take advantage of weaknesses in the system to hack it, payloads which are code sets that interact with the system, and auxiliary modules that perform functions, like scanning and sniffing. This framework helps in detecting a vulnerability, exploiting it, creating, and transferring payloads, and executing attacks. Currently, Metasploit has over 2000 exploits for various platforms including Android, Linux, Windows, Java, etc. It also hosts some exploit modules targeting ICS devices and protocols, like Programmable Logic Controllers (PLCs) and Modbus. However, this is limited to generic industrial components and currently, no such framework exists for the maritime industry for evaluating its systems.

D. *Shinolocker Ransomware Simulator*

Ransomware is a type of malware that, once it infects a system, will encrypt the files and prevent them from being accessed. Users will then be asked by the attacker to pay a ransom to decrypt the files and retrieve them. According to [14], in the year 2021, there was a 151% increase in the number of global ransomware attacks than the previous year and the numbers are predicted to rise in the coming years. For VDRs, where data is crucial and sensitive, a ransomware attack could lead to legal and regulatory issues in the event of an accident. As testing the VDR with real ransomware is dangerous, a ransomware attack on the VDR was carried out by means of a tool called ShinoLocker. ShinoLocker is a ransomware simulator developed by a security researcher, Shota Shinogi, and presented at Black Hat 2016 [16]. It works exactly like real ransomware, except that it does not ask for ransom. Once the payload has been executed, it encrypts all files of the specified type, for example, EXE, PNG, and JPEG, and displays a message, in this case, a transaction id, to retrieve the decryption key for accessing the files [15]. This tool is very useful for training and teaching purposes.

E. *Nmap (Network Mapper)*

Nmap is a network scanning and auditing tool. It will scan the network, find hosts, open ports and services for each host and its OS [17]. Nmap was used to identify the OS of the VDR PC and its version. It was also used to find open ports on the VDR to create test scenarios.

IV. HIGHLIGHTS FROM THE TESTING

After an intensive penetration test on the SuT, four key highlights were derived and presented in this section.

A. *Reverse Shell*

Reverse shells are interactive shell connections from a target machine to the attacking machine, that allows the attacker to access, transfer, manipulate and delete files. The first test was to determine if the attacker could obtain a reverse shell from the VDR PC to the attacking machine for viewing and manipulating files. Figure 1 shows the attack path and flow of commands. To create a reverse shell session, a reverse TCP shell payload was created using Msfvenom, a payload generator for Metasploit. With Msfvenom, users can specify a shell type, IP address, and port number, as well as a payload type (EXE, ELF, PHP) to target a system of a given architecture [18].

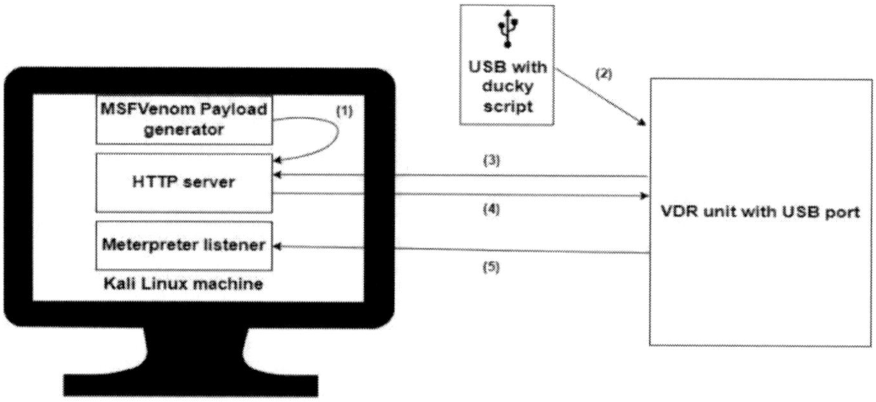

Figure 1. Attack path for creating a reverse shell.

Using Msfvenom, a reverse TCP shell payload was created to target Windows architecture using the local host IP address set as the IP address of the Kali machine. This payload then had to be transferred to the VDR for execution. To transfer the payload to the remote machine, an HTTP server was hosted on the Kali machine, and the payload was uploaded to it (see step (1) of Figure 1). Next, a ducky script was written such that once the USB device is plugged in, the HTTP server would download the payload to the VDR PC from the server. This can be seen in Steps (2) - (4) of Figure 1. Ducky script was written with five-second delays between each command, mimicking the keylogging of a human user in such a way that the VDR would be tricked even if it has a mechanism to flag fast key entries. The script was then encoded and written to an SD card.

During this time, Metasploit was running on the Kali machine with the exploit set as multi/handler; payload as meterpreter/reverse TCP, listening for any connection [19]. When the USB was plugged into Kali, a Meterpreter shell session was opened, i.e., Step (5) of Figure 1.

A complete list of steps for Figure 1 showing the path to the reverse shell:

(1) Payload generated (Msfvenom) and hosted in HTTP server
(2) Ducky Script written with commands to download payload
(3) Once the USB is plugged in, the command to download the payload
(4) Payload downloaded from server to VDR PC and executed
(5) Meterpreter listener receives a connection from VDR, and the session is opened.

Typically, shell sessions only grant local user access to the user. Thus, the privilege was escalated using the 'getsystem' command, which allowed the user to view files and folders. Additionally, other options in the Meterpreter shell were explored, such as viewing and accessing system logs, capturing webcam images, sharing screens, and listing processes. A hash dump of passwords produced 5 New Technology LAN Manager (NTLM) hashes, cracking it produced five passwords, out of which three were blank ones (including that of the 'Administrator' account), and the other two of 'Engineer' and 'Captain' accounts had simple passwords.

In a system like VDR, manipulating files using such a shell could be potentially dangerous and critical. An unauthorised or malicious insider could change the logs or files to create confusion during an accident investigation. Creating and using strong passwords is the first basic step in protecting any device from cyber-attacks. The guidelines on cyber security onboard ships document suggest using Multi-Factor Authentication (MFA) and changing default passwords to protect confidential data on safety critical systems [20]. It also recommends establishing a password policy with guidelines on password creation, updating and securing.

B. *Ransomware attack*

Ransomware attacks are one of the most common cyber incidents in the maritime industry and according to [22], ransomware is the leading source of cybersecurity threat risk to US ports and terminals. Maritime transport is a billion-dollar industry and ransomware attacks have risen over the past few years to take advantage of this. In the last five years, four major global shipping companies have been negatively affected by ransomware and their operations have been halted for weeks [21]. Recently, a Singapore-based offshore operator - Swift Pacific Offshore has reported a data breach that experts believe to be a ransomware attack [23]. To view the effects of a ransomware attack on the VDR, the ShinoLocker tool was used (see Figure 2). Since it was intended for training and teaching purposes, it appeared to be the most practical option without causing damage to the VDR.

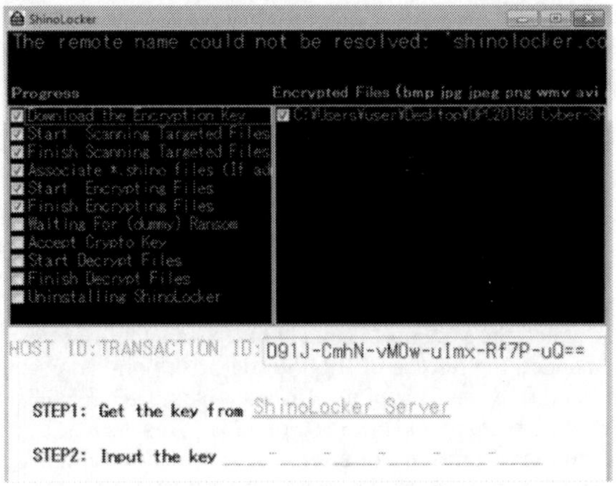

Figure 2. ShinoLocker Message Window.

To encrypt all PNG, JPG, TXT, and EXE files in the VDR, a ShinoLocker payload was created specifying those file types. The payload was transferred to the VDR in the same way as mentioned in the previous section, using an HTTP server hosted on Kali Linux machine. A ducky script was written to download the malware on to the VDR PC and then the script was transferred to the USB Rubber Ducky. As

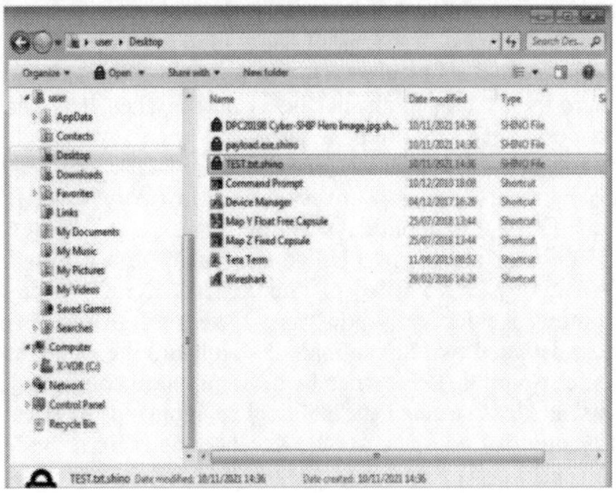

Figure 3. Encrypted Files.

soon as the USB device was plugged in to the VDR system, the malware started encrypting the files of the previously mentioned file types (see Figure 3).

There was a message like a typical ransomware message on the screen, but it did not ask for a ransom. In the message, there was an option to enter the decryption key obtained via the original tool using the transaction ID displayed on the screen after the malware infection (see Figure 4).

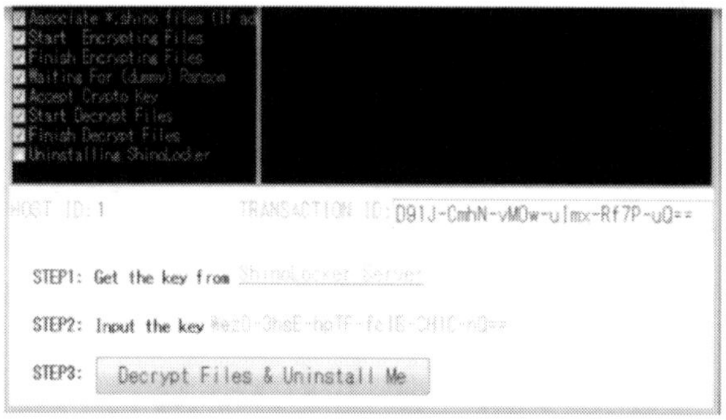

Figure 4. Decrypting Files.

Up until recently, the biggest motivation for ransomware attacks was money, but that is changing slowly. In January 2022, a Belarusian hacktivist group called 'Cyber Partisans' attacked the Belarus Railway systems using ransomware and encrypted the systems. They claim it as an act of protest and demanded the release of fifty 50 high-risk political prisoners in addition to banning Russian soldiers from using Belarusian trains as the ransom [24]. This shows that the definition of ransom in ransomware attacks is changing, and it is interesting to see if cybercriminals are likely to hold VDR data in exchange for ransom in a case where the VDR has critical evidence of a major incident.

C. *Hard Drive Erasure*

A third scenario involved erasing the disk contents and uninstalling Windows. This test was not performed as it would change the current settings of the machine and may destroy it. However, it could be easily accomplished with a USB Rubber Ducky and a few lines of code. The consequences of such an attack could be catastrophic on an autonomous vessel, where all configurations and settings are controlled by a machine. This is a denial-of-service attack where the system might not be available when it is needed the most or it might not be reliable.

Erasure or tampering of evidence data could lead to serious repercussions in investigations involving legal fines, human life, or geopolitical tensions. Almost a decade ago, on 15th February 2012, two Indian fishermen on a fishing boat 'St.Anthony' were killed off the coast of Kerala, India in a shooting incident mistaking the fishermen as pirates and India detained two Italian mariners on board the ship 'Enrica Lexie', an oil tanker, owned by a Milan-based company [25]. This incident strained the political relationship between the two countries. In this case, the Kerala police seized the VDR hard disk, however, it was alleged that the captain failed to preserve VDR data after the incident and the second officer of 'Enrica Lexie' stated that he did not press the VDR for recording [25].

D. *Eternal Blue Vulnerability*

While testing, an interesting result was obtained. The VDR PC was running Windows Embedded Standard 7 and a Nmap (Network Mapper) scan discovered that ports 139 and 445 were open. The VDR PC was found to be vulnerable to the Eternal Blue exploit that exploits remote code execution vulnerability in Microsoft SMBv1 Servers with vulnerability entry of CVE-2017-0143 in the Common Vulnerabilities and Exposures (CVE) database [26]. This vulnerability has a Common Vulnerability Scoring System (CVSS) score of 8.1 (HIGH) and the famous WannaCry attack used this exploit to spread its infection [27]. This could not have been found by only emulating parts of VDR firmware.

Even though the exploit module on Metasploit framework for Eternal Blue vulnerability was designed for 64-bit systems, and while the PC had a 32-bit operating system, the exploit module was run to see how the VDR would respond. The session was not opened as expected, however, VDR crashed with a blue screen of death and the machine needed to be manually rebooted. Since the Eternal Blue is a Random Access Memory (RAM) resident implant, once the system has been rebooted, it will function as normal again. As a result, the system may not be available when needed, and if the system is vulnerable to attacks like Eternal Blue, it may cause heavy damage.

V. Future Work and Discussions

Cyber security for maritime equipment is in its infancy, and there is little literature on voyage data recorders with even less research done on their security. Much of the literature available are reports of accidents involving VDRs, published by organisations like MAIB. Other articles analyse the investigation from a digital forensics point of view and suggest ways to improve the security of voyage data recorder data like the paper on the Costa Concordia shipwreck [4]. Data Integrity and Availability are critical properties in the Confidentiality, Integrity, and Availability (CIA) triad for devices, like Voyage Data Recorders. A study by [28] developed an algorithm of hash-based data recording where the time and date of the message are used to generate a key for authentication and a hash function is used to generate a key that combined with the original message can be used to check for message integrity. Research to improve the Remote Alarm Module (RAM) connected to the VDR would be good to alert the crew and people on the bridge if something is wrong in the system [29].

There is a need to improve VDR security from both technical and regulatory perspectives based on the little research conducted in this area. In the coming years, VDRs will become more connected, allowing new attack vectors, such as Wi-Fi access and poor network configuration, widening the attack surface. The encryption of critical data and the deployment of access control methods would help to protect the confidentiality of the evidence to an extent. The use of USB ports must also be restricted in addition to flagging when a USB device is connected to the system.

Using Sheep-dip protocol, where a dedicated computer that is isolated from the ship's network set up onboard, could also protect its systems from USB-based attacks. In this protocol, the removable media is plugged into the dedicated computer for scanning viruses and malware and preventing the spread of infection. This could be particularly useful in maritime systems where systems and charts are updated via USB drives.

The penetration testing of the systems could identify possible threats early on and allow them to be mitigated. At present, most of the testing is done manually by pen-testers who walk into a ship, scan the network, and inspect premises to find potential vulnerabilities. Considering the live networks and systems of critical shipping operations, this can be time-consuming and pose a high risk. In addition, manual penetration testing may miss certain vulnerabilities that are specific to a particular industry or system. An automated USB pen test tool, as demonstrated here, would make this job faster and easier. This is also more realistic than emulating parts of the VDR system [3]. As the paper [31] mentions, the main challenge in securing the maritime industry from cyber-attacks is that the common tools available currently may not be suitable or appropriate for testing due to the bespoke nature of the systems. Therefore, it is necessary to consider automated penetration testing and new vulnerability assessment framework tools that are specific to maritime systems and operations. This paper has done so with the use of the Rubber Ducky and scripts.

VI. CONCLUSION

This paper looked at investigating the security and accessibility of VDR data using an automated USB device. VDRs are safety-critical maritime systems that hold potential evidence in the occurrence of an incident. By performing an intensive penetration test, the authors were able to conclude that the data stored in the VDR is not secure and can be tampered with by a simple USB attack. Four main highlights of the testing were presented and each one discussed the consequences of the exploitation of those vulnerabilities. When VDRs become more networked and connected in future, the cyber-attack surface will expand, creating new attack vectors. Further research is needed to develop and standardize penetration testing methods for the shipping industry that will identify critical assets, uncover vulnerabilities, and report them in a way mariners could understand. It is also necessary to create information security policies and regulations for maritime systems, that will accommodate their industry-specific characteristics, to protect the data contained in these systems.

ACKNOWLEDGEMENT

This research was part of the Cyber SHIP lab project at the University of Plymouth. The authors are grateful to the project funder - Research England and our industry partners who supported our research by providing tools and equipment. The authors would also like to thank Juan Palbar Misas, Wesley Andrews and Rory Hopcraft from the University of Plymouth for their valuable comments and insights.

REFERENCES

[1] K. Tam and K. Jones, "Forensic readiness within the maritime sector," *2019 Int. Conf. Cyber Situational Awareness, Data Anal. Assessment, Cyber SA 2019*, no. June, 2019, doi: 10.1109/CyberSA.2019.8899642.

[2] International Maritime Organization, "Voyage Data Recorders," *Safety of navigation*, 2022. https://www.imo.org/en/OurWork/Safety/Pages/VDR.aspx (accessed 2022.10.21).

[3] R. Santamarta, "Maritime Security: Hacking into a Voyage Data Recorder (VDR)," *IOActive*, 2015. http://blog.ioactive.com/2015/12/maritime-security-hacking-into-voyage.html (accessed 2022.10.21).

[4] M. Piccinelli and P. Gubian, "Modern ships voyage data recorders: A forensics perspective on the Costa Concordia shipwreck," *Proc. Digit. Forensic Res. Conf. DFRWS 2013 USA*, pp. S41–S49, 2013, doi: 10.1016/j.diin.2013.06.005.

[5] Honeywell, "Industrial Usb Threat Report 2021," 2021. Accessed:2022.10.21. [Online]. Available: https://www.honeywellforge.ai/content/dam/forge/en/documents/cybersecurity/Industrial-Cybersecurity-USB-Threat-Report-2022.pdf

[6] N. Bowditch, "American practical navigator: an epitome of navigation and nautical astronomy," vol.1, pp. 72-73, 2019.

[7] IACS, "Recommendations on Voyage Data Recorder," no. 85, pp. 1–7, 2018.

[8] IMO, "Adoption of Revised Performance Standards for Shipborne Voyage Data Recorders Vdrs). IMO Resolution MSC 333(90)," 2012.

[9] N. Degnarain, "Decoding The Black Box: The 2015 US Disaster That Revolutionized Ship Crash Investigations," 2020. https://www.forbes.com/sites/nishandegnarain/2020/10/13/decoding-the-black-box-the-2015-us-disaster-that-revolutionized-ship-crash-investigations/?sh=2d39d9c3712f (accessed 2022.10.21).

[10] National Transportation Safety Board, "Sinking of the US Cargo Vessel El Faro," 2015, [Online]. Available: https://www.ntsb.gov/investigations/AccidentReports/Reports/SPC1801.pdf (accessed 2022.10.21)

[11] Hak5, "USB Rubber Ducky - Hak5," 2022. https://shop.hak5.org/products/usb-rubber-ducky-deluxe (accessed 2022.10.21).

[12] Hak5, "GitHub - hak5/usbrubberducky-payloads: The Official USB Rubber Ducky Payload Repository." 2022. https://github.com/hak5/usbrubberducky-payloads (accessed 2022.10.21).

[13] Rapid7 Inc., "Metasploit | Penetration Testing Software, Pen Testing Security | Metasploit," *Metasploit.Com*, 2019. https://www.metasploit.com/ (accessed 2022.10.21).

[14] Sonicwall, "Mid Year Upadte Sonicwall Cyber Threat Report," 2021, [Online]. Available: https://www.sonicwall.com/2021-cyber-threat-report/ (accessed 2022.10.21).

[15] "ShinoLocker - The Ransomware Simulator-." https://shinolocker.com/ (accessed 2022.10.21).

[16] "ShinoLocker - Malware Wiki." https://malwiki.org/index.php?title=ShinoLocker (accessed 2022.10.21).

[17] nmap.org, "Nmap: the Network Mapper - Free Security Scanner," *Https://Nmap.Org/*, 2021. https://nmap.org/ (accessed 2022.10.21).

[18] Offensive Security, "Msfvenom - Metasploit Unleashed," 2016. https://www.offensive-security.com/metasploit-unleashed/Msfvenom/ (accessed 2022.10.21).

[19] Offensive Security, "About the Metasploit Meterpreter - Metasploit Unleashed," *Offensive Security*, 2018. https://www.offensive-security.com/metasploit-unleashed/about-meterpreter/ (accessed 2022.10.21).

[20] BIMCO, "The Guidelines on Cyber Security Onboard Ships," Int. Chambber Shipp. Shipp., vol. 4, pp. 1–53, 2021.

[21] C. Cimpanu, "All four of the world's largest shipping companies have now been hit by cyber-attacks | ZDNet," *ZDNet*, 2020. https://www.zdnet.com/article/all-four-of-the-worlds-largest-shipping-companies-have-now-been-hit-by-cyber-attacks/ (accessed 2022.10.21).

[22] J. Walker, "Ports and Terminals Cybersecurity Survey," 2022.Available:https://sites-communications.joneswalker.com/38/1936/landing-pages/2022-cybersecurity-survey---lp.asp (accessed 2022.10.21).

[23] Maritime Execuritve, "Ransomware Attack on Swire Pacific Offshore Breaches Personnel Data."2021. https://www.maritime-executive.com/article/ransomware-attack-on-swire-pacific-offshore-breaches-personnel-data (accessed 2022.10.21).

[24] A. Greenberg,"Why the Belarus Railways Hack Marks a First for Ransomware | WIRED " 2022. https://www.wired.com/story/belarus-railways-ransomware-hack-cyber-partisans/ (accessed 2022.10.21).

[25] V. Golitsyn, J.-H. Paik, P. Robinson, F. Francioni, and P. Sreenivasa Rao, "Pca Case No. 2015-28 In The Matter Of An Arbitration-Before-An Arbitral Tribunal Constituted Under Annex Vii To The 1982 United Nations Convention On The Law Of The Sea The Italian Republic-V.-The Republic Of India-Concerning-The 'Enrica Lexie' Incident Registry: Permanent Court of Arbitration," 2020 [Online]. Available: https://pcacases.com/web/sendAttach/16500 (accessed 2022.11.09)

[26] MITRE Corporation, "Cve - Cve-2017-0144," *Cve*, 2015. https://cve.mitre.org/cgi-bin/cvename.cgi?name=cve-2017-0144 (accessed 2022.10.21).

[27] NIST, "Nvd - Cve-2017-0144," *National Vulnerability Database*, 2017. https://nvd.nist.gov/vuln/detail/CVE-2017-0144 (accessed 2022.10.21).

[28] K.-T. Seong and G.-H. Kim, "Implementation of voyage data recording device using a digital forensics-based hash algorithm," *International Journal of Electrical and Computer Engineering (IJECE)*, vol. 9, no. 6, pp. 5412–5419, 2019, doi: 10.11591/ijece.v9i6.pp5412-5419.

[29] J. Kang, B. Youm, D. Cho, H and H. Choe, "Development of Remote Alarm Module with playback functions in Voyage Data Recorder," 2009, [Online]. Available: https://ieeexplore.ieee.org/stamp/stamp.jsp?tp=&arnumber=5334244 (accessed 2022.10.21).

[30] G. Bassett, D. Hylender, P. Langlois, A. Pinto, and S. Widup, "DBIR Data Breach Investigations Report," 2022 [Online]. Available: https://www.verizon.com/business/resources/reports/dbir/ (accessed 2022.10.21).

[31] K. Tam, K. Forshaw, and K. Jones, "Cyber-SHIP: Developing Next Generation Maritime Cyber Research Capabilities," 2019, doi: 10.24868/icmet.oman.2019.005.

A Ship Honeynet Project to Collect Data on Cyber Threats to the Maritime Sector

Stephen James McCombie
Maritime IT Security Research Group
NHL Stenden University of Applied Sciences
Leeuwarden Netherlands
Email: stephen.mccombie@nhlstenden.com

Jeroen Pijpker
Maritime IT Security Research Group
NHL Stenden University of Applied Sciences
Emmen Netherlands
Email: jeroen.pijpker@nhlstenden.com

Abstract— **This paper discusses the development of a ship Honeynet. The criticality and fragility of the Global Maritime Transportation System (GMTS) has been clearly demonstrated during the COVID-19 Pandemic. At the same time, fleets are aging and their technology is aging with them and thus they are more vulnerable to cyber-attacks. This paper will describe a project aiming to gather information on current cyber-attacks on vessels using a Honeynet to gather data. Honeypots are Internet systems deployed for the sole purpose of being compromised to observe adversaries. Networks of Honeypots are termed Honeynets and, like network telescopes, are typically deployed on an otherwise unused address space. While Honeypot/Honeynets are not new, simulating all the different systems of a ship to research cyber attackers targeting them is a new concept. A ship in real life consists of multiple digital systems including for navigation, communication, safety, propulsion, cargo management and numerous other purposes. This paper will explain the concept of Honeynets and a ship Honeynet in particular, as well as their design considerations and benefits. This paper will also discuss the challenge of making the Honeynet digitally realistic and attractive for cyber attackers to interact with and drop targeted malware and other interesting artefacts.**

Keywords – Cybersecurity; Maritime Security; Cyber-Physical Security; Vessel; Honeynet; Honeypot; Cyber Deception.

I. INTRODUCTION

This paper will discuss the concept, development and use of a ship Honeynet to gather information on current cyber-attacks on vessels. This will be achieved by luring cyber attackers to interact with the ship Honeynet and capturing that interaction for later analysis. The criticality and fragility of our supply chains have been demonstrated during the COVID-19 Pandemic. This is particularly evident within the GMTS. The GMTS is a system of systems and includes not just vessels but also waterways, ports, and land-side connections, moving people and goods to and from the water. The role of GMTS in the global economy is significant with over 80% of the world's cargo transported by ship [2] and representing 70% of global trade by value [3]. At the same time, fleets are aging, and their technology is aging with them and thus they are more vulnerable to cyber-attacks. 38% of oil tankers and 59% of general cargo ships are more than twenty years old [4]. Supply chains themselves are increasingly vulnerable to cyber-attacks. This is particularly stark in recent years, "…European sources estimated a 400% growth in supply chain cyberattacks in 2021 compared to 2020" [5]. GMTS is clearly a key part of global supply chains and will be increasingly targeted by cyber threat actors. Since 2018, state sponsored threat actors from China (amongst others) have specifically targeted the maritime industry [6].

Honeypots are Internet systems deployed for the sole purpose of being compromised in order to observe adversaries. Networks of Honeypots are termed Honeynets and, like network telescopes, are typically deployed on an otherwise unused address space [1]. While Honeypot/Honeynets are not new, simulating all the different systems of a ship to research cyber attackers targeting them is a new concept. A ship in real life consists of multiple digital systems including for navigation, communication, safety, propulsion, cargo management and numerous other purposes. The Honeynet needs to simulate this.

Part of the process is to make the Honeynet to appear realistic to potential attackers and the paper identifies a number of features that would make the Honeynet more realistic and thus more likely to attract and engage attackers. The ship Honeynet is going to use a technique proposed by Luo et al. [7] called intelligent interaction. The paper also discusses methods to capture all interactions with those attackers including connection details, commands executed, files dropped, and other relevant activity.

The Honeynet data and any discovered attacker Tactics, Techniques and Practices (TTPs), will be used for a number of important purposes. To build industry awareness of this rising threat. To create research reports/publications. To report any identified vulnerabilities to vendors. Lastly to create realistic maritime cyber incident simulations for industry education and research into human factors.

The structure of this paper is firstly a description of the background of Honeynets, etc., followed by a description of the cyber threats to the maritime sector, then the project plan and design considerations for a ship Honeynet and, finally, the conclusions and future research.

II. BACKGROUND OF DECEPTION, HONEYPOTS AND HONEYNETS

Honeypots and the use of deception against cyber attackers date back to the 1980s. Astronomer Clifford Stoll in his seminal hacking tale, The Cuckoo's Egg, described when working as a part time system administrator at Lawrence Berkeley National Lab in the USA his efforts to uncover hackers who had penetrated his system [8]. This early Honeypot was born of his scientific approach to observe his attackers and get them to reveal more of themselves, "Do research...OK, I'll watch the guy and call it science" [9]. In 1999, the Honeynet Project was formed with 30 members from the, at that stage, small cyber security community. Amongst that group of 30 was Lance Spitzner and he described a Honeypot as:

"A ... security resource whose value lies in being probed, attacked, or compromised... It does not matter what the resource is (a router, scripts running emulated services, a jail, an actual production system). What does matter is that the resource's value lies in its being attacked" [10].

Common deployment strategies for Honeypots were described by Scottberg et al. [11]. They include: "Sacrificial Lamb", an isolated system that has no entry point to production systems; a "Hacker Zoo", an entire subnet of Honeypots with varied platforms, services, vulnerabilities, and configurations, which are isolated from production systems; a "Minefield", a number of Honeypots placed in forefront to serve as first attack targets; a "Proximity Decoy", a Honeypots deployed in close proximity to production systems; a "Redirection Shield External", that appear on production systems through port redirection and, lastly, a "Deception Port", simulating services (e.g., SMTP, DNS, FTP) on production systems.

III. Critical Cyber Threat to Maritime

As stated in the introduction the criticality and fragility of our supply chains is particularly evident within the Global Maritime Transportation System (GMTS).

In a 2019 report 'Shen attack: Cyber risk in Asia Pacific ports' – produced by the University of Cambridge Centre for Risk Studies, researchers described a hypothetical cyber-attack across the Asia Pacific against 15 ports using malware that jumped from ships to ports. They projected the loss could go as high as USD$110 Billion with the vast majority of that amount not being covered by any insurance [12]. Such a cyber-attack on this scale has not as yet been seen in the maritime sector, but we have seen numerous ports and ships impacted by attacks using ransomware, destructive malware, and the even hacking of Operational Technology (OT). These attacks have been initiated by both criminal groups and nation-state hackers. The well-known case of Maersk which lost over USD$200 million in 2017 in the NotPetya malware attack is a significant example [13].

In a non-cyber case in March 2020, the MV Evergiven blocked the Suez Canal and caused major disruption to the GMTS. While the incident was caused by human error rather than a cyber-attack it demonstrates the fragility of the GMTS costing some USD$9 Billion per day [14]. Such an incident could easily be deliberately caused by a cyber-attack. The threat actor could achieve this by compromising the navigation or propulsion systems of a ship or in a number of other ways. The aim of such an attack might be a part of a great power conflict (i.e., USA/China), a regional conflict (i.e., Israel/Iran), or by cybercriminals demanding ransom or shorting the stock market.

IV. Project Plan and Design Considerations for Ship Honeynet

A. *Project Plan*

The initial phase of the project to develop the ship Honey ship is as follows:

- Design of the ship Honeynet.
- Initial deployment in a test environment.
- Internal testing of the ship Honeynet.
- Penetration test by EC Council Certified Ethical Hacking (CEH) students.
- Initial deployment on the Internet.
- Examination of result of initial deployment and data gathered on cyber attacker activity.
- Analysis of cyber attacker information and artefacts gathered.
- Subsequent deployments with improvements.

B. *Architecture*

Ships are a complex network with a wide range of information and communication technologies onboard. Ships also have networked Operational Technology (OT) often directly connected to their IT networks.

Due to this significant complexity for the first version of the maritime Honeynet it was decided to just simulate the Integrated Bridge System (IBS) of a ship. This was to simplify the task for this initial version and also because of the critical nature of the IBS. The IBS acts as the main command and control of a vessel as it interconnects various digital devices used for navigation in open seas and is also connected to other on-board systems of a vessel, e.g., navigation and control, propulsion and machinery management system, cargo management system and safety management system, core infra structure systems, administrative and crew welfare systems, etc. [15]. Additionally, it also provides a gateway to the Internet.

The International Maritime Organisation (IMO) defines an IBS as combination of systems which are interconnected in order to allow centralized access to sensor information or command/control from workstations, with the aim of increasing safe and efficient ship's management by suitably qualified personnel [16].

The main components that are part of the IBS are Automatic Identification System (AIS), Electronic Chart Display Information System (ECDIS), radar, conning display, Bridge and Watch Alarm System (BNWAS) / Bridge Alert Management System (BAMS), Voyage Data Recorder (VDR), and autopilot. Sensors like compass, speed log, and echo sounder are also providing information to the system in the IBS [17]. In most cases there is Satellite terminal connected to provide the access through to the Internet.

The diagram in Figure 1 represents an architectural drawing of the ship Honeynet consisting of the following components ECDIS, Satcom, AIS, Long-Range Identification and Tracking (LRIT), VHF communications and VDR. These are the identified minimum components to run a realistic ship Honeynet. While not all the potential components of an IBS are represented the key systems are present.

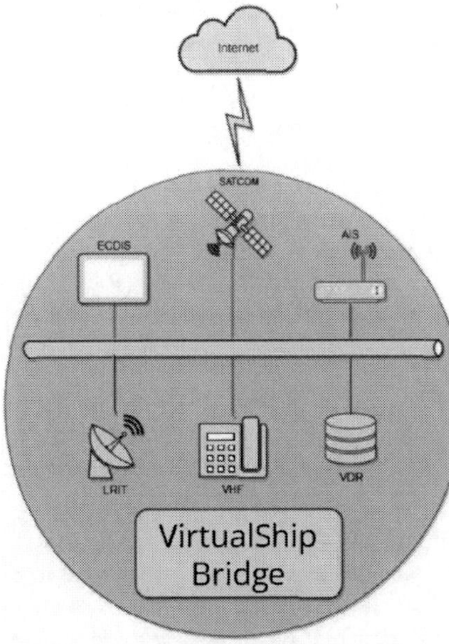

Figure 1. Minimal architectural drawing of the ship Honeynet. [18]

Figure 1 also describes the components that will each be hosted in so called docker containers. A docker container image is a lightweight, standalone, executable package of software that includes everything needed to run that application: code, runtime, system tools, system libraries and settings [19]. In practice, a container is easy to deploy and maintain. Utilising docker containers also provides security to prevent cyber attackers jumping from the ship Honeynet to the host system.

C. *Making the ship Honeynet an attractive target*

Considerations also needs to be made to make the ship Honeynet attractive and believable to potential cyber attackers.

To make the IBS attractive to cyber attackers as possible the following considerations will be taken into account [18]:

- Logical server location.
- Logical sailing route with realistic AIS data.
- Network speeds when using satellite should be slow.
- Network signs of life with traffic between systems.
- Logical entry point for cyber attackers i.e., Satcom, remote access portal etc.
- System architecture appropriate to type and size of ship.

The ship Honeynet is also going to use a technique proposed by Luo et al. [7] called intelligent interaction. The goal of intelligent-interaction is to learn the 'correct' behaviours to interact with clients from zero-knowledge about the maritime Honeynet.

D. *Entry point for ship Honeynet*

The entry point for a cyber attacker into the IBS is the satellite terminal for the first version of the ship Honeynet. Different vulnerability reports have revealed the misconfiguration of these types of remote management terminals are common. Leaving them open allows entry and also access to the network that sits behind it. So, when a cyber attacker is scanning the IBS they will find for example an open SSH port of the satellite terminal to attack and enumerate.

A specific example of a possible attack vector for the cyber attacker and a way of gaining access to the IBS can be done by emulating a Cobham SeaTel terminal. This type of terminal is being used as a gateway to the Internet. The Cobham SeaTel terminal has vulnerability regarding injection of malicious JavaScript using the devices TELNET built-in commands [20]. This way the attacker can gain access to the IBS directly from the Internet then move around the connected ship Honeynet in a realistic fashion.

E. *Broader scenario development for ship Honeynet*

The research team have gathered information on 152 maritime cyber incidents dating from 2001 to 2022. This is currently being formatted and will be published in December 2022. Analysis of those different cyber-attacks will inform scenario development for the Honeynet. For example, there was a malware attack targeting a deep draft Vessel travelling to the Port of New York in 2019 [21]. The malware in this example was transferred via USB drive. We would alter this ship cyber incident so the transfer could occur through the Internet gateway of the ship Honeynet since the introduction of malware via a USB is difficult to simulate within a ship Honeynet.

F. *Capturing the cyber attacker interaction*

An essential part of the maritime Honeynet is capturing the activity of the cyber attackers and storing it for later analysis. One basic but important element is capturing the source of the attack. The source refers to the origin of the attack and it includes the country and location. While source information such as IP addresses used by cyber attackers are often proxied to hide their origin or use anonymizing networks such as Tor they still may allow for attribution. Research on attribution has shown numerous methods of identifying the source of cyber-attacks [22]-[24]. This also includes examining the characteristics of the attack tools utilised.

Retaining the actual network traffic in the form of a packet captures is a preferred option for the project, but can cause storage issues if not managed carefully. Other network parameters and connection information will also be captured. Naturally all cyber attacker keystrokes and files will be captured.

G. Testing the ship Honeynet

NHL Stenden University of Applied Sciences teach the EU Council Certified Ethical Hacking program. Researchers working with students of that program will thoroughly penetration test the ship Honeynet for its functionality, realism and security. This will be an iterative process as new versions are created. Students involved will complete detailed surveys to identify weaknesses and areas for potential development in the ship Honeynet. Researchers will also evaluate the monitoring and data capture to ensure it is capturing all activity of the cyber attacker.

H. Secrecy and deception of the ship Honeynet

While it may appear an unusual approach to talk about the ship Honeynet if the aim is to trick cyber attackers it believing it is real. However, the nature of deception means that even if a cyber attacker reads this research they will not know when scanning the Internet and they find something that looks like a ship whether in fact it is a Honeynet or the real thing and may conclude that it is a Honeynet when in fact it is the real digital footprint of a ship. Research on cyber deception has shown it may significantly slow down their progress and negatively influence the decision making of a cyber attacker [25], [26].

V. CONCLUSIONS

While the design, development, and operation of a ship Honeynet is a quite complex project the benefit of intelligence that it would provide on current cyber attacker activity including modus operandi, motive and origin make it a worthwhile effort. The project itself will involve a series of ship Honeynets to build capability and to explore different aspects of the maritime sector.

A. Future Research

One area of further research is to focus is going to be on developing a more mature model that also represents both Information Technology and Operational Technology networks in ship environments.

This is a challenge because the maritime industry has a lot of standards for interconnecting components. The most relevant protocols are NMEA 2000, NMEA 0183, TCP/IPv6, and the latest one NMEA OneNet [27].

Other options include exploring simulating various types of ship environments such as container ships, cruise ships, tugboats, and executive yachts.

While a ship Honeynet in this case is used to study cyber attackers, it can also be a method to delay, frustrate and confuse them. This is an area studied under cyber deception but also an opportunity for further research in this area.

B. Benefits of the ship Honeynet

As stated, the ultimate purpose of a Honeynet is to be "probed, attacked, or compromised" by cyber attackers and by this process we learn more of the nature of those attacks, the threat they pose, the modus operandi of those attackers including their Tactics, Techniques and Practices (TTPs), their motives and other relevant features of their activity. This intelligence will be used for industry awareness, research reports/publications, reporting any identified vulnerabilities to vendors, and creating realistic maritime cyber incident simulations.

ACKNOWLEDGMENT

The authors would like to thank the contribution of the software engineering student group from Windesheim University of Applied Sciences, Rick Rijnierse, Erik Vedelaar, Stan van der Veen and Sami el Farj.

REFERENCES

[1] J. Franco, A. Aris, B. Canberk, and A. S. Uluagac, "A Survey of Honeypots and Honeynets for Internet of Things, Industrial Internet of Things, and Cyber-Physical Systems," *IEEE Communications Surveys and Tutorials*, vol. 23, no. 4, 2021, doi: 10.1109/COMST.2021.3106669.

[2] C. Bronk and P. deWitte, "Maritime cybersecurity: Meeting threats to globalization's great conveyor," in *Proceedings of the Annual Hawaii International Conference on System Sciences*, 2020, vol. 2020-January. doi: 10.24251/hicss.2020.240.

[3] W. Loomis, V. V. Singh, G. C. Kessler, and X. Bellekens, "Raising the Colors: Signaling for Cooperation on Maritime Cybersecurity," Oct. 2021.

[4] K. Tam and K. D. Jones, "Maritime cybersecurity policy: the scope and impact of evolving technology on international shipping," *Journal of Cyber Policy*, vol. 3, no. 2, 2018, doi: 10.1080/23738871.2018.1513053.

[5] G. Kessler and S. Shepherd, *Maritime Cybersecurity: A Guide for Leaders and Managers*, 2nd ed. Daytona Beach, Florida: Independently published, 2022.

[6] Mandiant, "Suspected Chinese Cyber Espionage Group (TEMP.Periscope) Targeting U.S. Engineering and Maritime Industries," Alexandria VA, 2018.

[7] T. Luo, Z. Xu, X. Jin, Y. Jia, and X. Ouyang, "IoTCandyJar: Towards an Intelligent-Interaction Honeypot for IoT Devices," *Black Hat 2017*, 2017.

[8] C. Stoll and J. W. D. Connolly, "The Cuckoo's Egg: Tracking a Spy Through the Maze of Computer Espionage," *Phys Today*, vol. 43, no. 8, 1990, doi: 10.1063/1.2810663.

[9] C. Stoll, "The Cuckoo's Egg: A True Story of International Computer Espionage,". 1989. Doubleday, New York. ISBN: 0-385-24946-2.

[10] L. Spitzner, *Honeypots: Tracking Hackers By Lance Spitzner*, vol. 52, no. 1. 2002.

[11] B. Scottberg, W. Yurcik, and D. Doss, "Internet honeypots: protection or entrapment?" in *IEEE 2002*

International Symposium on Technology and Society (ISTAS'02). Social Implications of Information and Communication Technology. Proceedings (Cat. No.02CH37293), 2002, pp. 387–391. doi: 10.1109/ISTAS.2002.1013842.

[12] J. Daffron and S. Ruffle, "Shen Attack: Cyber Risk in Asia Pacific Ports," 2019.

[13] L. Matthews, "NotPetya Ransomware Attack Cost Shipping Giant Maersk Over $200 Million," *Forbes*, 2017.

[14] J. M. Lee and E. Y. Wong, "Suez Canal blockage: an analysis of legal impact, risks and liabilities to the global supply chain," *MATEC Web of Conferences*, vol. 339, 2021, doi: 10.1051/matecconf/202133901019.

[15] M. S. Kaleem Awan and M. A. A. Ghamdi, "Understanding the vulnerabilities in digital components of an integrated bridge system (IBS)," *J Mar Sci Eng*, vol. 7, no. 10, 2019, doi: 10.3390/jmse7100350.

[16] BIMCO, "The Guidelines on Cyber Security Onboard Ships," *International Chamber of Shippinger of Shipping*, vol. 4, 2021.

[17] C. Hemminghaus, J. Bauer, and E. Padilla, "Brat: A bridge attack tool for cyber security assessments of maritime systems," *TransNav*, vol. 15, no. 1, 2021, doi: 10.12716/1001.15.01.02.

[18] R. Rijnierse, E. Vedelaar, S. van der Veen, and S. el Farj, "Ship Honeynet Student Project," Windesheim, 2022.

[19] S. Bistarelli, E. Bosimini, and F. Santini, "A report on the security of home connections with IoT and docker honeypots," in *CEUR Workshop Proceedings*, 2020, vol. 2597.

[20] The Mitre Corporation, "CVE-2018-5071," 2018.

[21] F. Akpan, G. Bendiab, S. Shiaeles, S. Karamperidis, and M. Michaloliakos, "Cybersecurity Challenges in the Maritime Sector," *Network*, vol. 2, no. 1, 2022, doi: 10.3390/network2010009.

[22] S. McCombie, "Threat actor-oriented strategy: knowing your enemy to better defend, detect and respond to cyber-attacks," *Journal of the Australian Institute of Professional Intelligence Officers*, vol. 26, no. 1, pp. 24–41, 2018.

[23] T. Rid and B. Buchanan, "Attributing Cyber Attacks," *Journal of Strategic Studies*, vol. 38, no. 1–2, pp. 4–37, Jan. 2015, doi: 10.1080/01402390.2014.977382.

[24] S. Goel, "Cyberwarfare," *Commun ACM*, vol. 54, no. 8, pp. 132–140, Aug. 2011, doi: 10.1145/1978542.1978569.

[25] K. J. Ferguson-Walter *et al.*, "The Tularosa study: An experimental design and implementation to quantify the effectiveness of cyber deception," in *Proceedings of the Annual Hawaii International Conference on System Sciences*, 2019, vol. 2019-January. doi: 10.24251/hicss.2019.874.

[26] K. E. Heckman, F. J. Stech, B. S. Schmoker, and R. K. Thomas, "Denial and Deception in Cyber Defense," *Computer (Long Beach Calif)*, vol. 48, no. 4, 2015, doi: 10.1109/MC.2015.104.

[27] K. Tran, S. Keene, E. Fretheim, and M. Tsikerdekis, "Marine Network Protocols and Security Risks," *Journal of Cybersecurity and Privacy*, vol. 1, no. 2, pp. 239–251, 2021, doi: 10.3390/jcp1020013.

Timely Maritime Cyber Threat Resolution in a Multi-Stakeholder Environment

Allan Nganga
Department of Maritime Studies
Western Norway University of Applied Sciences
Haugesund, Norway
e-mail: allan.kevin.nganga@hvl.no

Joel Scanlan
Department of Maritime Studies
Western Norway University of Applied Sciences
Haugesund, Norway
e-mail: josc@hvl.no

Margareta Lützhöft
Department of Maritime Studies
Western Norway University of Applied Sciences
Haugesund, Norway
e-mail: mhl@hvl.no

Steven Mallam
Department of Maritime Operations
University of South-Eastern Norway
Borre, Norway
email: Steven.Mallam@usn.no

Abstract— **In response to the growing maritime cyber threat landscape, the International Maritime Organization (IMO) developed guidelines on maritime cyber risk management, part of resolution MSC.428 (98). One of the guidelines' functional requirements calls for the development and implementation of activities necessary for the timely detection of a cyber event. This has seen the development of Maritime Security Operation Centers (M-SOCs), which give maritime operators and service providers better cyber visibility of vessel systems. In line with the conference theme on situational awareness, the position paper will explore this from the perspective of cyber threat information sharing and its necessity when it comes to enhancing awareness in multi-stakeholder domains. We propose a model that could form as a basis for future maritime cyber threat sharing from an M-SOC analyst's point of view. Gaps that could undermine the effectiveness of this structure are subsequently underscored and form the basis of future research to be conducted in this area.**

Keywords-maritime cybersecurity; situational awareness; information sharing; stakeholders; security operations center.

I. INTRODUCTION

The maritime sector is a complex ecosystem, bringing together stakeholders and organizations of varied sizes, maturity, complexity, and operational scope. With its increasing rate of digitization, and increased levels of connectivity in the near future, the threat environment is steadily becoming more hostile. Cyber-attacks are becoming more frequent with all actors in the digital value chain being targeted by criminal networks and hostile networks [1][2]. Against this backdrop, the IMO, in 2017 adopted resolution MSC.428(98)-maritime cyber risk management in safety management systems and MSC-Fal.1-guidelines on maritime cyber risk management. Recognizing the multi-stakeholder nature of the domain, the resolution called for administrators, classification societies, ship owners, operators, agents, equipment manufacturers, service providers, ports, port facilities and other stakeholders to work towards protecting shipping from current and emerging cyber threats [3] [4]. These regulations highlight that cyber security in the maritime domain is indeed a shared responsibility.

A benefit of stakeholder identification is that it helps in the clear defining of cyber threat information sharing structures and their participating entities [5]. One way of gaining increased cyber situational awareness necessary for the timely resolution of cyber threats is to exchange information with others [6]. It is within this context that we propose cyber threat information sharing as a discussion that needs to be had within the maritime domain.

As a build-up towards this, the position paper will take on the following structure: Section II gives a background on information sharing; Section III looks at legislation and guidelines that have steered information sharing in other multi-stakeholder domains; Section IV discusses information sharing initiatives within the maritime domain; Section V looks into M-SOCs; Section VI discusses the proposed model and the motivation behind its development; Section VII highlights key takeaways from the proposed work with identified implementation challenges framed as directions for future work; Section VIII concludes the paper.

II. INFORMATION SHARING

Information sharing has previously been defined as the act of voluntarily making information possessed by one entity available to another [7]. Within the context of this paper, the type of information we are most interested in is cyber threat information defined as any information that can help an organization recognize, assess, monitor, and respond to cyber threats. Examples of this include indicators of compromise, which are technical artifacts or observables that suggest an attack is imminent or is currently underway; tactics, techniques, and procedures used by threat actors; security alerts; threat intelligence reports; situational awareness data; best practices; and strategic analysis. Vessel mobility makes situational context information particularly important. Information sharing as used within this paper is the exchange of cyber threat information with trusted entities/stakeholders [8]–[10].

The choice of an information sharing model or structure can influence the effectiveness of information sharing between various stakeholders. Subsequently, various information sharing models have been proposed [5] [11].

One notable and highly adopted structure was established by the MITRE Corporation during the development of The Trusted Automated eXchange of Indicator Information (TAXII) [12]. TAXII defines a set of services, messages and protocols that aid in timely and efficient exchange of cyber threat information. As part of the work, three main information sharing models were defined namely hub and spoke, peer-to-peer and source-subscriber. Figure 1 below is reproduced from the work done by [12] and highlights these models.

In a hub and spoke model, a spoke shares information with the hub, which then re-shares this information with all other spokes. A peer-to-peer model is structured in such a way that any number of organizations can function as both producers and consumers of information. A source/subscriber model is one where an organization acts as a sole source of information for all subscribers. Respondents in a 2021 survey by [13] revealed that 58% of their threat intelligence came from peers.

III. MULTI-SECTOR INFORMATION SHARING INITIATIVES

The pivotal role played by information sharing when it comes to enhancing cyber resilience cannot be understated as is evidenced by multiple cross-sector initiatives related to this [14]–[16]. From a regulatory perspective, the United States of America (USA) passed the Cybersecurity Information Sharing Act (2015). This calls for concerned parties to develop procedures for sharing cyber threat information between different stakeholders. The European Union (EU) Network and Information Security (NIS) Directive calls for information exchange and cooperation among operators of essential services within sectors identified as critical. These include energy, transport, banking financial market infrastructures, health, drinking water supply and digital infrastructure.

Aviation regulation, such as European Civil Aviation Conference (ECAC) Doc 30-Part II [16] maps out information sharing relationships from the perspectives of various stakeholders, such as the nation-state, aircraft operators and software/system developers.

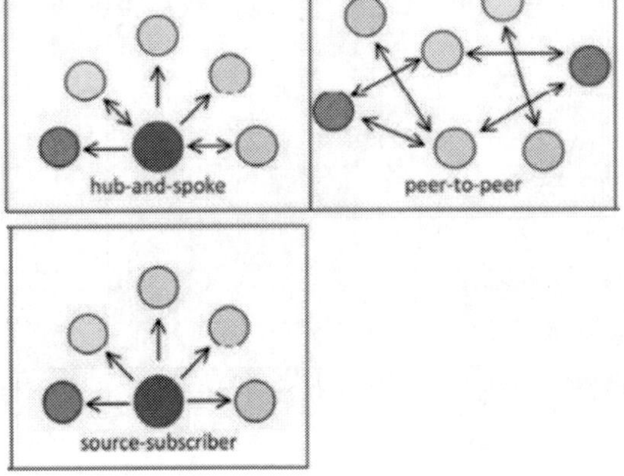

Figure 1: TAXII Information Sharing Model

The Forum of Incident Response and Security Teams (FIRST) recently released an updated version of the Traffic Light Protocol (TLP) that facilitates information sharing based on color categories. Information in the TLP: RED category can only be shared with individual recipients with no additional disclosure permitted. TLP: AMBER category authorizes limited information disclosure on a need-to-know basis within organizations and their clients. TLP: AMBER+STRICT restricts sharing to within the organization only. TLP: GREEN category enables limited disclosure within the recipient's community while TLP: WHITE has no limitation on sharing [17].

Of the sector-specific information sharing initiatives, one that has had considerable effort put in involves the development of Information Sharing and Analysis Centers (ISACs) and Information Exchanges [18][19]. Within their specific domains, these are intended to be trusted entities that promote information sharing and good practices related to cyber and physical threats and their mitigation. The United Kingdom (UK) Center for the Protection of National Infrastructure (CPNI) mapped out information exchanges for various sectors including transport, finance, water security, pharmaceuticals, and aerospace among others [20]. In compliance with the US Presidential Decision Directive-63 [21], the National Council of ISACS was established with various sector-specific ISACS, such as Automotive, communications, elections infrastructure, electricity, and financial services [22]. Likewise, the EU sees ISACs as a way of building a European cybershield [19].

IV. MARITIME INFORMATION SHARING INITIATIVES

Information sharing initiatives within the maritime domain have taken root in the form of legislation, regulatory guidelines, public and private sector collaborations, and funded research projects. These are subsequently highlighted:

A. *Legislation*

Within the EU, the maritime domain, an identified critical infrastructure sector, is required to adhere to the EU NIS directive [15], which calls for information exchange and cooperation among operators of essential services. Specifically related to the maritime domain, this directive requires incident reporting requirements to be met by identified stakeholders, such as companies, ships, port facilities, ports, and vessel traffic services. Additionally, the directive calls for a coherent approach in the satisfaction of reporting requirements by considering international codes and guidelines prepared by entities, such as the IMO.

B. *ISACS*

In compliance with the US Presidential Decision Directive-63 [21], which required the creation of sector-specific ISACS, the maritime domain has two established ISACs namely Maritime ISAC [23], and Maritime

Transportation System (MTS) ISAC [24]. The ever increasing cybersecurity concerns along the lower Columbia river prompted the Port of Vancouver (USA) and MTS-ISAC to launch the Lower Columbia River Maritime Information Exchange (LCR-MIX) to facilitate ease of communication, collaboration and cyber situational awareness among stakeholders [25]. Information sharing partnerships have been actualized by private sector entities, such as the Norwegian Maritime Cyber Resilience Center (NORMA Cyber) and MTS-ISAC who recently signed an agreement that will see both entities exchange maritime cyber threat intelligence information [26].

C. *EU ECHO Project (2019)*

As part of the EU funded ECHO project [27], the study by [28] adapted the user communities established by the Common Information Sharing Environment (CISE) [29]. It highlighted them as shareholders of sensitive cyber information sharing within the maritime domain. These user communities and their systems are Maritime safety and security; Fisheries control; Marine pollution preparedness and response in Marine environment; Customs; Border control; General law enforcement; and Defense.

D. *Danish Maritime Cybersecurity Unit (2019)*

The Danish Maritime Cybersecurity Unit developed the cyber and information security strategy [30] in which the Danish Maritime Authority (DMA) will serve as an exchange point between the Center for Cyber Security (CFCS) and various maritime sector stakeholders. The primary responsibilities of the DMA in this information sharing arrangement will be to communicate, procure, create, and validate IT security-related information between the parties, coordination tasks, organizing professional workshops and conferences related to specific IT security issues in the maritime sector.

The strategy [30] also recommends establishing the Maritime Cyber and Information Security Forum, which is coordinated by the DMA, and includes IT security representatives from Danish authorities who are directly involved in maritime activities. The forum is structured to serve as a platform for discussing how various security incidents have been managed by the parties involved and their experiences in managing the various situations. Long term goals of the forum will include identifying and addressing the possibilities of developing a digital hub where information security knowledge is made easily accessible and searchable by, maritime sector authorities and stakeholders.

E. *International Association of Classification Societies-IACS (2022)*

Recommendation 166 [31], UR E26 [32] and E27 [33] (cyber resilience of systems, for product suppliers) clearly define key vessel cybersecurity stakeholders and their responsibilities. The key stakeholders represented are the shipowner/company, ship designer/shipyard, system integrator, supplier, and classification society. One of the strengths of these regulations is that E26 and E27 become mandatory for new vessels commissioned after 1st January 2024 while remaining non-mandatory guidance tools for existing vessels. Additionally, the 2020 world merchant fleet statistics by Equasis [34] showed that 78% of vessels of a gross tonnage of more than 500 tonnes are classified under the IACS umbrella. An interpretation of the regulations yields TABLE I, which highlights stakeholder communication instances identified in the IACS regulations. In certain instances, there was no identified communication between certain stakeholders. For example, there is no direct communication between the ship and classification society. The ship owner has traditionally been responsible for ensuring the vessel complies with regulations and so it is assumed that the authors of this regulation factored that in and created communication between the classification society and ship owner instead.

While these regulations are designed for regulatory compliance, the communication pathways that they mandate between the various stakeholders can be exploited to establish dependable vessel threat information sharing structures.

V. M-SOCs

Entities in the maritime cyber resilience ecosystem that would benefit from increased information sharing are Security Operation Centers (SOCs). A SOC is a team primarily composed of security analysts organized to detect, analyze, respond to, and report on cybersecurity incidents. An internal SOC functions as part of the organization it is defending while an external one is contracted as a service provider [35]. An M-SOC is SOC that operates within the maritime domain. There has been a steady increase in the number of maritime operators who have either setup or contracted third party M-SOCs to enable them to have better visibility and cyber awareness of their vessels.

TABLE I:IACS STAKEHOLDER COMMUNICATION

	Classification Society	Ship Owner	Ship	System Integrator	Shipyard	Supplier
Classification Society						
Ship Owner	X					
Ship		X				
System Integrator	X	X	X			
Shipyard	X	X	X	X		
Supplier	X	X	X	X	X	

Examples of these include Norma Cyber [36], Marlink [37], Port-IT [38], Cyber-Owl [39], Port of LA [40], and Port of Singapore [41] among others.

These real-time monitoring units play a vital role in not only producing cyber threat information but also consuming the same when it comes from entities, such as equipment vendors and suppliers. It is, therefore, pivotal for M-SOC analysts to have complete domain awareness of the vessel cybersecurity ecosystem and information sharing complexities that exist between all the stakeholders within this ecosystem so that they can tailor their communication appropriately.

VI. PROPOSED VESSEL THREAT INFORMATION SHARING MODEL

Work on the proposed model was inspired by a similar outcome in the aviation domain and highlighted in the ECAC Doc 30-Part II regulation, which is currently active and enforceable [16]. In the case of this regulation, the authors developed three information sharing models from the perspectives of three critical stakeholders namely, nation state, operator, and software/system developer. Figure 2 shows the outcome of the process from the software/system developer perspective. The recommended actions of the software/system developer with regards to information sharing were then highlighted, which included identifying external stakeholders, information they would want to receive, communication channels to be used, vulnerability response/disclosure process, and finally assessing all the above with the identified stakeholders and regulators. Additionally, Figure 3 shows the outcomes of a similar process but from the perspective of the operator.

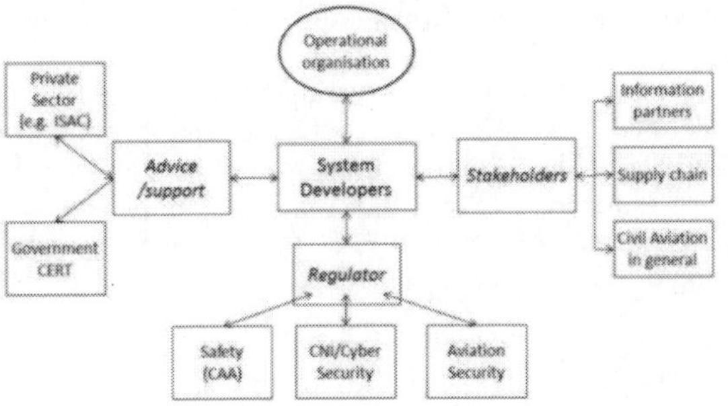

Figure 2: Aviation Information Sharing-Software/System Developer Perspective

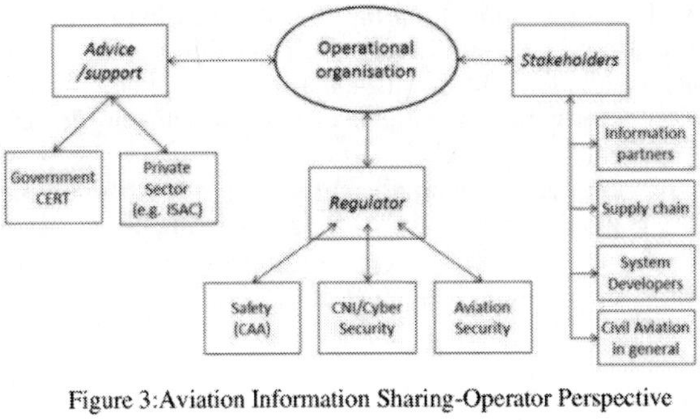

Figure 3:Aviation Information Sharing-Operator Perspective

Development of the proposed vessel threat information sharing model, shown in Figure 4, began by identifying the key stakeholders highlighted in the three IACS documents that focus on vessel cyber resilience, Recommendation 166 [31], UR E26 [32] and E27 [33] (cyber resilience of systems, for product suppliers). These were identified to be the classification society, shipowner, supplier, ship designer/shipyards and system integrator. The ship is the primary asset of focus and so has also been included. The next step involved establishing any instances of communication that are highlighted in each of the documents. As shown in TABLE 1, there are instances of communication between all stakeholders. Examples of statements in the regulations that guided this process include:

- E26: The Supplier shall design and document testing procedures suitable to verify the performance of measures adopted to fulfil relevant requirements (Test Plan)
- E26: The Shipyard or System Integrator shall incorporate the documentation provided by the Supplier into an overall Test Plan for the CBSs
- E26: The final Test Plans updated according to the actual CBSs configuration and implementation onboard shall be made available to the Classification Society.
- E26: The Shipowner shall retain onboard a copy of results of execution of tests and an updated Test Plan and make them available to the Classification Society.

The examples above, while only representing a small portion of the regulations, already highlight how the development and maintenance of a test plan involves all stakeholders. The directional arrows in the model are a direct interpretation of the stakeholder communication responsibilities. Because the model has not been evaluated, we opted to leave them as is to act as a guide. Testing of the model will determine the actual cyber threat information sharing responsibilities between stakeholders, which may lead to a variation in the direction of communication.

The increased adoption of M-SOCs as highlighted in Section V means that that they will be a key source of real-time vessel threat information. Interviews we have conducted with a few M-SOC vendors, part of on-going work to be published in future, reveals that most are currently operating as a service provided to ship operators to help them increase asset visibility from a cyber security perspective. The service level agreement between them would therefore mean that any cyber threat information that the M-SOC gathers from the vessel would be shared with both the operators and the vessel. We therefore position them in the model between the operator and the vessel. The M-SOC is highlighted in a different shade because they are not one of the key stakeholders identified in the IACS guidelines used above. However, from a threat information perspective, they are a primary stakeholder. Additionally, the green dotted outline encompassing the M-SOC, ship owner and ship shows the current limited scope of information sharing due to the limiting nature of service agreements.

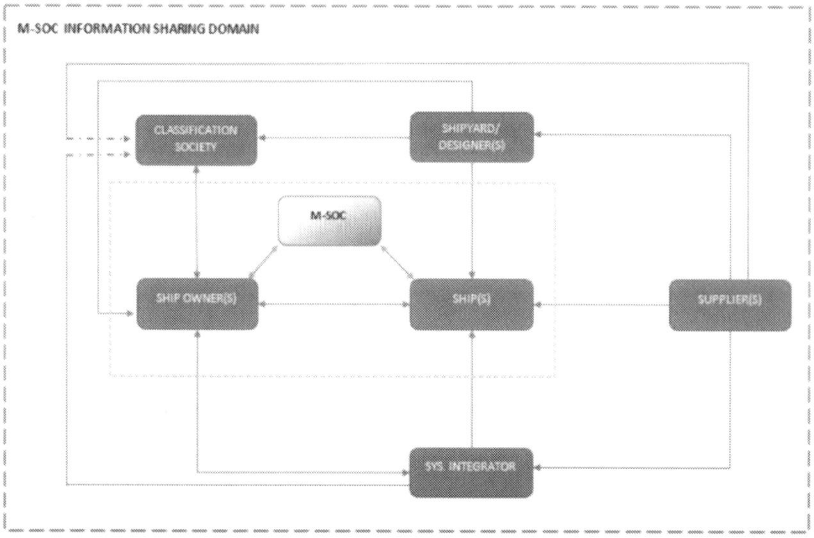

Figure 4: Proposed Vessel Threat Information Sharing Model

It is important to highlight the assumptions made when developing this model. The first assumption is that all the vessel resilience stakeholders identified in the guidelines are also key when it comes to sharing of threat information. It is possible that some stakeholders may have been left out of the model or some have been included who are not critical in the process. As an example, we added M-SOCs in the model because they are a key producer of real-time vessel cyber threat information. Closely related to this is also the fact that stakeholder cyber resilience responsibilities vary during the lifecycle of a vessel from design, commissioning, construction, and operation [32]. However, as the model is yet to be tested, the assumption made is that there is uniform responsibility, something that we anticipate will change once validation of the model begins.

The second assumption made is that pre-existing mandated communication between stakeholders, albeit currently for regulatory compliance, would make it easier to establish threat information communication pathways. It is assumed that it is easier to build upon a pre-existing relationship rather than proposing an entirely new one where none existed before. It is for this reason that the connections between stakeholders are made this way. However, we acknowledge that this could change once testing the viability of the model begins.

While the guidelines identify the stakeholders as distinct separate entities, it is assumed that the same happens in actual operation where it may not always be the case. There are examples of shipyards also providing system integration services to their clients, which would therefore lead to a merging of those two entities in the model presented [42]. However, we have opted to maintain all stakeholders as distinct separate entities as highlighted in the guidelines.

VII. KEY TAKEAWAYS AND FUTURE RESEARCH DIRECTIONS

The key contribution of this position paper is the proposal of a maritime vessel cyber threat information sharing model. This model differs from previous maritime information sharing initiatives highlighted in Section IV in that this is more specific to vessel cyber resilience and focuses on the stakeholders considered critical to the secure posture of the same. Its development was motivated by similar work done in the aviation domain as highlighted in Figure 2 and Figure 3 contained in the presently active ECAC Doc 30-Part II regulation [16].

Having the information sharing model allows us to be more targeted in what we want to uncover with regards to the state of maritime information sharing because we now have well defined stakeholders to start with and hypothesized relationships which testing will help us refine. Additionally, we also aim to explore the following implementation challenges that we feel would impede the successful adoption of such a model:

A. *Identifying Information Sharing Stakeholder gaps*

While the stakeholders involved in vessel cyber resilience have been identified, research on their roles with respect to threat information sharing is still a significantly under researched area with the potential of revealing glaring gaps that could undermine the information sharing process. For example, a 2021 study [43] conducted by the US transport department identified gaps in vulnerability and exploit information sharing between various transportation stakeholder groups, such as:

- Indirect communication between equipment manufacturers and Infrastructure Owner Operators (IOOs), which occurs mostly through contractors, distributors, and intermediate agents

- Equipment manufacturers lacking procedures to manage unsolicited reports from security researchers; manufacturers reporting of the long time taken to disseminate patches to all devices
- IOOs believing vulnerabilities are a problem that equipment manufacturers should take ownership of and address in case any problem arises.

In order to overcome this challenge and optimize cyber information sharing within the maritime sector, future research will focus on understanding communication gaps, and variations in information sharing perceptions between the stakeholders presented in the model. This will also help determine the validity of one of the assumptions made during development of the model whereby it is easier to build threat information pathways on top of pre-existing stakeholder communication.

B. *Stakeholder Specific Actionable Cyber Threat Information Needs*

Actionable cyber threat information has previously been defined by multiple researchers as constituting multiple dimensions. Research by [44] established that actionable information is determined by correctness, relevance, timeliness, usefulness, and uniqueness. [45] defined actionable threat intelligence based on timeliness, prioritization, implementation, resolution, relevance, integration, automation, trustworthiness, and context. The European Union Agency for Cybersecurity (ENISA) [46] highlighted that actionable information has to be Relevant, Ingestible, Accurate, Complete, and Timely within the context of the particular recipient organization or stakeholder. An acknowledged consequence of the highlighted dimensions is that different stakeholders will have varying perspectives on what constitutes actionable threat information. Indeed, this is reflected in surveys conducted by [13] who established that less than 50% of respondents considered the intelligence they received as being accurate and actionable with timeliness being the worst rated by only 29% of respondents. In the same study, only 33% of respondents acknowledged having effective processes for handling actionable threat intelligence from external sources. Actionability of threat intelligence was also ranked, at 61%, as the most essential element during calculation of risk scores.

Overcoming this challenge will require further research into how the various stakeholders define what constitutes actionable cyber threat information and exploring how the same fosters their participation in the information sharing ecosystem. It also ensures that everyone contributes in the information sharing process to reduce the problem of free-riding [5][44].

VIII. CONCLUSION

This position paper began by introducing information sharing and its role in enhancing cyber resilience in multi-stakeholder domains. Specific to the maritime domain, various information sharing initiatives were highlighted through articles of legislation, funded projects, and regulatory authority guidelines. The IACS regulations [31]–[33] are the closest that the maritime sector has in terms of a communication structure between the various vessel cyber resilience stakeholders. However, these were tailored towards compliance with regulatory requirements rather than to be used as cyber threat information sharing structures.

Nevertheless, the increasing adoption of SOCs in the multi-stakeholder maritime domain necessitates the need to have efficient cyber threat information sharing structures, which are critical to vessel safety, security, and timely resolution of cyber incidents. We believe that the communication pathways proposed by the new IACS regulations, enforceable for newly contracted vessels as from January 1st, 2024, provide an excellent starting point as a stable structure. Further research therefore needs to be done to ascertain their usability and applicability for cyber threat information sharing within the vessel cyber resilience domain.

REFERENCES

[1] P. H. Meland, K. Bernsmed, E. Wille, J. Rødseth, and D. A. Nesheim, "A retrospective analysis of maritime cyber security incidents," *TransNav*, vol. 15, no. 3, pp. 519–530, 2021.

[2] J. D. Scanlan, J. M. Styles, D. Lyneham, and M. H. Lutzhoft, "New Internet Satellite Constellations to Increase Cyber Risk in Ill-Prepared Industries," in *70th International Astronautical Congress (IAC)*, 2019, pp. 1–12.

[3] IMO, "Guidelines on Maritime Cyber Risk Management." IMO, pp. 1–6, 2021.

[4] IMO, "Maritime Cyber Risk Management in Safety Management Systems." IMO, p. 1, 2017.

[5] T. D. Wagner, K. Mahbub, E. Palomar, and A. E. Abdallah, "Cyber threat intelligence sharing: Survey and research directions," *Comput. Secur.*, vol. 87, pp. 1–13, Nov. 2019.

[6] U. Franke and J. Brynielsson, "Cyber situational awareness – A systematic review of the literature," *Comput. Secur.*, vol. 46, pp. 18–31, Oct. 2014.

[7] A. Y. Akbulut and J. Motwani, "Integration and Information Sharing in E-Government," in *Encyclopaedia of Networked and Virtual Organizations*, IGI Global, 2008, pp. 729–734.

[8] C. S. Johnson, M. L. Badger, D. A. Waltermire, J. Snyder, and C. Skorupka, "Guide to Cyber Threat Information Sharing." National Institute of Standards and Technology, Gaithersburg, MD, p. 43, 04-Oct-2016.

[9] A. Albakri, E. Boiten, and R. De Lemos, "Risks of sharing cyber incident information," *ACM Int. Conf. Proceeding Ser.*, vol. 10, pp. 1–10, Aug. 2018.

[10] ENISA, "Incentives and Challenges for Information Sharing in the Context of Network and Information Security." ENISA, p. 56, 2010.

[11] L. O. Nweke and S. Wolthusen, "Legal Issues Related to Cyber Threat Information Sharing among Private Entities for Critical Infrastructure Protection," *Int. Conf. Cyber Conflict, CYCON*, vol. 2020-May, pp. 63–78, May 2020.

[12] J. Connolly, M. Davidson, and C. Schmidt, "The Trusted Automated eXchange of Indicator Information (TAXII™)." Mitre Corporation, p. 10, 2014.
[13] Ponemon, "Fourth Annual Study on Exchanging Cyber Threat Intelligence: There Has to Be a Better Way." Ponemon, p. 63, 2021.
[14] DOJ and DHS, *Cybersecurity Information Sharing Act of 2015 Procedures and Guidance | CISA*. 2015.
[15] EU, *Directive (EU) 2016/1148*. 2016, p. 30.
[16] ECAC, *ECAC Doc 30, Part II-Cyber Threats to Civil Aviation*. 2018, p. 71.
[17] FIRST, "Traffic Light Protocol (TLP) Version 2.0," 2021. [Online]. Available: https://www.first.org/tlp/. [Accessed: 23-Oct-2022].
[18] ENISA, "Information Sharing and Analysis Centers (ISACS)-Cooperative Models." ENISA, p. 51, 2017.
[19] ENISA, "Cross-Sector Exercise Requirements." ENISA, p. 40, 2022.
[20] A. Powell, "Information Sharing in the UK," 2010.
[21] National Telecommunications and Information Administration, *Presidential Decision Directive 63 on Critical Infrastructure Protection: Sector Coordinators*. US, 1998.
[22] NCI, "National Council of ISACs," 2022. [Online]. Available: https://www.nationalisacs.org/. [Accessed: 23-Oct-2022].
[23] MSC, "Maritime Security Council," 2020. [Online]. Available: https://www.maritimesecurity.org/. [Accessed: 23-Oct-2022].
[24] MTS-ISAC, "Maritime Transportation System ISAC," 2022. [Online]. Available: https://www.mtsisac.org/. [Accessed: 23-Oct-2022].
[25] MTS-ISAC, "Port of Vancouver (LCR-MIX)," 2022. [Online]. Available: https://www.mtsisac.org/post/port-of-vancouver-usa-launches-cyber-security-information-sharing-group-for-lower-columbia-river. [Accessed: 23-Oct-2022].
[26] NORMA_Cyber, "MTS-ISAC and NORMA Cyber," 2022. [Online]. Available: https://www.normacyber.no/news/the-mts-isac-and-norma-cyber-strengthen-information-sharing-ties. [Accessed: 23-Oct-2022].
[27] echonetwork, "ECHO," 2022. [Online]. Available: https://echonetwork.eu/. [Accessed: 23-Oct-2022].
[28] J. Rajamäki, I. Tikanmäki, and J. Räsänen, "CISE as a Tool for Sharing Sensitive Cyber Information in Maritime Domain," *Inf. Secur. An Int. J.*, vol. 43, no. 2, pp. 215–235, 2019.
[29] EMSA, "Common Information Sharing Environment (CISE) - EMSA - European Maritime Safety Agency," 2009. [Online]. Available: https://emsa.europa.eu/cise.html. [Accessed: 23-Oct-2022].
[30] Danish_Maritime_Cybersecurity_Unit, "Cyber and Information Security Strategy for the Maritime Sector." Danish Maritime Authority, p. 13, 2019.
[31] IACS, "Rec 166-Recommendation on Cyber Resilience." IACS, p. 57, 2022.
[32] IACS, "UR E26-Cyber Resilience of Ships." IACS, p. 32, 2022.
[33] IACS, "UR E27 Cyber Resilience of On-board Systems and Equipment." IACS, p. 14, 2022.
[34] Equasis, "The 2020 World Merchant Fleet." Equasis, p. 105, 2020.
[35] C. Zimmerman, *Ten Strategies of a World-Class Cybersecurity Operations Center*, vol. 1. MITRE, 2014.
[36] NORMA-Cyber, "Norma Cyber," 2022. [Online]. Available: https://www.normacyber.no/en/home. [Accessed: 23-Oct-2022].
[37] Marlink, "Maritime cyber security solutions and services," 2022. [Online]. Available: https://marlink.com/solutions/cyber-security/. [Accessed: 23-Oct-2022].
[38] Port-IT, "Port-IT," 2022. [Online]. Available: https://www.port-it.nl/about/history/. [Accessed: 23-Oct-2022].
[39] CyberOwl, "Cyber Owl - Cybersecurity analytics for operational assets," 2022. [Online]. Available: https://cyberowl.io/. [Accessed: 23-Oct-2022].
[40] Port_of_LA, "Port of Los Angeles Launches First-of-its-Kind Cyber Resilience Center," 2022. [Online]. Available: https://www.portoflosangeles.org/references/2022-news-releases/news_012422_csc_ibm. [Accessed: 23-Oct-2022].
[41] maritime_gateway, "Singapore opens cyber security operations centre," 2019. [Online]. Available: https://www.maritimegateway.com/singapore-opens-cyber-security-operations-centre/. [Accessed: 22-Sep-2022].
[42] Vard, "VARD," Jan-2022. [Online]. Available: https://www.vard.com/. [Accessed: 24-Oct-2022].
[43] M. C. Ramon, A. T. Dodson, S. R. Institute, and I. Cambridge Systematics, "Transportation Cybersecurity Incident Response and Management Framework: Final Report." United States. Department of Transportation. Federal Highway Administration, p. 196, 01-Jul-2021.
[44] O. Al-Ibrahim, A. Mohaisen, C. Kamhoua, K. Kwiat, and L. Njilla, "Beyond Free Riding: Quality of Indicators for Assessing Participation in Information Sharing for Threat Intelligence," Feb. 2017.
[45] Ponemon, "Third Annual Study on Exchanging Cyber Threat Intelligence: There Has to Be a Better Way." Ponemon, p. 47, 2017.
[46] ENISA, "Actionable information for security incident response — ENISA." ENISA, p. 79, 2014.

Reducing the Cyber-Attack Surface in the Maritime Sector via Individual Behaviour Change

Konstantinos Mersinas

Information Security Group
Royal Holloway, University of London,
Egham, Surrey, TW20 0EX, UK
Email: konstantinos.mersinas@rhul.ac.uk

Chupkemi Divine Chana

Information Security Group
Royal Holloway, University of London,
Egham, Surrey, TW20 0EX, UK
Email: divine.chupkemi.2019@live.rhul.ac.uk

Abstract — **The maritime sector has been a target for cyber-attacks during the past years. Humans play a significant role in cyber security in a dual fashion; on the one hand, human error allows for the majority of attacks to be successful, as in the case of ransomware attacks via phishing, and on the other hand, appropriate security behaviours can serve as a strong line of defence. We advocate that security needs to transcend awareness and materialise as behaviour of individuals. The question that we attempt to answer is which conditions are necessary for individuals to follow specific information security behaviours, and how to translate these conditions into a tool of practical value for the maritime industry with the intention of minimising the attack surface. Our suggestion comprises of a) identifying the characteristics of the maritime sector with regards to cyber security behaviour, b) introducing and adapting models of behaviour change from behavioural economics and psychology into maritime cyber security, and c) in the next stage of the research, creating an Artificial Intelligence (AI) based tool for individual cyber behaviour change for enterprise centres, ports and ships.**

Keywords – maritime security, cyber security, behaviour change, security training.

I. INTRODUCTION

Cyber-attacks evolve and spread worldwide becoming an increasingly crucial issue in the maritime industry, resulting in individual and organisational impact; these threats have been documented within the sector [4][15][37]. Emerging recommendations aim at unifying and enhancing the security posture of the maritime industry [18][27]. This endeavour includes a focus on training; for example, the International Maritime Organization (IMO) develops model courses for various seafarers' competencies, including maritime cybersecurity related digital skills, under the International Convention on Standards of Training, Certification and Watchkeeping (STCW) [23]. It is also being recognised that human errors and behaviours are related to the majority of cybersecurity and security incidents. Therefore, personnel training is crucial for security hygiene.

There are three main obstacles, however, in achieving security hygiene via training. First, the maritime sector status quo, by large, does not provide the necessary training conditions or the training opportunities needed for personnel. Second, the sector has inherent complexity due to the interconnectivity of various systems, often including legacy ones, along with being a regulation-dense field. And third, training via traditional approaches has questionable effectiveness long-term, due to the way of delivery (e.g., a classroom setting), the frequency of occurrence (e.g., taken once or annually), its generalised nature, i.e., that it is usually not tailored to individuals' needs, and most importantly, the fact that human and circumstantial limitations are not taken into consideration.

The combination of the aforementioned environmental, sector-specific, and training factors indicates the need to investigate the underlying reasons for security awareness training ineffectiveness and to propose an innovative means for training personnel and achieving policy compliance. In this paper, we provide the theoretical basis upon which a practical solution for behaviour change will be built. The authors have developed a prototype which leverages artificial intelligence to automate security awareness and behaviour change as well as ensure personnel can easily access, assimilate, and comply with the many different regulations inherent to the industry. The finalisation of the AI-based tool comprises the next step of our research.

We advocate that the measurable and important factor in creating security hygiene is behaviour. That is, awareness on its own does not necessarily translate into corresponding (secure) actions. Thus, the goal needs to be how to shape behaviours and form secure and safe habits amongst personnel. The rest of the paper is organised as follows. In Section II, we present the challenges which relate to secure behaviours in the maritime sector. Section III presents challenges for changing security behaviours and Section IV provides the proposed solution along with the future steps needed. We conclude in Section V.

II. CHALLENGES IN THE MARITIME SECTOR

The majority of cybersecurity incidents including human errors are generally considered to be a result of behavioural and other factors, such as lack of knowledge, human cognitive limitations, and the lack of time and motivation (World Economic Forum, [28]). To that end, it is only natural to expect cybersecurity professionals to ensure, as high priority, the effective management and mitigation of cyber threats related to human actions. In the following sections we take a closer look at some of those threats in the context of the maritime industry.

A. The maritime training environment

Human behaviour, typically in the form of unintentional actions by individuals without sufficient security training or awareness has been identified as the most significant security incident cause [28, p. 45], and human weaknesses are reported to cause more than three-fourths of data breaches in organisations, in general [20]. For example, clicking on phishing links in emails or accessing false websites despite warnings from an anti-virus have been usual ways for attackers to install malware. Similar percentages hold for shipping accidents caused by human errors directly or indirectly [13]. The authors are not aware of maritime-specific studies on human-generated cybersecurity breaches. Sen analyses the vulnerability of cybersecurity in the maritime industry and reports the over-reliance on outdated technology and security tools as a major issue [32]. The global fleet has an average ship lifespan of more than 20 years [21][45] and Information Technology (IT) and Operational Technology (OT) systems are usually not upgraded regularly, if at all, resulting in, e.g., legacy operating systems which are no longer supported.

The focus on technology, outdated or not, also diminishes the importance and increases the risk of human-related security incidents. In particular, the traditional view that firewalls, antivirus software and other technical controls are sufficient to deal with cyber-attacks, is still existent across sectors, including the maritime sector. The disproportionate focus on technical controls has indeed, on the one hand, significantly enhanced the effectiveness of these controls and, to an extent, possibly diminished the role of humans in security. On the other hand, it has driven attackers to target human weaknesses. For example, it is highly unlikely that attackers target the underlying cryptographic algorithms to gain access to a system, but most likely they would utilise social engineering attacks [7].

The sector has a heavily operational nature which does not provide a conducive environment with enough opportunities for personnel training [35]. Training usually takes place at ports, or is expected from personnel at the expense of their leisure time [24]. Importantly, seafarers are reported to have excessive workloads, lack of sleep and job-related worries [40]. In combination with being away from their families, these factors contribute to suboptimal decision-making, subjective risk perceptions and increased susceptibility to social engineering attacks. Therefore, the nature of the maritime environment can increase the attack surface and a higher level of susceptibility to human error.

B. Sector characteristics and challenges

The maritime sector is becoming digitised, with increasing interconnectivity of ship and port systems. A first issue, however, is that ships tend to have long life cycles estimated to be on average between 20.3 years [45] and about 30 years (25 years life expectancy and 5 years build time) [21], which result in legacy systems that are difficult to maintain and patch [32]. Moreover, legacy systems need additional controls in place to compensate, e.g., for the lack of support to outdated versions, which add complexity and cost overheads. Additionally, the different life cycles of IT and OT systems result in company overheads in managing risks.

Companies which operate internationally are known to face a significant compliance challenge, due to multiple region-related requirements [27], as in the case of the Maritime Transportation Security Act of 2002 (MTSA) in the U.S. which required that ports and vessels perform a number of vulnerability assessments, access control, screening and other procedures [6]. Another example of country-specific stricter-than-IMO requirements is that of ballast water treatment, where although the IMO deferred the implementation of the requirements to 2019, at the time, the U.S. issued their own regulations and implementation schedule [3].

As defined by the IMO, maritime cyber risk relates to the extent to which a technology asset could be endangered by a potential circumstance or event, resulting in operational, safety, or security failures due to corrupted, lost or compromised information or systems [23]. However, in the maritime sector there is a combination of navigational, IT and OT critical systems, threats to which can also be detrimental. To that end, the maritime industry recognises the need for cybersecurity compliance measures for effective mitigation of evolving threats, some of which include the IMO resolution MSC.428(98) maritime cyber risk management in safety management systems [42], ISA/IEC 62443-4-2 security for industrial automation and control systems [43], and ISO/IEC 27005 information security risk management [44].

The case of the A.P. Møller-Maersk ransomware attack which incurred losses approaching $300m [12] is well known in the sector. The Evergreen container ship that blocked the Suez Canal hindered international trade and impacted the world economy. The Suez Canal Authority demanded $916m for compensation, salvage costs and reputational losses from the shipping company (later lowered the demand to $550m) [5]. Although the Evergreen case was not a cyber-attack, it illustrates the impact of maritime incidents and the potential impact of cyber incidents [39].

Compliance challenges and the interconnectedness of cyber physical systems, that is, the intersection of IT, OT and the human interface, increase the complexity of maritime security. Indicative of OT systems are cargo, fuel and utility management, vessel propulsion, mooring and docking, operations for cranes and equipment; IT systems include all navigation, communication and monitoring systems and sensors. Finally, the human interface angle includes port and vessel operators, deck and engine crew, support officers, office employees, technical superintendents and various service providers [31].

These factors pose challenges for personnel, some of which include managing multiple projects simultaneously in limited time [24] with an increased risk of errors and managing a continuously rotating personnel. The question, thus, is how to ensure that staff understand and comply with the various standards and codes of practice, participate in effective training, and behave accordingly. The combination of the aforementioned characteristics and challenges, make the maritime sector a unique cyber security environment.

C. *Security behaviour change*

The IMO identifies that the human element is a significant and complex multidimensional and that 'consideration of human element matters should aim at decreasing the possibility of human error as far as possible' [22]. Additionally, insights from other sectors expand the scope of the human element by combining security with safety, as in the case of the International Atomic Energy Agency practices [14]. However, the way to minimise human error is not straightforward and is largely context-dependent. Limitations of training and practices to be avoided, for example, a blame culture towards seafarers and shore-based personnel, are identified in maritime; indicatively, the IHS Markit and BIMCO report highlights the need to 'look deeper' into the human element [16]. The behaviour change interventions that we propose are in line with this needed 'deeper look'.

There are specific reasons for traditional training not being as effective as policy-makers and security professionals would like it to be; some of these reasons are inherent in human nature while others are environmental or circumstantial. First, as humans, we have limited cognitive capacity and we can absorb, remember and utilise certain amounts of information. Second, only a fraction of the information is available to an individual when they have to make a decision; that is, access to information is partial, or worse, information is unknown. Finally, the available timeframes for making a decision or collecting information is limited by definition. These limitations were identified by the economist Herbert Simon and were termed as 'bounded rationality' [33].

The criticality of time is amplified in the maritime and other sectors, where often personnel have to make fast operational, security and safety related decisions. The aforementioned factors are not to diminish the influence of knowledge and understanding in optimising decision-making, and more so in organisational contexts [34]. However, they portray the inherent issues related to training and whether this training can have significant long-term effects.

We can think of a behaviour change mechanism (or intervention) as having a messenger, a message and a receiver. The message includes a particular threat (including likelihood and impact) and a suggested solution to be accepted or rejected by the receiver (including the level of difficulty of the solution or the skills of the receiver and how effective the solution is expected to be). For example, a threat could be typosquatting the URL used by ship operators to access live ship traffic maps and the solution could be providing a set of actions that ship crews need to undertake, in order to avoid such attacks.

The receiver, e.g., personnel, have a subjective perception of the threat, of their ability (self-efficacy) to follow the suggested solution, and of the solution itself (response efficacy). The so-called 'intervention design' needs to utilise the individual's strengths and be customised to the individual's competence level, professional role, and even cultural background, so that the individual is convinced about the importance of the threat and is subsequently persuaded about the efficacy of the proposed solution. Depending on the context, *who* conveys the message (e.g., senior management, officers etc.) also influences receivers' acceptance decision. The goal is to consider and balance these factors in a way that individuals accept messages and comply with the proposed security behaviour, e.g., adhering to a security policy.

One of the main approaches to change behaviour in psychology and health sciences, and one that has recently been introduced to cybersecurity, is fear appeals. A definition of fear appeals is that they are *'persuasive messages designed to scare people by describing the terrible things that will happen to them if they do not do what the message recommends'* [41, p. 329]. Overall, responses to fear depend on two main factors. On the one hand, we have context-dependent stimuli, which are objective. On the other hand, we have behavioural responses which – to an extent – depend on individual traits and characteristics [1], possibly both cognitive and physiological. The latter point reinforces our initial argument that any behaviour change intervention should be individualised to match the subject's needs and characteristics. *Figure 1* depicts an abstraction of conveying a message to, for example, personnel.

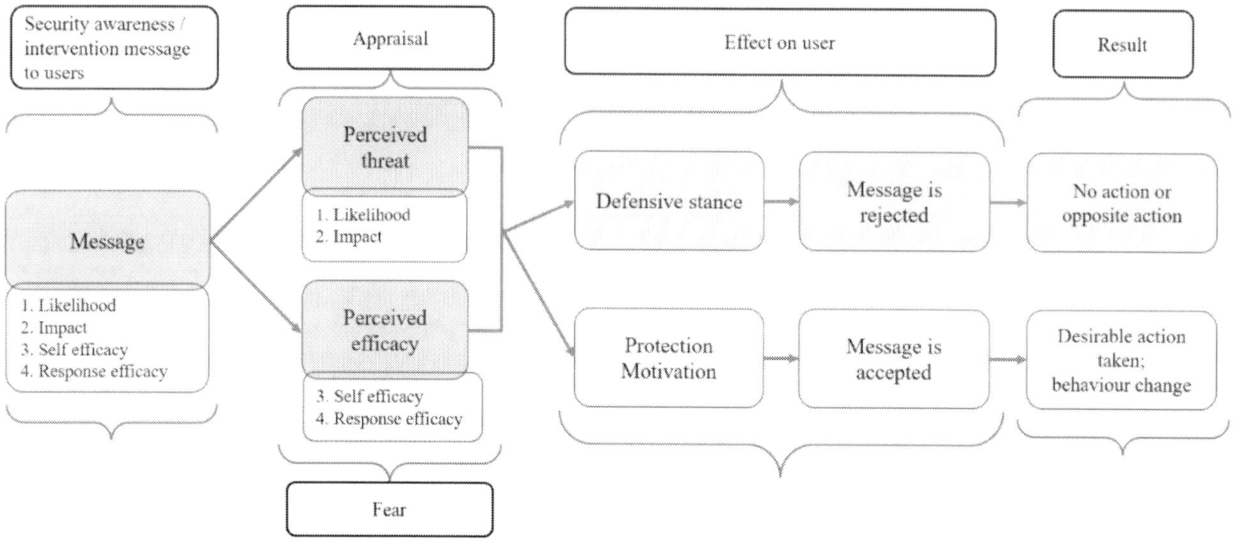

Figure 1. Behavioural intervention model for personnel (adapted from [29] and [38]).

III. BEHAVIOUR CHANGE CHALLENGES

A. *Defining secure behaviour*

It is not straightforward what constitutes secure behaviour. As a first step, desired behaviours need to be identified. 'Following IMO's guidelines on maritime cyber risk management on board ships.' is a generic and perhaps not fully constructive goal. Understanding which behaviours work, e.g., for personnel, and why, is a more promising approach. In fact, some of the guidelines might be impractical or not in line with the daily reality of personnel and, thus, full and consistent compliance should not be expected from users, by default, without considering situational circumstances.

For instance, reading and memorising vast amounts of international cyber security standards related to technologies that are crucial to the operation of numerous maritime systems is not necessarily a reasonable expectation. Personnel have a number of tasks to perform, their attention is focused on their own work and cybersecurity is not their priority. So, what is expected of personnel needs careful examination and dissemination.

B. *Balancing and utilising emotion and reason.*

The balance of emotion and reason in appeals to individuals is key for conveying a message. And, equally, considering the individuals' responses is important. For example, [38] suggests that cognitive responses are the desired reactions to communicated threat messages, rather than emotional ones. However, defining 'reason', 'rationality' and adjusting the level of emotional appraisals is not an easy endeavour [2]. Indicatively, the factor of fear plays an important role, as well as the various types of rationality [26].

Additionally, in the maritime sector, we have critical OT systems and safety risks, which can attract the attention of individuals more, if contrasted to cyber security risks. Thus, fear appeals, unless they are linked to safety and OT risks, might not be sufficiently salient in the perception of personnel.

C. *Selecting and weighing the behavioural intervention variables to be modelled.*

According to [30], the perceived level of threat, along with the individual's perceived efficacy to cope with this threat, are the main predictors of whether people take protective actions or not. Additionally, [10] proposes motivation, appropriate triggers, simplicity of solutions, peer pressure and social acceptance as the main factors which influence behaviour change, and the Hook model also utilises triggers, along with rewards for personnel and their investment in an action [9]. The majority of research literature on behaviour change originates from health sciences, e.g., studies on alcohol consumption, smoking, poor nutrition or lack of exercise, and people fail to change their behaviour even when facing life-threatening conditions. The core variables for behaviour change in a maritime security setting are yet to be identified empirically.

D. *Considering security culture.*

Including security culture as an 'environmental' factor in the equation is another angle. Security culture can be considered as the set of shared values, beliefs and practices relating to cyber security in an environment, e.g., in an organisation [8]. The benefits of cyber security and safety culture have been reported in the literature [19]. Situational circumstances can affect message acceptance; e.g., social norms, peer pressure or herding behaviours, say, in a ship environment. A new employee observes her colleagues' behaviour and will most likely follow aspects of this behaviour. It is, thus, important to consider security culture and environment-dependent factors, and model them to a sufficiently adaptable level, so that a generic model and a context-specific implementation are balanced.

IV. PRACTICAL BEHAVIOUR CHANGE FOR THE MARITIME SECTOR

Taking into consideration context, technology and personnel-related challenges in the maritime sector and the underlying psychological and behavioural reasons for people's non-compliance we propose a practical solution. Namely, the authors propose an AI-based individualised assistant which a) is customised to the particular environment of implementation, e.g., by analysing and codifying the existing – and being updated with new – guidelines on maritime cyber risk management, security policies and standards, and b) learns the individual's personal characteristics, behaviours, and knowledge gaps, and directs them to relevant information in a focused fashion. For example, the tool will know which policies and procedures are required for the person's role and rank and will learn which knowledge gaps the person has; it can then prompt the individual with targeted information.

The idea of our solution aims in minimising the susceptibility of individuals to security (and safety) errors by providing training and support with practical information, and prompting hints to maritime staff, in a timely manner. In this paper, we provide the theoretical basis upon which the idea of this digital assistant will be built. The current state of the solution achieves an AI-based analysis of maritime security policies, guidelines, and standards, and can be trained through them to direct individuals and assist with their security-related enquiries. Next steps include a constant training of the tool, based on maritime security policies, guidelines, and standards, user behaviour and user characteristics (with user consent), so that a holistic 'understanding' is achieved by the tool, and the tool can consequently assist in complex and emerging situations and needs of the individual and the company.

Limitations, technical details and future research

The goal of this part of the research is to set the basis for the future development of our intervention technologies for security behaviour change. However, the approach has its limitations; as a matter of fact, a significant part of the literature in this area has similar limitations and in particular, a lack of experimental verification of certain aspects of models and theories [29]. This is an open problem which we plan to tackle through our future research, in two ways. First, via lab-based experiments where we can measure individuals' reactions in a 'clean' environment, with clear conditions to be tested; and, thus, examining both individual traits and situational circumstances. Second, with field experiments in maritime context, where we will be able to measure the specific characteristics of individuals, but also of the environmental and the social conditions, i.e., aspects of the security culture. The aforementioned research activities will inform and shape the development and finalisation of the AI-based tool.

In more detail, there is a need for large-scale gathering and analysis of security policies, standards, and guidelines of interest. With the aim of developing agents that are capable of systematically identifying, extracting, and quantifying sentences and paragraphs, these documents will be prepared and trained using techniques such as clustering, semantic analysis, and similarity analysis from Natural Language Processing (NLP). In parallel, in collaboration with industry partners, further research will be conducted to identify Key Monitoring Points (KMPs), as well as potential Threat Entry Points (TEPs), in such an OT dominated environment.

The identification of KMPs (e.g., a ship's satellite-related software) and TEPs (e.g., a connection point that allows for malware to be injected) will serve as a baseline and paradigm on which behavioural protocols are designed (similarly to traditional protocols, but aimed at affecting users' actions through statements, reminders, advice, extracts from policies, and other interventions). Algorithms are derived from translating measurable behaviours and are fed with selected actions (events or group of events) to trigger targeted behavioural interventions based on the protocol's threshold or trigger point. The algorithm's output will, in most cases, be determined with the help of trained Machine Learning (ML) agents from NLP training of available documents (policies, procedures and standards of interest). These agents are able to extract the most appropriate text or point personnel to the right document.

Many additional questions emerge from this study. Namely, fear is an evolutionarily useful emotion, initially related to survival. We would like to further explore the degrees of fear in relation to less-strong individual traits like risk aversion, uncertainty avoidance and loss aversion. Moreover, another goal is the experimental testing of behavioural responses to fear in a maritime security context. There are also ethical considerations of having human participants in experimentally tested fear conditions. Beyond these considerations, the 'fear-level matching' that simulates a real-world threat, e.g., data loss due to ransomware attacks, is a challenge on its own. Another aspect of future work is the empirical identification of behavioural interventions best-suited for maritime environments.

V. CONCLUSION

The vulnerability and susceptibility of the maritime sector can be significantly minimised via investing in the human factors of cybersecurity. Humans can become a significant 'line of defence' in the sector, if equipped and trained appropriately. In order for this approach to be successful, both the individual traits of personnel and the environmental, contextual factors need to be considered. In this paper, we present the theoretical background and propose a practical approach for effective behavioural interventions, at a high level. A combination of adapted behavioural theories and collected data can inform the creation of a practical tool to reduce personnel time and effort for accessing knowledge, and which can gradually form security behaviours, reducing the cyber-attack surface in the sector.

REFERENCES

[1] R. Adolphs, The Biology of Fear. Current Biology, 23(2): p. R79-R93, 2013.

[2] D. Ariely, Predictably irrational: The hidden forces that shape our decisions. New York, 2008.

[3] P. Benecki, *"Compliance Challenges," The Maritime Executive,* 22 March 2018. [Online]. Available from: https://maritime-executive.com/magazine/compliance-challenges 2022.09.22

[4] BIMCO. *The guidelines on cyber security onboard ships*, 2017. [Online]. Available from: http://www.icsshipping.org/docs/default-source/resources/safety-security-and-operations/guidelines-on-cybersecurity-onboard-ships.pdf?sfvrsn=16 2022.09.27

[5] BBC. *Ever Given: Ship that blocked Suez Canal sets sail after deal signed,* 2021. [Online]. Available from: https://www.bbc.com/news/world-middle-east-57746424 2022.09.22

[6] C. E. Carey, Maritime Transportation Security Act of 2002 (Potential Civil Liabilities and Defenses). Tul. Mar. LJ, 28, p.295, 2003.

[7] P. Carpenter and K. Roer, The Security Culture Playbook: An Executive Guide To Reducing Risk and Developing Your Human Defense Layer. John Wiley & Sons, 2022.

[8] A. da Veiga and J. H. P. Eloff, A framework and assessment instrument for information security culture. Computers & Security, 29(2), pp. 196–207. doi:10.1016/j.cose.2009.09.002, 2010.

[9] N. Eyal, Hooked: How to build habit-forming products. Penguin, 2014.

[10] B. J. Fogg, A behavior model for persuasive design. In Proceedings of the 4th international Conference on Persuasive Technology (p. 40). ACM, April 2009.

[11] Gov.uk. *Ship security,* 2022. [Online]. Available from: https://www.gov.uk/guidance/maritime-security 2022.09.24

[12] A. Greenberg, *"The Untold Story of NotPetya, the Most Devastating Cyberattack in History," Wired.com. 22 August* 2018. [Online]. Available from: https://www.wired.com/story/notpetya-cyberattack-ukraine-russia-code-crashed-the-world 2022.09.24

[13] C. Heij and S. Knapp, "Predictive Power of Inspection Outcomes for Future Shipping Accidents – An Empirical Appraisal with Special Attention for Human Factor Aspects." Maritime Policy and Management, 2018, 45 (5), 604-621, 2018.

[14] International Atomic Energy Agency. *IAEA, Safety Culture Practices for the Regulatory Body,* 2020. [Online]. Available from: https://www-pub.iaea.org/MTCD/Publications/PDF/TE-1895web.pdf 2022.09.28

[15] Institute of Engineering and Technology, IET, Code of practice – cyber security for ports and port systems, 2016.

[16] HIS Markit, Safety at Sea and BIMCO cyber security white paper. Safety at Sea, p.15, 2019.

[17] R. Hopcraft, Developing Maritime Digital Competencies. IEEE Communications Standards Magazine, 5(3), pp.12-18, 2021.

[18] R. Hopcraft and K. M. Martin, Effective maritime cybersecurity regulation–the case for a cyber code. *Journal of the Indian Ocean Region*, 14(3), pp.354-366, 2018.

[19] R. Hopcraft, K. Tam, J. D. P. Misas, K. Moara-Nkwe, and K. Jones, Developing a Maritime Cyber Safety Culture: Improving Safety of Operations. Maritime Technology and Research, 5(1), 2023.

[20] ENISA, ENISA threat landscape report 2018: 15 Top Cyber-Threats and Trends. Heraklion: European Network and Information Security Agency (ENISA). doi: 10.2824/622757, 2019.

[21] International Maritime Organisation. IMO, Resolution MSC.287(87) – Adoption of the International Goal-based Ship Construction Standards for Bulk Carriers and Oil Tankers, 2010.

[22] International Maritime Organisation. IMO, MSC-MEPC.2 – Guidelines for the Application of the Human Element Analysing Process (Heap) to the IMO Rule-making Process, 2013.

[23] International Maritime Organisation. IMO, Resolution MSC.428(98) — Maritime Cyber Risk Management in Safety Management Systems, 2017.

[24] K. D. Jones, K. Tam, and M. Papadaki, Threats and impacts in maritime cyber security. Engineering & Technology Reference, 1(1). doi: 10.1049/etr.2015.0123, 2016.

[25] K. Mersinas, M. Bada, and N. Tzoumerkas, Security behavior change ethics: implications for research and practice [Unpublished manuscript]. Information Security Group, Royal Holloway, University of London, 2022.

[26] K. Mersinas, T. Sobb, C. Sample, J. Z. Bakdash, and D. Ormrod, Training Data and Rationality. In ECIAIR 2019 European Conference on the Impact of Artificial Intelligence and Robotics (p. 225). Academic Conferences and publishing limited, October 2019.

[27] Missionsecure, *A Comprehensive Guide to Maritime Cyber Security,* 2020. [Online]. Available from: https://www.missionsecure.com/resources/comprehensive-guide-to-maritime-security-ebook 2022.09.24

[28] World Economic Forum, *The Global Risks Report,* 2022. [Online]. Available from: https://www.weforum.org/reports/global-risks-report-2022 2022.10.01

[29] L. Popova, The extended parallel process model: Illuminating the gaps in research. Health Education & Behavior, 39(4), pp.455-473, 2012.

[30] R. W. Rogers, A protection motivation theory of fear appeals and attitude change. *The Journal of Psychology*, 91(1), pp.93-114, 1975.

[31] I. Progoulakis, P. Rohmeyer, and N. Nikitakos, Cyber Physical Systems Security for Maritime Assets. *Journal of Marine Science and Engineering*, 9(12), p.1384, 2021.

[32] R. Sen, Chapter 9. Cyber and information threats to seaports and ships. McNicholas, MA, Maritime Security, 2, pp. 281-302, 2016.

[33] H. A. Simon, Theories of bounded rationality. In C. B. McGuire and R. Radner (eds.). Decision and Organization, pp. 161-176, 1972.

[34] H. A. Simon, Bounded rationality and organizational learning. Organization Science 2(1), pp. 125-134, 1991.

[35] D. Smith, *Cybersecurity challenges for the Maritime Industry. SeaRates,* 2022. [Online]. Available from: https://www.searates.com/blog/post/cybersecurity-challenges-for-the-maritime-industry 2022.09.22

[36] B. Svilicic, J. Kamahara, M. Rooks, and Y. Yano, Maritime Cyber Risk Management: An Experimental Ship Assessment. *Journal of Navigation*, 72(5), pp.1108-1120, 2019.

[37] TRANSAS, *Connected ships and cybersecurity. Frank J Coles CEO,* 2016. [Online]. Available from: https://docs.wixstatic.com/ugd/9491c8_5fbc6ff941df40f8a5b90d703de4a64b.pdf 2022.09.22

[38] K. Witte, Fear as a motivator, fear as inhibitor: Using the EPPM to explain fear appeal successes and failures. The Handbook of Communication and Emotion, 1998.

[39] E. Wong, F. Chan, I. Kim, and J. Lee, Canal Blockage: Legal Risks and Liabilities Framework on the Global Supply Chain

from Suez Canal Blockage by Ever Given. *SSRN Electronic Journal*, 2022.

[40] B. Tetemadze, M. Carrera Arce, R. Baumler, and I. Bartusevičiene, Seafarers' wellbeing or business, a complex paradox of the industry. TransNav: *International Journal on Marine Navigation and Safety of Sea Transportation*, 15, 2021.

[41] T. M. Wilkinson, Nudging and manipulation. Political Studies 61, 341–355, 2013.

[42] IMO, Resolution MSC.428(98) — Maritime Cyber Risk Management in Safety Management Systems, 2017.

[43] ISA/IEC 62443 - Industrial Automation and Control Systems Security by the International Electrotechnical Commission

[44] ISO/IEC 27001:2018 – International Organisation of Standards, International Electrotechnical Commission, Information Security Management Systems.

[45] International Chamber of Shipping, Review of Maritime Transport. United Nations Conference on Trade and Development (UNCTAD), Geneva, 2016.